P9-CQX-822

History: Its Purpose and Method

The Author: Gustaaf Johannes Renier (1892-1962)

Professor Renier was born in Holland, 25 September 1892, and died in London, 4 September 1962. He was educated at Flushing and Louvain Schools, and at the Universities of Ghent and London. He had a long and varied career: London correspondent for Dutch newspapers, 1914-1927; author and translator, from 1927; Lecturer in English History, University College, London, from 1934; Reader in Dutch History, University of London, from 1936; Literary Adviser to the Netherlands government in London, 1939-1945 (World War II); and Professor of Dutch History and Institutions, University of London, 1945-1957 (Emeritus, from 1957). He was a corresponding member of the Royal Academy, Amsterdam; Fellow of University College, London, 1948; and an Officer of the Order of Orange, Nassau, 1947. Professor Renier's publications included (among others) *The English: Are They Human?* (1931); *The Dutch Nation, An Historical Study* (1944); *The Criterion of Dutch Nationhood* (1946); and numerous translations into English from the Dutch, French, and German.

Professor Renier's *History* is the attempt of a working historian to "look at the place of history in the world of men"—a "statement of the place of history among the departments of human knowledge," and a description of "the historian's work as it actually takes place." Renier was concerned to rescue his profession from the danger to which it had been subjected—he contended—by those "professionals of history who wish to raise their subject to the rank of a universal philosophy, or to degrade it to the task of fact collecting." "The task of explaining history," Renier rightly insisted, "is too often left to philosophers who make puns upon the semantic avatars of the word history. History reveals its nature only through the familiarity of daily practice." *History* presents just such a revelation.

In the very best sense Professor Renier was an able "philosopher of history"—but he would eschew such a title. He wanted only—he said—that it might be said of him what Hegel once said of Ranke: "Das ist nur ein gewöhnlicher Historiker." And so he was—"Just an ordinary historian!"

By G. J. Renier

The English: Are They Human?

Great Britain and
The Establishment of the Netherlands

The Dutch Nation

Oscar Wilde

Robespierre

William of Orange

 ROSE—Reprints of
Scholarly Excellence

Certain good books should be, like the rose, not only hardy perennials in their intrinsic worth and usefulness, but also perennial in their availability. The purpose of the ROSE series is to make available such choice books from the past that are not otherwise available.

ROSE is intended primarily to meet the needs of the university classroom. Volumes are included in the series upon the recommendation of professors in the classroom who indicate a need for a currently out-of-print text. When investigation indicates that a reprint is warranted and available, ROSE reprints the text in an attractive and durable, yet affordable, format—equal or even superior to the original in quality.

Roses come in many varieties. So do books in the ROSE series. ROSE is not restricted to any one subject area but will reprint classics from any and all classes—the humanities, the sciences, the arts. But each is a "rose" of a reprint—preeminent among its kind, rare, of scholarly excellence.

History
Its Purpose and Method

by

Gustaaf Johannes Renier
(1892-1962)

*Late Professor of Dutch History and Institutions
at the University of London*

Mercer University / ROSE
Press
Macon, Ga. 31207

All Mercer University Press books are produced on acid-free paper
which exceeds the minimum standards set by
the National Publications and Records Commission.

Library of Congress Cataloging in Publication Data

Renier, Gustaaf Johannes, 1892-1962.
History, its purpose and method.

(ROSE)
Reprint. Originally published: London: Allen & Unwin, 1950.
Includes index.
1. History—Philosophy. 2. History—Methodology. I. Title. II. Series
D16.8.R38   1982   901   82-3522
ISBN 0-8655 4-036-5   AACR2

FOREWORD

LET us, till the moment arrives for hammering out a definition of the word history, and for parting company with those who do not care to accept it, agree upon a non-committal formula. Let us say that history is the discipline or study which is concerned with the human past. And let us look at the place of history in the world of men.

In his last published work the poet Paul Valéry gave utterance once more to the loathing of history which obsessed him for many years. "L'histoire," said the poet[1] in this ultimate comminatory tirade, "est le produit le plus dangereux que la chimie de l'intellect ait élaboré. Ses propriétés sont bien connues. Il fait rêver, il enivre les peuples, leur engendre de faux souvenirs, exagère leurs réflexes, entretient leurs vieilles plaies, les tourmente dans leur repos, les conduit aux délires des grandeurs ou à celui de la persécution, et rend les nations amères, superbes, insupportables et vaines."[2]

The task of the apologist would be too easy if he had to deal solely with attacks of this nature. Of course, history ill-told and ill-applied can be dangerous. Any tool is dangerous in the wrong hands. Moreover, like so many people who write about history, Valéry was not clear about the meaning of the word. He proclaimed as a discovery that the pace of occurrence is growing, and that old mental habits are inadequate when we attempt to name events and to correlate them. This, surely, does not pension off the historian. New developments call for new histories, and will receive them.

The welfare of history as a department of human knowledge is exposed to dangers more serious than rhetorical ignorance. Scientists distrust a discipline which, they mistakenly imagine, adopts an unwarranted attitude of certainty, proclaims resignation and gradualism, precludes open-mindedness and enterprise. At other moments they demand from historians the use of

[1] For translation, see Appendix II, p. 258.
[2] *Regards sur le Monde actuel, et autres Essais*, 1945, p. 43. For putting history to a bad use, see Geyl, *Napoleon*, 1949, pp. 183 *sqq.*, 395.

statistical methods and sociological formulations which cannot be provided. A better understanding of the function and methods of history would turn scientists into friends of the historical discipline. But there is no doubt that the professionals of history who wish to raise their subject to the rank of a universal philosophy, or to degrade it to the task of fact-collecting, have fostered the distrust of the outside world.

The decision to attempt this statement of the place of history among the departments of human knowledge, and to describe the historian's work as it actually takes place, was born from conversations with my distinguished colleagues in the Senior Common Room of University College, London. It has become clear to me that, while the limits between human disciplines are continually being redrawn, and while society expects a justification for the material support it gives to those who elaborate and teach knowledge, such a statement has to be made. Moreover, history must be defended from a danger greater than any I have yet mentioned.

There are people, and in some countries they are endowed with immense power, who look upon history as the instrument by which society can forecast its future. According to the extreme Marxists the task of history is to discover the laws that have ruled the behaviour of human societies, and that will, therefore, rule their future behaviour. They demand from history that it shall work out a sociology. But they are already in possession of the only true sociology, and they know, therefore, how the historian will formulate his laws. They are informed in advance of the wording of the report they will receive from the historian who carries out his terms of reference. He is expected to fill in the details of a picture of which the general outline has been laid down. Thus also did Bossuet know the results of his investigation of the past before he sat down to write his discourse upon universal history; it was to be the story of the acts of Divine Providence performed through the wired puppets who thought of themselves as captains and as kings. Such friends are dangerous. For the historian who fails to please them communists have raillery and vituperation, while he and they still live in a free society. What would be the independent historian's fate under the dispensation of which they dream is no secret.

Yet it will be my endeavour to prove that history does indeed perform a social task. But it is an independent task, and faithfully performed whatever the historian's personal bias, whatever the conclusions he wishes to draw from the events he must narrate. This paradox will explain itself, I hope, when we study the actual methods used by the historian in the course of his work. The task of explaining history is too often left to philosophers who make puns upon the semantic avatars of the word history. History reveals its nature only through the familiarity of daily practice. This is why practising historians should express their views upon the function and the methodology of their subject. Yet they, like every human being, have a philosophy of their own. Mine is derived from the great historian Henri Pirenne, who was my first master. It was confirmed by the study of the writings of the Anglo-Saxon. pragmatists William James, F. C. S. Schiller, Alfred Sidgwick, and John Dewey.[1] From them I learned that we can know, but that we never finally know whether we have reached knowledge. In this modest realization I think I find myself upon common ground with my friends

[1] I have made no attempt to give a survey of the works of those who have written about history. A systematic history of the methodology of history remains to be written. Collingwood's *The Idea of History* (1946) gives such a survey in outline, but his conception of history is too one-sided to make his contribution really valuable. When here or there I refer to the views of my predecessors, my intention is not in the first place to obtain the support of their authority. I find it necessary, upon occasion, to underline the fact that my notions have occurred to other minds before they struck mine. André Gide makes a similar observation in his diary: ". . . cette habitude que j'ai de citer toujours ceux à qui ma pensée s'apparente . . . j'ai plaisir, et plus elle est hardie, à penser qu'elle habita déjà d'autres esprits. On me dit que j'ai tort. Peu m'importe. J'ai trop grand plaisir à citer, et me persuade, comme Montaigne, que ce n'est qu'au regard des sots que j'en parais moins personnel" (*Journal*, January 10, 1923, p. 752. See also his entry for August 4, 1922, p. 739). My only claim to novelty is one of arrangement and of emphasis. I have permitted myself a considerable number of references to the works of pragmatist philosophers. I am aware that Mr. Michael Oakeshott points out that there are no authorities in philosophy, and that references are of little value for the philosopher, because, as a philosopher, he is not a scholar. "There is no book which is indispensable for the study of philosophy," he says (*Experience and its Modes*, p. 8). But, precisely because I am not a professional philosopher, I think it wiser to inform the reader of the origin of my doctrines.

the scientists. Even so it remains my ambition that it will be said of the author of this book, as Hegel once said of Ranke: "Das ist nur ein gewöhnlicher Historiker."[1]

[1] My colleague A. J. Ayer, professor of philosophy at University College, London, has read several chapters of the typescript of this book and has given me valuable advice. F. G. Young, professor of bio-chemistry in the University of Cambridge, has patiently perused the whole typescript and has discussed with me my views on scientific method. I have been greatly assisted by his stimulating criticism.

G. J. R.

CONTENTS

9

Part One

WHAT IS HISTORY?

Chapter I

THE STORY THAT MUST BE TOLD

THE purpose of this chapter is to suggest that history fulfils a social need, and that this is its essential function.

§ 1

HUMAN INDIVIDUALS AND THE MEMORY OF THEIR PAST EXPERIENCE

For every human being the memory of his individual experiences is a matter of supreme importance. To it he owes his sense of identity and possibly his consciousness, without it he can take no important decision, he cannot improve his condition, he cannot survive. How does he use it?

To call man a thinking animal is to attribute an undue importance to one of the many operations among which he divides his time. If thinking had been their sole pursuit, men would have been defeated in the struggle for primacy by ants and other animals with a civilization more ancient and more completely organized than theirs; they would have been beaten by intelligent animals with quicker and preciser reactions, like rats. The main concern of men is to cope with situations by the performance of deeds. As a rule thinking stands in the way of action, which, on many vital occasions, such as those in which there is immediate danger, has to be instantaneous. More often than not, thought is unnecessary. For men are guided by drives or internal stimuli like hunger, thirst or the craving for rest. Many of their actions are conditioned responses[1] to a sensation, and take place without the intervention of the higher centres in the brain. Sequences of acts of this nature are habits. Men are creatures of habit. While they behave in this elementary fashion, their minds are occupied, not by the process of reaching beliefs and establishing them on

[1] Often referred to as conditioned reflexes. See Menninger, K. A., *The Human Mind* (1930), pp. 157–62. See also Ogburn, W. F., and Nimkoff, M. F., *Handbook of Sociology*, 1947, pp. 83 *sqq.*, and Sidgwick, A., *Fallacies* (1901), p. 34.

firm foundations, not, in other words, by the comparing of ideas which alone deserves the name of thinking, but by images that may be of interest to the psychologist, but not to the logician, by musings and day-dreams.

Men, or their ancestors, have learned long since that there were occasions when it paid them to delay action and to watch. The discovery of the use of reflection and contemplation must have been an important moment in their evolution. They know, now, that they must sometimes "stop to think."[1] When trouble arises they try to reconstruct the conditions which occasioned it. When they are faced with the need for taking a difficult or important action, they first recall experiences previously undergone in circumstances that show some resemblance with those of the present situation; then they make sure in their minds that these resemblances are genuine, and they also note the differences between the present situation and their past experiences. Having done this, having exercised their thought, they allow their action to be guided by the resulting knowledge. We see, then, that thinking, or reasoning, is of a practical nature, that it is a preliminary to action. We also see that an awareness of our past experiences is an essential part of the thinking process.[2] Without it we are unable to construct ideas about the consequences of our actions. R. G. Collingwood says much the same thing when he tells us that "knowing yourself means knowing what you can do; and since nobody knows what he can do until he tries, the only clue to what man can do is what man has done."[3]

The more complex human life grows, the more frequent will

[1] On stopping to think: Schiller, F. C. S., *Must Philosophers Disagree?* (1934), p. 173; the same, *Our Human Truths* (1939), pp. 193 *sqq.*; Dewey, J., *Experience and Nature* (1929), pp. 313-4; the same, *How We Think* (1910), p. 12; the same; *Essays in Experimental Logic* (1916), pp. 2, 11, 12.

[2] On the value of past experience: Dewey, J., *Essays in Experimental Logic*, p. 73; "Thinking is a reconstructive movement of actual contents of experience in relation to each other" (*ibid.*, p. 176). "Thinking is comparing with the past" (Schiller, F. C. S., *Logic for Use*, 1929, p. 51). See also *ibid.*, pp. 199 *sqq.*, 223. "Our source of confidence is the resemblance or analogy we discover between the case in question and other cases where the event has already occurred" (Sidgwick, A., *The Process of Argument*, 1893, p. 39). See also Dewey, J., *The Quest for Truth* (1930), pp. 258-60.

[3] *The Idea of History* (1946), p. 10.

be the need for coping with difficult and novel situations, the more frequent also the need for thinking—or for inference and reasoning.[1] Whenever the human individual thinks, he calls up past experiences which are stored in his memory. From the first moment of our individual existence our brain keeps impressions of our sensations, and as the number of these increases, they meet previously stored memories with which they are automatically compared; if there is some resemblance they are grouped and preserved with them. Whatever view is taken of the human soul, memory is acknowledged to be a physiological function. It operates somewhat oddly, stores the impressions it receives at different levels, so that it disgorges its treasure with varying ease and speed, sometimes reluctantly or not at all. Memory can be defective in its recording, its retention, or its reproduction.[2] Nevertheless, we are constrained to accept as a postulate that it is a trustworthy keeper of the records of our personal sensations, provided we try, by exercising it, and by depriving it of reasons for playing us false—an act which is not beyond the powers of a sane and intelligent person—to put it on its best behaviour.[3]

It is, undoubtedly, of the greatest practical importance that our memory shall function accurately. When a man is on the point of crossing a busy thoroughfare he is faced with one of those crucial situations in which he must "stop to think." If, at that moment, his memory deceives him, and informs him that according to previous experiences motor-omnibuses always move at 3 miles per hour, and if, in crossing the road, he acts upon the false knowledge which results from the comparison of the present situation with the alleged past experiences, a bus may arrive at a speed of 10 miles or more, with the result that the deluded individual will fail to reach the opposite side of the street.

[1] These three words are sometimes used with slightly different connotations: there is no need for us to adopt this complication which finds no justification in the practice of life.

[2] Menninger, *op. cit.*, pp. 158–9. Nothing that is said in this or in other places of my book should be taken as implying the belief that the phenomenon of retention has been satisfactorily explained by students of the nervous system. They are still speaking in terms of symbols and metaphors.

[3] Schiller, *Logic for Use*, pp. 372–3.

§ 2

HUMAN SOCIETIES AND THE STORY OF THEIR PAST EXPERIENCES

Do societies, like individuals, refer to past experiences when facing complex or difficult situations? In answering this important question we must avoid reasoning by analogy. Some sociologists have allowed themselves to be lured by the supposed resemblance between society and the human body into parable and symbolism till they substitute imagery for reasoning. The relation between human individuals and human societies is not one of analogy: it is factual.[1] Obviously, there can be no societies without the individuals that compose them, though communist Marxists often talk and usually behave as if their ant-heap contained no ants. But equally, no human individual exists without a society that rears him in his early years and gives him, long after he has ceased to be defenceless, a chance to develop his personality by utilizing the possibilities of specialization held out by social life.

Are the societies to which men belong by birth, nations, civilizations, the all-embracing society of mankind, merely the sum of their human components, or are they, as ancient modes of thinking revived by holist metaphysics and Gestalt psychology bid us believe, the sum of these components plus an extra element which they possess in their capacity of whole or configuration? For our present enquiry the difference is of no importance. The conception of society as a bare sum-total gives us satisfactory results, while any interpretation that integrates societies more thoroughly would strengthen our case.

The fact that human beings are, necessarily, at the same time, physiological and psychological units as well as members of society, implies that every one of their actions possesses a personal and a social aspect. But while the actor is aware of the personal aspect, he is much less conscious, perhaps entirely unconscious, of the social aspect of his actions. This is clearly the case in the acts of procreation and feeding, and in the satisfaction of all our

---

[1] "It is impossible to think of men otherwise than as living in societies," Dewey, *Experience and Nature*, p. 175.

natural appetites. One might say, speaking metaphorically, of course, that in the ordinary activities of life society uses these appetites of the individuals for its own purposes. But even the collective acts of societies, those affecting their political life, which they usually entrust to élites, to delegates, to leaders— these too are to a large extent performed unconsciously, and not seldom for apparently personal reasons. Did not Graham Wallas remark in one of his books that no man who was driven solely by an impulse towards public service could possibly submit to the drawbacks of a parliamentary or ministerial existence? The politician could not carry on unless moved by ambition, exhibitionism or the lust for power, by impulses that are psychological and private, as well as by a desire to perform a social service.

When acting socially, i.e. when performing acts that clearly concern the society to which they belong, men usually behave as they did when acting privately: their responses to situations are conditioned, and they follow habits which are embodied in customs and institutions. One need not be an Englishman to do a thing merely because it is "done." Men respond to the stimulus of immediate social peril without having recourse to reasoning. In 1672 the Dutch community, in 1940 the British community, saved their lives by refusing to draw logical conclusions, and by ignoring the fact that they were beaten according to the rules of the game. In circumstances like these, combative impulses get hold of the individuals who compose a society, and hypnotic suggestion goads them into irrational but useful action. As a rule, however, when situations arise that are complex or unusual, and therefore baffling, men will reflect and contemplate, they will recall experiences previously undergone, and compare them with the present predicament, before they act upon the resemblances and differences they detect as a result of this comparison.

Aristotle praises the teaching provided by actual experience,[1] but he looks upon the precedent set by experience as a norm. Such an attitude throws the good back into the golden age,

[1] *Politics*, 1264a. Ayer, A. J., in *Language, Truth and Logic* (2nd edition, 1947, p. 50), says "being rational entails being guided in a particular fashion by past experience."

invites us to go and dwell there, and is pure "escapism." It is a denial of progress and of the possibility of progress. Now present-day physicists are inclined to believe that the physical universe is running down, and is, therefore, regressing. Physicists will get over this phase, because human optimism is indomitable. We shall be informed, one day, that the physical universe is tending to assume the nuclear equipoise that appears to our senses as nickel.[1] Anyhow, there is no regression yet in the world of life: living tissue still tends to adopt shapes which possess increasing possibilities of generic survival. Biologists still believe that evolution is progress. In the third aspect of the world as we know it, the social sphere, there also is progress. Pain can be soothed more easily than in the past,[2] and no heroism is needed to have a stone removed from one's bladder as in the days of Samuel Pepys. The cultural possessions of societies tend to be shared by an ever-increasing proportion of their members. An ill-educated proletarian of today knows more about the universe than did a Roman patrician. The delusion that happiness should be reserved for the few is on the wane. Even in this dangerous middle of the twentieth century the notion of progress is sufficiently potent for the worship of precedent to have become a pathological symptom which is met only in the artificially restricted world of reactionaries. Constitutional lawyers may still quote precedent as though it possessed authority,[3] but all

[1] My friend F. G. Young, professor of biochemistry, suggests that a considera-tion of the nuclear packing fractions indicates that, provided infinite time is avail-able, atomic nuclei of all species should change into those of nickel.

[2] This is a social event; it implies no physiological modification in man.

[3] "I do not for a moment suppose that the experiences of the past, personal and social, are of no importance. For without them we should not be able to frame any ideas whatever of the conditions under which objects are enjoyed nor any estimate of the consequences of esteeming and liking them. But past experi-ences are significant in giving us intellectual instrumentalities of judging these points. They are tools, not finalities. . . . We are not, then, to get away from enjoyments experienced in the past and from recall of them, but from the notion that they are the arbiters of things to be further enjoyed. . . . It is not for a moment suggested that we can get away from customs and established institutions. . . . What is needed is intelligent examination of the consequences that are actually effected by inherited institutions and customs, in order that there may be intelligent con-sideration of the ways in which they are to be intentionally modified in behalf of generation of different consequences," Dewey, *The Quest for Certainty*, pp. 258–60.

others look upon the wisdom of our fathers, those unclean, complex-ridden sufferers from avitaminosis, as a poor guide indeed. Would it not come to us as a shock if we discovered one day that we were no wiser than our fathers? We have learned so much they did not know; we have learned to forget so much that they believed; the existence of witchcraft, the direct intervention of Providence in the course of nature, the inevitability of sin. If we believe with Bacon that "histories make men wise"[1] it is mainly because we accept the view expressed in the Dutch proverb: "a donkey does not twice hurt itself on the same stone." Meanwhile, the reactionary need not part company with us: past experience is even more important in his scheme of life than in ours. We need it for comparison, he wishes to copy it.

Societies have not the same facilities as individuals for the automatic recall of past experience. They have no organic memory that can store experiences and produce them when required.[2] This is why, from time immemorial, men have had to tell each other and their descendants the narrative which keeps these experiences available for comparison as a preliminary to unusual action. The narrative of past experiences, active and passive, is for societies what memory is for their individual members.

We must bear in mind, at this point, what has already been said about the use societies appear to make for their own purpose of the activities of their members. Individuals often serve society unknowingly. We need not therefore expect, and least of all at the early or uncritical stage of social development, that the tellers of the tale of the past realized that they were contributing to social memory. They were moved, in all probability, by the pure delight they took in narrating memorable events. Thus the narrative was told, remembered, retold, and handed on. At first,

[1] *Essays*: "Of Studies." While believing in progress, or at least in its possibility, we need not hold the view that it is constant. It is more likely that it proceeds in waves, maybe in jerks, and undergoes frequent regressions.

[2] We may, without having the temerity to reject it, disregard Jung's collective unconscious, because its manifestations are too uncertain for safe recognition in specific cases, because it is too unequally distributed among the members of the human society, because its contents are not readily available for comparison with novel situations.

it must have been almost useless as a method for saving past experience from oblivion. Anyhow, occasions for taking non-habitual collective action must have been less frequent in primitive societies. Primitive men no doubt told their tale in verse, an elementary form of expression in which copious use is made of mnemotechnic devices like rhythm, rhyme, and assonance. They recited their epics, their legends, their sagas, sang songs in which tradition was mishandled, and allowed every liberty to the play-element which encouraged adornment and invention. Their tale satisfied family pride, local patriotism, and religiosity. Psychological motives such as a desire to improve upon the end of the narrative, to give it a sharp edge by introducing witty antitheses, encouraged further departures from fact.[1]

Gradually, and without interrupting the flow of epic and legend, prose came into its own. In prose form is not a dictator, it does not modify the material for its own end. The change must have occurred at a time when men were becoming aware that the narration of their past experiences had a social purpose and when they felt the need of improved methods for securing the assistance of the gods. As the narrative became utilitarian, it was entrusted to professional compilers. What they wrote was history. They were historians.[2]

In the classical world, the habit of noting down the experiences of societies was almost everywhere connected with ritual pre-occupations: the religion of Greeks and Romans was practical, and showed little concern with doctrine. The gods were jealous and irritable, they displayed no benevolence. The only way to conciliate them was to find the right formula, the precise gestures and words that gave them pleasure and compelled them to intervene in one's favour. This is why, at a time when the city was the largest homogeneous social unit, every city kept a book that was a ledger of transactions with the gods. Such rites were performed at such a moment, such were the results. Droughts,

[1] Cf. Bernheim, E., *Lehrbuch der Historischen Methode und der Geschichtsphilosophie* (1908), pp. 349 *sqq.*, 384 *sqq.*, 494 *sqq.* Bauer, Wilhelm, *Einfuehrung in das Studium der Geschichte* (1928), pp. 281–7.

[2] "L'objectif le plus immédiat de l'histoire est de sauver de l'oubli les faits du passé," Halphen, L., *Introduction à l'Histoire* (1946), p. 12.

earthquakes, plagues, sieges, victories and defeats were noted, and the efficacy of any formula would jump to the eye.[1] Beliefs being what they were, it was considered essential that the notes should be complete and accurate.

Utilitarian history, as I have already mentioned, did not put an end to poetic history. But it gave rise to a new form of history, in which the concern with accuracy became united with the pleasure taken in knowing the past and recounting it. Professional historians like Herodotus, less single-minded than the ritual annalists, made their appearance. As time went on, the minds of men acquired greater suppleness and penetration; men's interests grew wider, the range of their curiosity increased, and the past experiences they narrated became more varied. Histories appeared that were more complex and more intelligent. Let us not conclude from this that the nature of history changed. Different witnesses in a court of law tell their story differently; the policeman is stereotyped and ritualistic, the educated witness is more personal, the cultured witness, in countries where the rules of evidence permit, can throw light upon motive. Nevertheless the substance of their testimony is, as a rule, the same.

The historians' concern for accuracy satisfied itself for ages by the taking of elementary precautions, and centuries passed before the idea was born that the evidence upon which their narrative was based must be subjected to methodical probing. The system which has become known as the historical method was not invented by historians. They learned it from the philologists who evolved their critical rules at the time of the Renaissance for the purpose of dealing with classical and sacred texts. The historical method, first formulated by the learned French Benedictines of the seventeenth century, made immense progress in the nineteenth. Research has now become, not a science, but something that resembles it, something which the Finnish philosopher Grotenfelt once called "eine nicht ganz reine Wissenschaft." But even at this early stage we must for one moment interrupt our survey to formulate the vital principle that

---

[1] Bauer, *loc. cit.*, Bernheim, *op. cit.*, pp. 24–5. Fustel de Coulanges, *La Cité Antique* (1855), pp. 194–202. Some of the basic doctrines of this great book are out of date, but it is still a reliable guide on many subjects.

criticism or method is not history, but its servant, and that he who tells the story of the experiences of human societies or of human beings living in a society is an historian, whether he is critical or not. We must reject with the utmost emphasis views like those of Collingwood which can be held only if one excludes from the ranks of historians men of the calibre of Tacitus. There is good history and there is poor history, but even the worst history is history.

As the narrative, like the life of those who told it and of the societies that demanded it, grew more complicated, it became more blended with elements that were not purely narrative. At the same time the historian responded with increasing readiness to society's urgent demand for specific points of comparison taken from past experience. These developments had a considerable effect upon the nature of the historical narrative. For one thing, they increased the extent to which non-narrative elements became mixed with the narrative. We must realize, of course, that the notion of "pure narrative" is self-contradictory. Even in the days when men first left the uncritical stage of epic story-telling, and liberated the historical narrative from the play-element and the satisfaction of rudimentary cravings, they were unable to cleanse it from subjectiveness. For the barest statement of fact implies the expression of a view about that fact, a statement of theory.[1] Whenever we make an assertion, we say something about the nature of a person or a thing, in other words, something about its relations to other things. If we call a man a hero—as Alfred Sidgwick remarks[2]—we mean that he may be expected to act heroically. This is a statement which implies a belief in causation. For "predicates are shorthand registers of causal assertions." We shall say more about causation at a later stage. What matters at present is that the most innocent statement, ventured in its right place in the chronological sequence, contains implications which go far beyond narrative in its bald, common-sense acceptation. Any narrative, every narrative,

---

[1] Sidgwick, A., *The Use of Words in Reasoning* (1901), pp. 205–14.

[2] *Distinction*, pp. 198–9. "All intelligent observation contains an attempt to explain the observed phenomena, . . . all explanation involves generalization" (Sidgwick, *The Process of Argument* (1893), p. 103).

implies explanation, a reference to causes, motives, effects and results. To say that a narrative of past experience is needed implies that there will also be an explanation.

This mixture of explanation and narrative will be found in the plainest fairy-tale. "And because the wicked fairy resented the fact that she had not been invited, she said . . ." Now, obviously, in noting this essential characteristic of the story we do not adopt the view that a story is told for the sake of the explanations it contains.[1] Nor are explanations what society asks from the historian; it requires from him a statement, as accurate as possible, of the facts of past experience. If the historian cannot fulfil his task without giving explanations in the same breath no one will mind. Nor will he be deemed guilty of neglecting his social task if the nature of his explanation is less convincing, less compelling, than the facts of which his narrative is composed.[2] My butter is rolled into lumps or shaped into discs, it may form a cube, a parallelepiped, or a cylinder; but what I want is the chemically describable mixture of substances that goes by the name of butter, although I have the right to prefer one rather than the other shapes in which my dairyman can present it.

The confusion between unavoidable explanation and indispensable narrative is closely connected with another equally natural terminological confusion between generalizing and theorizing. Every story-teller generalizes. He narrates occurrences, i.e. things that have happened. But the plainest occurrence is really a series of simpler occurrences.[3] Napoleon lost the battle of Waterloo: what a collection of occurrences, psychological, ballistical, tactical, strategical, logistical, is summarized in this

---

[1] As is asserted by so many theorists who suffer from what Sidgwick calls "the logical mentality which delights in pushing to the extreme" (*Fallacies*, p. 103).

[2] "As soon as a fact is named or described, or conceived in this or that way, it is seen in the light of theory, and theory may be mistaken" (Sidgwick, *Process of Argument*, p. 15). Collingwood, for one, believes that the historian's task is to show how the present has come into existence (*The Idea of History*, p. 104). Anyhow, I can for once quote Hegel with approval: "das Denken können wir aber einmal nicht unterlassen" (*Philosophie der Geschichte*, Einleitung, c.). Halphen considers that the least philosophical history is still, and of necessity, explanatory, because if it is not it becomes "une informe compilation" (*op. cit.*, pp. 15–16).

[3] Sidgwick, *The Process of Argument*, pp. 114–15. For a distinction between occurrence and event, see below, II: i: § 2.

generalization! "The company director lit a cigar." This implies that he helped himself to a cigar, bit off the tip, or cut it off, or merely punched it; he struck a match (or a lighter) or somebody offered him a light; he puffed several times, and uttered a little sigh of pleasure as he took out the cigar and looked at its farther end; meanwhile, he expelled several distinct clouds of smoke. The narrative would never reach its end if it had to enter into these details, every single one of which can in turn be analysed into further details. On a larger scale we can say: "The early Georges made use of their position as kings of Great Britain to further their ambitions as electors of Hanover." This generalization is still a statement of fact. It is neither the formulation of a "law" nor the expression of a philosophy of life.

Every narrative knows two *tempi*. At times it moves rapidly, states as little as possible apart from the events it has to recount, and comes nearest to the theoretical form of narrative, the skeleton of which is chronological: "then, then, afterwards, meanwhile." This is the kinetic aspect of history. Sometimes it becomes necessary to slacken the speed, and the narrative becomes almost, or entirely, descriptive and static. When all these elements are present we have a story. The purely kinetic portion of the story is a narrative. One speaks of a bald narrative, not of a bald story.

The story, as we know, plays in the behaviour of societies the part played by memory in the behaviour of individuals. Figuratively speaking one can therefore call history the memory of societies. A recent Dutch writer denies this, and says that history is not memory (*geheugen*), but recollection (*herinnering*). Memory is comprehensive, recollection is constructive; memory is a museum, recollection is the discerning visitor who knows what to look at, what to pass by. This author forgets that memory is itself selective, but this is not relevant. The historian's task is to preserve. It must be left to other agents to make use of the material collected and presented by him. The confusion is one of the many that result from attempts to saddle history with tasks that are not its own.[1]

[1] Schilfgaarde, P. van, *De Zin der Geschiedenis* (1946), Vol. I, pp. 82–91. For the same reason we should reject Schopenhauer's view that history is the intelligent

The practical problems that face any society change constantly. Novel situations have to be coped with, different indications will be required, new kinds of guidance from the collective past will be needed, and historians will have to retell the story from a new point of view. They will have to look more closely at certain aspects of the past which previous generations could afford to neglect, while past occurrences that fascinated and preoccupied their ancestors appear to them fairly, or entirely, irrelevant. When noblemen mattered in the life of communities, whose professional defenders and rulers they were, when noblemen based their claims to pre-eminence upon the purity of their blood and lineage, the marriages and family fortunes of noblemen loomed large in the stories which men thought it worth their while to learn and to retail. Now genealogy is a modest and subsidiary ancillary discipline of history, and our interests are focused in other directions.

Sometimes the story, refocused under the influence of new preoccupations, demands new investigation and gains greatly in accuracy as a result. Arthurian legends formed part of the dynastic propaganda of Henry VII, and at the beginning of the seventeenth century learned people in England still generally believed in the historicity of Brute, ancestor of the Britons, and in the Trojan origin of their dynasty. Camden was careful not to reject this tradition too openly; Selden would appear still to have accepted it. But during the reign of James II the rising opposition to absolutism encouraged writers to apply their critical sense to the demolition of these legends.[1] The experiences of the Dutch during the occupation of their country by the Nazis caused them to take a totally different view from that prevalent till then of

---

self-consciousness of mankind (quoted Bernheim. *op. cit.*, p. 172) or Droysen's similar opinion that history is "das Wissen der Menschheit von sich, ihre Selbstgewissheit" (quoted Bauer, *op. cit.*, p. 18). Just as in the individual there can be no consciousness without memory, so there can be no social consciousness without the historical awareness of past experiences. But one should never look for a complicated explanation where a simpler one is adequate. This is an elementary rule of methodology.

[1] Bush, D., *English Literature in the Earlier Seventeenth Century* (1945), pp. 214–15.

the French occupation between 1795 and 1813.[1] We can follow, through the nineteenth century, the parallelism between national-istic, institutional and social preoccupations on the one hand and the rise of history in the manner of Thierry, Hallam, Schmoller—to take but three instances out of the many tendencies and schools that were prominent in that century. "Every age has its own particular conception of the essence and of the tasks of history," says Bauer.[2]

How actually does society turn to the historian and ask him for the information it requires? It stands to reason that there can be no exact reproduction of the process by which the individual on certain occasions "stops to think" and becomes the immediate recipient of a parcel of recollections despatched by his memory, takes his decision, and acts upon it. For, as I have observed, social activities have a way of looking after themselves, and the indi-vidual is usually unconscious of the fact that he is serving society while he is following his own inclination. What happens is that, as a social being, not as an historian, the historian becomes conscious of numerous issues that face the society to which he belongs. While reading his newspapers, conversing with his friends, in his contacts with colleagues in the common room of his college, in carrying out his duties as a citizen, he acquires interests and curiosities. They guide him when he chooses the subject into which he will research till he is ready to compose a story based upon his discoveries. While he works, questions will arise in his mind—and again, these questions express his preoccupations as a member rather than as a servant of the community—which will determine the detail of his work. His story will therefore become a series of answers to questions in which society asks for guidance. In his autobiography Colling-wood turns this system of question and answer into a veritable philosophy of knowledge.[3] He may be right, but we must

[1] When men in the Low Countries became less certain that God created the Netherlands Dutch and Belgian, Geyl retold the history of these countries in a way that made clear the unity of their origin and the accidental way of their separation. See his *Revolt of the Netherlands* (1934) and my *Criterion of Dutch Nationhood* (1946). [2] *Op. cit.*, p. 17.

[3] *An Autobiography* (1939), chapter V. I have been assured by archaeologists that the subject to which Collingwood devoted his attention happened to lend

remember that, so far, we have learned to know history as an activity based upon knowledge, and not as a form of knowledge.

§ 3

THE COLLECTIVE PAST AND THE HUMAN INDIVIDUAL

The assertion that in telling his story the historian is in the first place a social agent does not meet with ready reception, least of all among historians. Some people show a justifiable distrust of the Spenglerian doctrine which debases history to the role of a servant of politics, and is an easy preliminary to the contempt for intellectual independence common to fascists and communists.[1] They ought to realize that honest social service belongs to a different category; those who perform it are not precluded from following the argument whichever way it leads them. Others refuse to admit that history performs a social task because they are idealists who hate the thought that their discipline should be cultivated for utilitarian ends. They serve history as a lofty mistress, and wish to pursue knowledge for its own sake. They may, with Halphen, call the purpose of history: "expliquer les faits dont nous sommes témoins,"[2] or they may think with R. C. K. Ensor that "the fascination of history is that it tells you (or should tell you), how in the world of fact things actually did come about."[3] They are, among humanists, what the advocates of the theory of art for art's sake are among the artists.

The slogan *l'art pour l'art* admirably formulates what should be the individual artist's ideal. He makes his contribution to society by providing it with beautiful things that will ennoble the minds of his contemporaries. This service, like other social actions—as I have already pointed out—is performed unin-

itself most particularly to his epistemological method, and that he might have been less successful with it in other fields. Collingwood did, of course, not invent the method of question and answer. Fustel de Coulanges advocated it in 1885.

[1] "Historical science will only then satisfactorily perform its task as the servant of politics, when it takes into account the demands which politics make upon it." E. Otto, "*Het Gevaar der Historische Vergelijking,*" in *Nederland,* a Nazi review published during World War II in Holland (August 1943).   [2] *Op. cit.,* p. 7.
[3] *Why we Study History* (Historical Association Publication 131, 1944), p. 3.

tentionally. A conscious attempt to formulate or to illustrate social conceptions through the medium of art will lower the quality of the artist's work. Mr. I. A. Richards takes the same view when he says in his *Principles of Literary Criticism* that "the arts are the supreme form of communicative activity," but that "the artist is entirely justified in his apparent neglect of the main purpose of his work."[1] Like the artist, the historian can serve society while remaining single-minded in his concern with his subject. John Dewey considers that this is the case for every intellectual discipline: it is "instrumental in function," and at the same time "an enjoyed object to those concerned in it."[2]

Another pragmatist philosopher, F. C. S. Schiller, would show less tolerance towards the single-minded priest of Clio. "The attitude described as 'dispassionate' enquiry," he writes, "is really one of high internal tension, and, when we look closely into it, the profession of dispassionate neutrality towards vital problems always turns out to be a cloak for a lurking interest that is ashamed of the light of day."[3] Schiller was a crotchety gentleman. We may concede to him, however, that the quest for pure knowledge is sometimes less pure than those engaged in it would like to believe, and that it is not free from a stiff admixture of pride.[4]

Some of the great historians of a previous generation had no hesitation in confessing that they worked because they loved their work. Henri Pirenne wrote in 1897 that history is as ancient as poetry, and, like poetry, corresponds to a need in our nature—"un besoin dans notre nature"[5]—and the Leyden Professor Bussemaker declared in his inaugural lecture that history fulfils an undeniable need.[6] It would be difficult to deny that a knowledge of the past satisfies some of our profoundest longings. May we not trust life sufficiently to admit that it is good for men

[1] 1934, pp. 29 and 32.   [2] *Science and Experience*, pp. 204–5.
[3] *Logic for Use*, p. 355. See also his *Must Philosophers Disagree?* pp. 174–5.
[4] I prefer the frank confession of V. H. Galbraith, who wrote, in *Why we Study History*, p. 7: "The study of history is a personal matter, in which the activity is generally more valuable than the result." A hedonistic doctrine, and somewhat *fin de siècle* for the 1940's.   [5] *Revue Historique*, 1897, p. 51.
[6] *Over de Waardeering der Feiten in Geschiedvorsching en Geschiedschrijving* (1905), p. 35.

to have their own way, if they harm no one in the process? Yet, as soon as we venture into a serious explanation of the psychological grounds of this love of the past, we meet with disapproval on the part of practising historians.[1] Is their reluctance as wholesome as they would like to make themselves believe? I shall make use of a few Freudian categories in the following pages. They are descriptive of certain tendencies that lurk within all of us, and can be used even by those who prefer to reject the Freudian explanation of their origin.[2]

Writing about Rousseau, Hazlitt says that "he seems to gather up the past moments of his being like drops of honey-dew, to distil a precious liquor from them," and he calls this "the greatest charm of the *Confessions*."[3] All men take an interest in their own past, and like to recall it, even if they do so less skilfully than Rousseau. When this interest is excessive it is accompanied by other pathological symptoms and is called narcissism. But even the so-called normal will recognize within themselves the operation of narcistic longings for the resurrection of their past experiences. Who has not sniffed the smell of a late-autumn bonfire in an urban park and known a wistful but acute recall of the bonfires of childhood? From this there is but one step to the birth of an interest in the larger past in which our own is embedded. Monuments, customs, and institutions among which we live belong to our extended self, and they are our contact with the collective past. We are, all of us, unconscious *unanimistes* of the school of Jules Romains—I think particularly of *La Mort de quelqu'un*, *Les Copains*, *Poèmes unanimistes*, and of his other works dating before the famous series in which his doctrines are raised to the level of a sociological theory, *Les Hommes de bonne Volonté*. Our beings throw out tendrils in complicated ramifications, not only into space, but into time.[4] All past

[1] One can admire the work of Marx without being a Marxist, and one need not be a blind follower of Freud to recognize the greatness of his mind. The most remarkable aspect of modern psychological practice is entirely ignored by its detractors: it is invariably on the side of respectability and self-control, and is thoroughly ethical.

[2] See my paper on "History and Ourselves," in *Economica* (November, 1948).

[3] *Essay* "On the Past and Future."

[4] Laurence Sterne formulated the theory of the individual's "circle of importance" in 1759, in *Tristram Shandy*, I, 13, para. 2.

is my past, and I want to recapture it for my own satisfaction. Here is the real meaning of Croce's "all history is contemporary history," not metaphysical, but psychological. The narcistic component of our soul complacently looks at itself in the course of what it considers to be an objective quest for truth.

The anxious treasuring of past personal experience as a precious component of the beloved self, and the way in which it grows into something wider, receives a fine illustration in the work of Marcel Proust. While tasting a tea-soaked sponge cake Proust has recaptured dormant sensations which send him out "à la recherche du temps perdu." He feels that experiences through which he has passed, which have made him what he is, still belong to him, and can be resurrected by the use of associations with present sensations. In looking for his own past he becomes absorbed in the past of a social group to which he belongs, or in which, at any rate, he moves. Being a pessimist, he sees in "le temps retrouvé" nothing but faded gilt, decay, mortality. But this matters little to us. What matters to us in Proust is his quest, which is the quest of all of us. Its result is a highly individual work of art, but the longing that inspired it is universal.

Those who turn to the human past as it may be supposed to have occurred, to the contents of the historian's story, extract from it pleasures of great diversity. The personages in Hans Heinz Ewers's novels and short stories, *Nachtmahr*, *Vampir*, etc., seek in the contemplation of the past the satisfaction of cravings that lie beyond the borderline of sanity. One meets these cravings in milder forms, and I have diagnosed them in gentle-minded people who would shudder at the thought of actually sharing the delights of a degenerate King of Spain witnessing from his balcony the burning of a wretched heretic, but who are prepared, from their lofty seat in present-day England, to day-dream without moral disapproval about the Inquisition, about the tortures inflicted upon Catholics by the Dutch Beggars in 1575, or about the writhings of John Foxe's martyrs.

Even where there is no such mental satisfaction of the secret weakness known to psychologists by the name of algolagnia, visits to the past are often what Petrarch describes as *iniqui temporis oblivio*, psychologists as "fugues," and ordinary people

30

as "escapism." Now the fugue satisfies a profound need in us, a need which becomes dangerous only when it is excessive and results from an unmistakable arrest in our psychological development! The most startling experience in every human life is birth, the emergence, in the most frightening manner conceivable, from the safety of the maternal womb into the inhospitable and hostile world of individual existence. It is no exaggeration to say that every human being harbours a secret longing to return to the pristine foetal state. In its diseased form this longing becomes a death-wish. In ordinary life it manifests itself in scores of ways, of which the fugue or escape from practical and present-day life is the only one that interests us here. All this is well-known to the practical psychologist. I think this doctrine is Freud's greatest contribution to human knowledge,[1] although, for the peace of mind of those who dislike him, I may recall that it has been described, long before Freud thought of it, by the English author Samuel Butler.[2]

Where is the distinction between the permissible and the dangerous, the wholesome and the morbid, in these matters? It is indicated by the way in which the individual who seeks relief is affected by his escape into the past. If it keeps him imprisoned in an ivory tower and makes him a stranger in his own world, it is bad. That from which he returns invigorated and ready to face his own period and to perform what he conceives to be his duty is a legitimate holiday. It answers to the requirement formulated by Dewey: "Piety to the past is not for its own sake nor for the sake of the past, but for the sake of a present so secure and enriched, that it will create a better future."[3]

"A need in our nature," said Pirenne. There are other needs

---

[1] Freud, S., *Jenseits des Lustprinzips*, is the first formulation of a doctrine which was later elaborated and perfected, i.a. in his *Inhibition, Symptoms and Anxiety* (1927), cf. Rank, Otto, *The Trauma of Birth* (1929).

[2] "The agony and settled melancholy with which unborn children regard birth as the extinction of their being," *Note Book I*, p. 289. "Birth and death are functions of one another," *ibid.*, pp. 15–16. Embryos fearing life as we fear death, *Note Book II*, p. 100; "a man's pre-natal accidents are more important to him than his post-natal," *ibid.*, p. 108, also p. 190. The shock of birth and death, *ibid.*, pp. 188–90. See also *Erewhon* on "The World of the Unborn." These notes were written in the 1870's and 1880's.

[3] *Human Nature and Conduct, an Introduction to Social Psychology* (1922), p. 21.

that can be most usefully canalized to the great benefit of our souls into the social service called history. One of the most frequent symptoms of arrested psychological growth is the complex which makes men excessively tidy and great lovers of worldly goods. Chemistry, with its concern for precise weighing and measuring, offers an excellent chance of "sublimation" for this deviation. Collecting, a useful occupation in the young, presents the grown-up with another safety valve. What form of collecting could be more useful socially than the bringing together of manuscripts, archaeological remains, or card-indexes, and the methodical arrangement of these objects, which accompanies the historian's preliminary research? It is preferable to the collecting of match-box labels or of company directorships.

To close without exhausting it the list of impulses satisfied by the study of the past I shall mention men's universal concern with other men. History is the story of human beings, and nothing else. "Nur der Mensch ist Objekt der Geschichtswissenschaft," says Bernheim. The deeper our human understanding, the better our history; the broader our historical knowledge, the richer our psychological insight.

Chapter II

NOTHING BUT A STORY

THE reader of the previous chapter may not find it impossible to accept my submission that the story of the experiences of men living in societies is what we call history. Will he also agree with the converse proposition that history is the story of the experiences of men living in societies? The conversion of subject and predicate is a risky manipulation.[1] It can, at most, provide us with an hypothesis that has still to be made plausible through further investigation. This is what I shall now attempt, while trying to work out a definition of the word history.

§ 1

A DEFINITION

Scientists, I have often noticed, fight shy of definitions. If not actually trained in the deadly formal logic of the schools, they have heard its echoes, and are under the misapprehension that a definition is a verbal operation used for the purpose of capturing the "essence" of the thing defined. At the same time the experience acquired through the practice of their craft has warned them that "essence" may well be a pretentious synonym for "appearance." Actually, definition is merely an instrument for use in discussions.[2] If properly formulated, it can become an efficient tool for clear thinking. No definition can be final, no definition can avoid making use of terms not yet defined. Definition is a pair of pins which people prick into a map to mark the beginning and the end of the road they can agree to follow together. Scientists should not be afraid of little pins with

[1] Schiller, Formal Logic (1931), pp. 161–2.
[2] Schiller, Logic for Use, pp. 19–20. "To render its subject more familiar is the first business of definition," ibid., p. 22. Cf. also Schiller, Our Human Truths, p. 342. A definition should be "flexible, corrigible, relative . . . and never for show" (Schiller, Formal Logic, p. 72). Cf. also Ogden and Richards, The Meaning of Meaning (1923), p. 209: "All definitions are essentially ad hoc" and "the ability to frame definitions comes for most people only with practice" (p. 243).

coloured heads. It would be absurd to perpetuate our methodological Babel through fear of so unpretentious and innocuous
a gadget.

Our definition should lend itself to frequent use, and this will
be easier if it is simple and unambitious. Purpose should not be
mentioned in it, and controversial matter as little as possible.
In defining history we must guard against pandering to the
inclination of certain professionals to exclude from the ranks
of historians people whose outlook, personality, or style of
writing they dislike. Indeed, we must agree with the remark of
the historian Firth that "history is not easy to define."[1]

A definition must not be too ambitious: the next section of
this chapter will deal with attempts to turn history into a universal
philosophy of life. This is one of the main dangers that beset our
discipline. There exists another danger, which comes from those
who want to degrade history to the mere collecting of past
events. A further section of this chapter will be devoted to the
discussion of their nefarious attempt to ignore the social function
of history. In adopting a position between these two extremes,
in stating that history is a story, nothing more and nothing
less, I have reached one of the points in my survey where some
readers must part company with me. They can quote authority
in support of their own views. It will be found, however, that
definitions offered by the supporters of the broader view suffer
from obscurity and unwieldiness, and from all the sins a work-
manlike and pragmatist definition tries to avoid. As for the
supporters of the narrower view, their lack of social awareness
makes them an anachronism in the tragic, titanic age in which
we live.

The knowledge that history is a story was revealed to me by
Henri Pirenne, who was not only a great historian but a giant
among teachers. In his class on "The Encyclopaedia of Medieval
History," he liked to practise the maieutic art of Socrates. "What
is history?" he asked one day. I replied—for I was a raw youth:

[1] Quoted in Williams, C. H., *The Modern Historian* (1938), p. 4. As a warning
to ambitious historians who wish to annex the universe to their discipline I reproduce at the end of this volume two definitions of history by great German
theorists, Bernheim and Bauer, and I give them in their untranslatable original.

"The study of the development of mankind."—"Et la philosophie de l'histoire, qu'en faites-vous?" he barked. Keeping
only my word "mankind," he coaxed us into constructing the
definition he had in mind. "L'histoire est le récit des faits et
gestes des hommes en tant que vivant en société—history is the
story of the deeds and achievements of men living in societies."[1]
With minor modifications it is still the definition to which I
adhere.

The definition of history as a story could be justified by an
impressive array of authorities. I shall mention one or two not
so much as an argument than as social credentials for Pirenne
and myself. "L'histoire est le récit des choses dignes de mémoire,"
says the dictionary of the French Academy. G. M. Trevelyan
says that the historian's first duty is "to tell the story," and that
"history is, in its unchangeable essence, a 'tale'."[2] Taine, a great
brewer of generalizations, whom no one could accuse of indifference to ideas, wrote: "Pour que l'oeuvre soit vivante comme
la nature, il faut que, comme la nature, elle ne comprenne que
des événements et des actions"; he became more explicit even,
and added: "N'oublions pas que l'histoire est surtout une narration."[3] F. S. Oliver abounds in my sense; not only does he want
the historian "to tell his story straightwise," but he also asks
him "not to cumber it with preachings and moralizings of his
own." He instructs him to "eschew argument."[4] The Dutch
historian Huizinga admits that the most current meaning attached
to the word "history" (*geschiedenis*) is "the story of something
that has happened," and G. N. Clark, who will not admit that
history is a story, goes a long way, nevertheless, in the right
direction.[5] Even Croce distinguishes between *la storia* and *la*

---

[1] *Encyclopédie de l'Histoire du Moyen Age*, Lecture notes, unpublished.

[2] Quoted in Williams, *op. cit.*, pp. 56–7.

[3] *Essai sur Tite-Live* (1855), pp. 355–6. Raymond Aron, in *Philosophie de
l'Histoire* (1938) is even more positive in his rejection of the over-ambitious
definition: "La sociologie se caractérise par l'effort pour établir des lois (ou du
moins des régularités ou des généralités) alors que l'histoire se borne à raconter
des événements dans leur suite singulière" (p. 190: see also p. 142).

[4] *The Endless Adventure*, Vol. III (1935), pp. 3–17.

[5] Huizinga, J., *Over een Definitie van het Begrip Geschiedenis*, Royal Academy of
Amsterdam, Lit., 68, B, 2 (1929). He says that "history is the spiritual form in
which a civilization gives to itself an account of its past," and this, of course, is

dissertatione o il ragionamento storico.[1] These references and quotations are, as I said, not intended as arguments in support of my thesis. The argument is provided by the fact that if history is less than a story it cannot fulfil its social function, while if it is more it competes unnecessarily with other disciplines, speaks in an uncertain voice, and brings confusion rather than guidance.

It is with an eye to the social function of history that instead of Pirenne's "faits et gestes—deeds and achievements," we shall say that history is the story of the experiences of men. These experiences are, of course, passive as well as active; men require a knowledge of what life has done to them, as much as they must know what they themselves did when faced with certain situations. We shall also accept Pirenne's view that history is concerned with men "living in societies" only.[2] But has this qualification much practical importance? It means that, in theory, a human being living entirely by himself is of no interest to the historian. Did Robinson Crusoe on his island before the arrival of Man Friday stay outside history? Only if no traces of his sojourn had ever been found, if his life on the island had not been conditioned by his previous experiences as a social being. It can be argued that a biography contains elements that cannot be described as experiences of men living in societies. But do even those who live in the ivory tower, like Gauguin, those who would have liked to pretend they did, like Oscar Wilde during some stages of his career, present in their personality facets that are genuinely non-social? Do they not all their life undergo social influences and exercise some? Statesmen and reformers obviously belong to history, but might certain aspects of their existence, their sex-life, for instance, be ignored as irrelevant to history? Can anything that ever happened to a man who played a public

not a rejection of the definition of history as a story. See also Huizinga's conception of history in *De Wetenschap der Geschiedenis*, pp. 33–4. Clark, G. N., *Historical Scholarship and Historical Thought* (1944), says of history: "Narrative is its characteristic instrument; there is no kind of historical method into which narrative does not enter as a component, and every good historian is something of a story-teller" (pp. 20–1).   [1] *Il Concetto della Storia* (1896), p. 45.

     [2] Acton says: "History is a generalized account of the personal actions of men, united in bodies for any public purposes whatever," *Historical Essays and Studies*, p. 305.

part be said not to have influenced the performance of that part? It will be wise to admit that, in all its aspects, biography belongs to history.

What shall we say of the story of the arts? The fact that economic circumstances brought about the production of such large numbers of paintings in the Dutch Republic during the seventeenth century obviously belongs to history. But one might argue that the influence exercised by Van Goyen upon the treatment of landscape by his son-in-law Jan Steen does not interest the historian.[1] Dante belongs to history. His Divine Comedy expresses the plaint of Christendom deprived of its law and deprived of a head. But the slow formation of his genius, his suffering from love, his way of handling his material, can be neglected by the historian, and left to the student of literature.[2] In the history of literature judgments of value are not an adventitious matter, as in ordinary history: the passing of aesthetic judgments belongs to the essential tasks of the historian of literature. Some aspects of sport offer us a better illustration of past experiences that do not belong to history. The ever-unpredictable R. G. Collingwood wrote that "to know who played centre-forward for Aston Villa last year is just as much historical knowledge as to know who won the battle of Cannae."[3] I find it difficult to agree; this piece of information seems to me to be no more concerned with the experiences of men living in societies than the development of headplay or the rise and decline of the off-side rule in Association football. Now shares in football clubs as an investment, or the fact that in England sport, for most people, means looking on, while play is for a small minority only, the social and economic influence of football pools in the 1930's and 1940's, or the fairly recent date at which sports appeared as a dominant feature in English public schools—these, it seems to me, are events which historians cannot ignore.[4]

One restrictive qualification must be added to Pirenne's

[1] Renier, G. J., *The Dutch Nation* (1944), pp. 94–100.

[2] See Renaudet, in *La Fin du Moyen Age*, Vol. VIII of "Peuples et Civilisations," p. 252.

[3] *The Philosophy of History*, an Historical Association Leaflet, No. 79 (1930), p. 4.   [4] Renier, G. J., *The English: are they Human?* (1931), *passim*.

definition. Men have lived in societies ever since they were men. Their ancestors were social beings. The life of *homo sapiens* is said to have covered 300,000 years so far. During most of that time, however, the societies to which men belonged were not sufficiently differentiated for their experiences to lend themselves to historical narrative. Other methods are required to deal with them. Events that took place during all but the end of that time are detected in a manner very different from the way in which events that appear in ordinary history are found out. The subject had therefore better be left to the discipline known as pre-history, while history proper deals with those men only who lived in societies that were civilized. The word civilized is used here in a non-committal way; it suggests without pedantic insistence that, for better or for worse, states had emerged, and that the period covered begins some 6,000 or 7,000 years ago.[1]

We have now worked out the following definition of history: it is the story of the experiences of men living in civilized societies. One further remark about the word "story," which occupies such a prominent position in our definition. We saw in the previous chapter that every story contains an admixture of theory and of preconceived notions. Narrative is like gold: it can be used only in the form of an alloy. To say this does not imply that the additional element which turns the narrative into a story contributes to the performance of its major or social function, or that it is actually the more important part of the story. The historian, as we shall see in the next section, is not entrusted with the task of explaining the past. But to tell the story as it should be told he must understand the events he narrates; he must be able to explain them to his own satisfaction. A bare knowledge of the events of Napoleon's life is insufficient for the purpose of the historian. He must also know the place of these events in Napoleon's life, and their effect upon other events.

[1] Bernheim considers that pre-history belongs to history, but he agrees that for practical reasons it must be left to its own specialists (*op. cit.*, pp. 46–7). Those who are satisfied that the past presents a picture of continued progress, the Marxists, for instance, with their insistence upon the part played by technology, will not attach great importance to the appearance of states, and will wish to begin history much earlier than is here suggested. For a moderate and reasonable presentation of the Marxist case see Gordon Childe's short book, *History* (1947).

Why did Napoleon order the murder of the Duke of Enghien? At what time can he be said to have begun working at his own downfall? When did he reach the zenith of his career? I think it was when he signed the Peace of Amiens, but others say it was during the glorious days of Tilsit, in 1807. There is the question whether, as Sorel believes, Napoleon's foreign policy was a continuation of that of the French Revolution, or whether, as Holland Rose affirms, there is a complete break between the two. It is impossible to tell a satisfying story if one has not honestly made up one's mind about points such as these. Also, like any story, that told by the historian can be static (Vol. I of Sorel's *L'Europe et la Révolution française*, or Vol. I of Halévy's *Histoire du Peuple anglais au XIXe Siècle*), or kinetic, like the other volumes of these two works.

§ 2

METAPHYSICS AND CLAIRVOYANCE

Like Maximilien de Robespierre and Joseph Stalin, history has its right deviationists and its left deviationists, but, being liberal, it does not liquidate them. The enemies on the right wish to reduce the historian's task to the gathering of facts; a section of this chapter will be devoted to them. Meanwhile, we shall deal with the extremists on the left, those who try to burden history with the problems of the universe.[1] Pirenne has warned us against the danger of making a confusion between history and sociology, and of drowning history in sociology.[2] "La philosophie et la morale ne sont point les parties essentielles de l'art de l'historien," said Anatole France, who meditated all his life upon the problems of history.[3] The much quoted German philosopher, Wilhelm Dilthey (1833–1911) attributes a purpose to historical study, which is "to come to know scientifically and methodically what in art we understand imagi-

---

[1] Haec decies repetita placebit (Horace, *Ars Poetica*, v. 365). Even those readers who will not take so indulgent a view of my repetitiveness are asked to remember that I am a schoolmaster.

[2] "Une Polémique historique en Allemagne," in *Revue Historique* (1897), p. 56.

[3] Essay on "M. Thiers, Historien," in *La Vie Littéraire*, Vol. I, p. 244.

natively, the nature of the human mind."[1] The great Italian thinker Benedetto Croce says that philosophy and history are identical.[2] Why, in that case, not simplify our vocabulary? The Dutch theorist Van Schilfgaarde, who begins by admitting that history is a story, adds that it is a story with a meaning and a purpose, for it is the story "of a struggle between idea and chaos," it is "the revelation of righteousness."[3] And thereby history becomes annexed to a system of metaphysics. But metaphysics, as Anatole France remarks in *Le Jardin d'Epicure* (1894), has no substance. Its name, "after-physics," is due to the fact that in a famous ancient encyclopaedia it was dealt with immediately after the section devoted to physics. It consists of methodical musings about essence, being, and the absolute. Its devotees tend to endow with reality the abstract terms that are the playful inventions of language.

Let us explore the mentality that refuses to distinguish between history and philosophy, as it reveals itself in the work of its most distinguished British exponent, the late R. G. Collingwood, who, by his own admission, identified "the idea of history" with "the idea of spiritual life or process."[4] We shall naturally pay special attention to his book *The Idea of History*, published posthumously in 1946, but we must remember the existence of finer productions like *The Idea of Nature* (1945), also posthumous, but somehow not so deplorably unfinished as the other work, as well as his *Autobiography* (1939) and his *Roman Britain and the English Settlements* (1937). These are the books by which he deserves to be judged. Unhappily, the dimensions of *The Idea of History*, which has to be isolated for the purpose of the present survey, are less than those of the mind which produced it. Even so, this book contains the finest attempt at a synthesis in the field of historical methodology produced by an English writer. Collingwood possessed intellectual courage, the kind of courage that allows a man to change his mind, and he had the privilege of working in a university where the minds of men are not crushed.

[1] Hodges, H. A., *Wilhelm Dilthey, an Introduction* (1944), p. 32.

[2] *Theory and History of Historiography*, p. 61.

[3] *De Zin der Geschiedenis*, Vol. I, pp. 303-4. See my review in *History* (February–June 1948, pp. 129-30).   [4] *The Idea of History*, p. 184.

His work sets high standards of value, and though I consider his conception of history to be dangerous, and differ from him in most respects, I look upon him as a fine thinker and a writer of sound English prose.

It will be necessary in the first place to say a few words about two authors to whom Collingwood owes much and perhaps too much: Croce and Oakeshott. Croce is another of those authors who, like Dilthey, are quoted more often than read. His Italian is very difficult, and the English translations of his work are atrocious. Moreover, an attempt to formulate his doctrines is like an effort to embrace Proteus.[1] Croce is too vital and nimble to become the life-long servant of a formula. But he *is* devoted to an attitude. And he is condemned, by the accident of his birth, to use a language which lends itself somewhat easily to rhetoric. There is nothing out-of-the-way in some of his statements. "History separated from the living document and turned into chronicle," he says, "is no longer a spiritual act, but a thing, a complex of sounds and other things. But the document also, when separated from life, is nothing but a thing like another, a complex of sounds or of other things."[2] Could one not paraphrase this passage in these words: do not write history without using documents, or you will produce hot air; do not use documents without interpreting them intelligently and imaginatively, or you will produce something even worse? What doctrine could be sounder? But Croce's attitude is one of undue emphasis upon the second proposition. He advocates the imaginative approach till he creates the impression that he believes in nothing else. "The deed of which the history is told must vibrate in the soul of the historian." Is not Croce advising the historian to go into a trance and to live through the deed that has to be recounted, and does he not promise secure knowledge as a reward? "How could that which is a present producing of our spirit ever be uncertain?" he asks.

Once we fail to distinguish between the historical narrative

---

[1] Who constantly changed his shape. The comparison falls to pieces when we remember that although Proteus knew all things past, present and future, he was loath to tell what he knew.

[2] *Op. cit.*, pp. 20–1.

41

and its factual content, and delight in the linguistic accident which has caused men to call both by the name of history,[1] we are easily led to the Crocean identification between past and present, and we lay ourselves open to the influence of fairy-tales about a four-dimensional world in which past history can be influenced by those who contemplate it from the observation post that is called the present. I do not accuse Croce of having told such stories, but of wearing a mantle under which aberrations of that kind can find refuge. The alliance between philosophical idealism and history advocated by him leads to the verbiage and verbalism we meet in the work of my compatriot Van Schilf-gaarde, and in the lucubrations of Eric Dardel, in *L'Histoire Science du Concret*. In this stimulating but exasperating little book which is continually on the verge of saying something worth while, we meet statements like "il n'y a pas d'objet en soi, isolé du sujet qui l'objective" (p. 10), and "le préjugé moderne qui ne tient pour réel que l'objectif se traduit en histoire par une hyper-trophie des modes les plus extérieurs du devenir" (p. 11). What would become of the historical discipline if it were practised by people who genuinely held views of this nature? Dardel tells us that an historical understanding of the world corresponds to an identification of Being and Meaning (p. 19), and that this can be achieved by the judicious forgetting of facts which are not sig-nificant in themselves. To detect which facts possess this insig-nificance—do facts, then, exist after all?—we need *la rectitude du coeur* (p. 33). Although this dictum appeals to me, I think it leads to anarchism. And so, like Croce and the Croceans, Dardel advocates *l'histoire vécue*, history that has been lived. "If, from history conceived as an abstract construction, we return to history lived as a concrete presence in the world, at *this* moment and in *this* place, we witness a complete change in the light projected upon Being within the framework of time" (p. 57).

No doubt, as I have already attempted to do, the dicta of Croce and his devotees can be translated into ordinary language. In the process they become remarkably prosaic. But anyone who attempts to take them literally will be flying in the face of good sense. The Croceans try to turn the historian into a clairvoyant

---

[1] A discussion of this accident in the next chapter of this work.

or a traveller along a twisted time-stream where chronology is of no account.

Croceanism, as the perversions of the doctrine show, is a dangerous school. Collingwood was exposed to another danger; his personal predilection induced him to adopt a philosophic doctrine which led directly to the placing of certain recognized historians upon the index. This was the philosophy propounded by Mr. Michael B. Oakeshott, of Cambridge, whose book *Experience and its Modes* (1933) was called by Collingwood "the high water mark of English thought upon history."[1] I shall not attempt to summarize the doctrines of Mr. Oakeshott or to pass judgment upon their value; his idealistic philosophy makes him a citizen of a country where I could find no home. All I can do is to point to certain features of his doctrine which have particularly impressed themselves upon Collingwood's mind. Meanwhile I confess that I like *Experience and Its Modes*, even if it were only because its author asks history to give him "a narration of a course of events"(p. 143).[2] Oakeshott's theory of experience leads directly to the Croce-Collingwood method of making the past live again in the mind of the historian.

How, by the doctrine of Oakeshott, can the historian get hold of past events, since "an event independent of experience, 'objective' in the sense of being untouched by thought or judgment, would be unknowable; it would be neither fact nor true nor false, but a nonentity" (p. 93)? Shall we conclude, then, that there are no geological events? Meanwhile, it is clear from this quotation that the historian desirous of possessing himself of an event will have to make it cease being "independent of experience"; he must make it dependent upon experience. The difficulty is that according to Oakeshott, " 'experience' stands for the concrete whole which analysis divides into 'experiencing' and 'what is experienced.' Experiencing and what is experienced are, taken separately, meaningless abstractions; they cannot, in fact, be separated" (p. 9). I am ever impressed by the number of things which idealists reject as "meaningless abstractions."

[1] *The Idea of History*, p. 159.

[2] It is well written, it has warmth, the author is sincere in his belief that when he sits at the window the room behind him has no existence.

Idealism breeds unbelief. But that is another story. We know that the historian will have to experience the past event if he is to capture it. He must bear in mind that "the claim of any form of experience to be more elementary than judgment, in whatever form it is preferred, turns out to be contradictory" (p. 20). In other words the historian, seeing "experience as a single homogeneous whole," will also perceive it "as thought or judgment" (p. 26). We are now coming very near to the need for "thinking the thoughts of the past," which is, as we shall see, the doctrine dear to Collingwood. Meanwhile, just to make things a little less easy, Mr. Oakeshott asks us to revise our notions about the past. There is a "practical past . . . from which the present has grown," which "has been influential in deciding the present and future fortunes of man," and this is not an historical past (p. 103). History, on the other hand, "is the past for the sake of the past" (p. 106). Perhaps Mr. Oakeshott had to write these things because he is an idealist philosopher. But he is also a scholar and a gentleman, and that is no doubt why he says that what is known as history is "what evidence obliges us to believe" (p. 108). We shall find the same matter-of-fact recognition of the obvious, after much indulgence in clairvoyance and ecstatic immediacy of apprehension, when we read Collingwood. But we shall also find in Collingwood deplorable echoes of Mr. Oakeshott's *prolegomena* to the establishment of an *index librorum prohibitorum*. Thucydides, says Mr. Oakeshott, is not only a peculiar, but also "a defective historian" (p. 131). Which does not entirely deprive Thucydides of the title of historian, and makes him luckier than Tacitus at the hands of Collingwood.

"As a contributor to historical literature," says Collingwood, whose views we are now ready to discuss, "Tacitus is a gigantic figure; but it is permissible to wonder whether he was an historian at all." This explosive utterance occurs on p. 38 of his *Idea of History*, the manifesto of history's left extremists in England.[1] Around a framework of subtle and abstract principles, Collingwood constructs a building of curious shape and vast dimensions. He deliberately restricts history to the history of thought. "The historian has no direct or empirical knowledge of his facts, and

[1] Montesquieu and Gibbon do not fare much better at his hand.

no transmitted or testimoniary knowledge of them" (p. 282). How, then, can he know the past? The answer is deliberate; we are given it again and again: The historian knows the past by re-enacting it in his own mind. This is done by thinking the thoughts of men who lived in the past (pp. 39, 209, 301, etc.). Is it unkind to mention in immediate juxtaposition with this statement another dictum, that "the right way of investigating minds is by the methods of history" (p. 209)? After all, Collingwood's book is posthumous. Yet this circular reasoning is not the result of negligence: it is inherent in Collingwood's metaphysical approach. For he also says: "The historian is looking for processes of thought. All history is history of thought" (p. 215). And, in another place: "The life of man is an historical life because it is a mental and spiritual life" (p. 93).

What warrant is there for this limitation of the idea of history? The reasonable, indeed the rational attitude, would be to accept as history that which has been recognized as such through the ages, or, if we are to be meticulous in our use of words, that which has been called "history" through the ages. It will be legitimate to ask what are the characteristics of the body of writings that have become known as history. But to construct an abstraction, to annex for it the common name of "history" —sheer misappropriation of the people's linguistic funds!—why should this provide anyone with a criterion for the excommunication of recognized historians? And yet, if we take Collingwood for guide, we shall have to submit to a number of further restrictions. "It is not knowing what people did, but understanding what they thought that is the proper definition of the historian's task" (p. 115), and therefore history is "nothing but the re-enactment of past thought" (p. 228).

Let us not seek consolation in the thought that we are wandering in the land of speculation. Collingwood's principles are meant to be applied. "So far as man's conduct is determined by what may be called his animal nature, his impulses and appetites, it is non-historical; the process of those activities is a natural process. Thus, the historian is not interested in the fact that men eat and sleep and make love and thus satisfy their natural appetites; but he is interested in the social customs which they create by their thought as a framework within which these appetites find satisfaction in ways sanctioned by convention and morality" (p. 216). Does this not exclude Drummond's work upon the food of our ancestors, although metabolism depends upon the nature of food, glandular functions upon metabolism, and behaviour in part at any rate upon glandular functions?

History is not exclusively the history of philosophy, as one might imagine after reading some of Collingwood's statements. "There can be history of warfare. . . . Economic activity, too, can have a history. . . . Again, there can be a history of morals. . ." (p. 310). But, always, these things must issue from thought (p. 304). No doubt this is because "wrong ways of thinking are just as much historical fact as right ones." Nevertheless, the cynic might feel inclined to ask whether the history of warfare necessarily presupposes the existence of right, or even wrong, thought, and whether its very existence does not frequently presuppose the absence of all thought. To this the answer would seem to be that "when an historian says that a man is in a certain situation, this is the same as saying that he [i.e. that man] thinks he is in this situation" (p. 317). Is it the same thing? What if our man is blissfully unaware of the situation, if he does not know that he has been poisoned—not by the thought-act of a fellow man, of course, but by the non-historical fact (see above!) that he has just eaten poisoned mushrooms, absent-mindedly, entirely without thinking of what he was doing? Does the historian escape from this predicament by being told that "the rational activity which historians have to study is never free from compulsion" (p. 316)? Certainly not: even with Oakeshott's identification of experiencing and the thing experienced, we are not always sure whether Collingwood speaks of past thought or of the historian's thought, and in the present case compulsion appears to apply to the historian, not to my mushroom eater.

There is an answer, a somewhat unexpected one. Collingwood does not give it in so many words, but he was groping for it. It is provided by the *unanimiste* philosophy of Jules Romains.[1] The deeds and thoughts of all men are subtly intertwined. Therefore "non-historical" deeds, deeds that are innocent of

[1] § See 3 of my previous chapter.

all thought, are so intermingled with historical thought-actions that they reach our knowledge whether we want it or not. Far-fetched? May I refer the sceptical reader to Collingwood's p. 316, where, in support of another argument, the following words appear? "A healthy man knows that the empty space in front of him, which he proposes to fill up with activities for which he accordingly now begins making plans, will be very far from empty by the time he steps into it. It will be crowded with other people all pursuing activities of their own. Even now it is not as empty as it looks. It is filled with a saturate solution of activity, on the point of beginning to crystallize out. There will be no room left for his own activity, unless he can so design this that it will fit into the interstices of the rest." Surely the historian will not be able to isolate his legitimate prey from this luxuriant overgrowth, and deeds unsanctified by thought will share the privilege of being re-enacted!

Collingwood saw the light, but did not follow it. Instead he remained severely logical. If our animal nature was to be excluded from history, there was even more reason for excluding "the processes of nature." Knowledge of them "is not historical knowledge" (p. 302). Now it happens that early in the fifteenth century a change occurred in the habits of the Gulf Stream which began to carry its rich maritime pastures nearer to the Low Countries. The herrings followed their food and migrated to the North Sea. The result was a boom in fishing, the building of many more fishing-vessels, the use of these, during the off-season, for carrying goods, and a vast development of the trade of the Counties of Holland and Zeeland. But even if one attributes the behaviour of the Gulf Stream to a decision of Herbert Spencer's Grand Fetish, it is not human thought, and therefore not history.

Let it be said in justice to Collingwood that his views on method are entirely consonant with his doctrines about the subject matter of history. He labours diligently for the identification of the experiencing and the object experienced. The past and the historian are one, for history is "a process to which the historian himself is integral as at once part of it and the self-knowledge of it" (p. 181). The way in which this is worked out is not easy to follow. It amounts to this: the historian must re-think the thoughts of the past, and his own thought is to meet this past thought and become one with it. The historian's mind must offer a home to this revived thought, and his own thought "must be, as it were, pre-adapted to become its host" (p. 304). How are we to prepare for this exquisite symbiosis except by going into a trance? In Collingwood's nomenclature the resulting clairvoyance is called "the historical imagination."[1] As introduced to us, it appears to possess uncommonly robust characteristics. It is "a self-dependent, self-determining, and self-justifying form of thought" (p. 249). With historical imagination thus solidly entrenched in the realm of metaphysics, we might expect its revelations to be unassailable, with the result that all history must coincide with history as re-thought by Collingwood. Surely, all genuine historians must necessarily be in agreement? But Collingwood has an escape clause. If one historian is fit to re-enact some subject at a given moment, this does not mean that others are capable of the right re-thinking at the same time. No historian should be "working against the grain of his own mind." Later, he may feel called to deal with the subject he wisely avoided at one time, but by then it will have changed out of all recognition (p. 304.) Meanwhile, echoing Oakeshott once more, Collingwood wishes to check imagination by submitting its revelations to the control of evidence. And, since "in history we demand certainty" (p. 270), this control will have to be very probing, if conclusions that are merely provisional are to be excluded.

Among English historians the reputation of Collingwood stands high. Nevertheless, their allegiance to him is somewhat shaky, if we are to judge by the case of a former Regius professor. Having read Collingwood's paper on "Human Nature and Human History," printed in 1936 (and now reprinted in *The Idea of History*), this historian declared, in 1938, that it was, from a philosophical point of view, a statement of his own general position. Accepting the definition of history as the history of ideas, because "historical events . . . cannot be separated from what we call mind," he proceeded to exclude from the ranks of historians all those who consider that ideas are the result of his-

[1] See below, III: ii: § 3, for imagination as an instrument of historical method.

torical events. A little later, however, the enthusiastic disciple made a rather drastic reservation. "History is *full* of the dead weight of things which have escaped the control of the mind, yet drive man on with a *blind* force."[1] What an obliterating admission!

After this excursion into the occult[2] we shall ask the Provost of Oriel to administer a sober corrective. "To me," said G. N. Clark in his inaugural lecture as Regius Professor of Modern History in the University of Cambridge, "it seems that no historical investigation can provide either a philosophy, or a religion, or a substitute for religion. If in this I express only a personal opinion, I think I should have a general consensus of the working historians with me if I confined myself to the simpler conclusion that we work with limited aims. We try to find the truth about this or that, not about things in general. Our work is not to see life steadily and see it whole, but to see one particular portion of life right side up and in true perspective."[3]

The exclusion of sociology and of the philosophy of history from history is more than a matter of methodological convenience. To grant these subjects rights of citizenship within our discipline would alter its texture and its function. Sociology, the systematic study of the social life of men is, like the kindred subjects social psychology and anthropology, a humanistic science, a systematization of observations made by men about men. All such disciplines remain subjective in their generalizations, their syntheses are influenced by the temperament, the antecedents, the outlook of those who practise them. Moreover, they have complicated techniques of their own. They must be left to the specialists who apply them. With philosophy we would introduce into history all the uncertainties that are the inevitable concomitant of trained intelligence, varieties of interpretation, and conflicts of doctrine. As long as men philosophize

---

[1] Powicke, F. M., *History, Freedom and Religion* (1938), pp. 6 and 19. *My italics.*

[2] In chapters vii and viii of the *Voyage to Laputa* Swift shows us Gulliver using the methods of Collingwood with great effect, although the historical knowledge acquired by necromantic re-enactment is depressingly meagre.

[3] *Historical Scholarship*, p. 11.

under regimes that are not totalitarian, they will pay little heed to the wisdom of Alfred J. Ayer, who informs them that "there is nothing in the nature of philosophy to warrant the existence of conflicting philosophical parties or 'schools'."[1] They will continue to disagree. But our stories of the past need not differ from each other in their factual contents. Does this mean that totally objective history is possible? Certainly not. It means that where events are concerned, and nothing else, men can put their heads together and weigh evidence. Conflicting versions will have common elements, and on these agreement can be achieved. It will be provisional agreement, of course, since in the realm of the intellect all things are forever provisional.

§ 3

ACCURACY AND ANTIQUARIANISM

The story needed by society has to be as accurate as possible. This relative accuracy is secured by the application of methods that will be described at some length in the second and third parts of this book. The story has, moreover, to be told from an ever-changing angle, determined by the questions which society puts to the historian. Again, the facts required for this refocusing of the story can be found out only by the same methods. This preliminary investigation is known as "historical research." Apart from being indispensable for the performance of the historian's task, research provides him with an invigorating contact with some of the realities to which he devotes his existence. He handles documents and other relics dating from the very period of which he intends to tell the story, he sees the hand-writing of some of the men with whom he deals, reads their letters, lives their lives almost at first hand. Moreover, as we have noted before, research provides a worthy satisfaction of the collector's instinct that lives in most of us. Research certainly makes one a better historian; it probably makes one a saner man.

Unhappily, there is harboured in what is known as the historical world a delusion which causes those it infects to misunderstand

[1] *Language, Truth, and Logic* (1936), p. 209.

the function of research. Some of the denizens of the historical world—they are our extremists on the right—have persuaded themselves that, in history, research is the thing that really matters; they have a predilection for the word "scholar," and readily apply it to the research worker. But scholarship implies infinitely more than the finest kind of research. The critic and novelist E. M. Forster defines a scholar as "the man who chooses a worthy subject and masters all its facts and the leading facts on the subjects neighbouring."[1] Not all scholars belong to the world of history, but wherever he is found, the scholar is a man who is at the same time familiar with the technique of preliminary investigation and capable of presenting its result in a palatable way. The historical scholar is both research worker and historian.

There is no need to defend history proper by adopting towards research the attitude of a former Master of Balliol, Benjamin Jowett, who once exclaimed, in the course of a conversation with Logan Pearsall Smith: "Research! Research! A mere excuse for idleness; it has never achieved, and never will achieve, any results of the slightest value!"[2] After all, as Logan Pearsall Smith tells us, Jowett was the inventor of the tutorial system, and imagined that it was threatened by the endowment of research. We might, however, consult a few experts whom no one could accuse of having neglected research, or of being afraid of it, and whom the sternest purist could not call "bad scholars."

The foremost methodologists agree that research is merely the servant of history. "It must be emphasized," wrote Bernheim, "that research (*Quellenforschung*) is only a means to an end, only a preliminary operation."[3] "Supposing," writes Bauer, "that good luck or favourable circumstances cause a man to discover sources which throw a sharp light upon parts of our discipline which have thus far remained in the shade, and supposing also that he publishes those sources. What has he done for history? He has rendered ancillary services. Otherwise humanists like Poggio, who from dusty monastery libraries have dragged into

[1] *Aspects of the Novel*, p. 19,

[2] Logan Pearsall Smith, *Unforgotten Years* (1938), p. 169. For Jowett's distrust of research see also an excellent passage in F. C. S. Schiller, *Must Philosophers Disagree?* pp. 176-7.   [3] *Op. cit.*, p. 252-3.

the open and published a Quintillian, an Ammianus Marcellinus, must be called the greatest historians of all times. He who does not also give shape to the material does not achieve the ultimate and the greatest that exists in our subject—der erreicht das Letzte und Grösste auf unserem Gebiete nicht."[1] We shall see in a moment that Langlois and Seignobos take the same view.

Henri Pirenne was obviously thinking of those Germans who, towards the end of last century, tried to identify research and history, when he wrote: "Historical criticism, or if one prefers, historical erudition (*l'histoire érudition*) is not the whole of history. It does not exist for its own sake. Its sole purpose is the discovery of facts. Nor has it for its task to set these facts in motion, to establish causal relations between them, to reconstruct by means of them the past in its living reality. Criticism provides materials for what is properly called history, narrative history (*l'histoire proprement dite, l'histoire récit*). Once this task is accomplished, criticism goes no further. Important and indeed essential though it be, its role remains subordinate. Once the authenticity of texts has been established, the sources criticized, the chronology of events fixed, there still remains the task of making history (*de faire l'histoire*)."[2]

It is sometimes said of a work of pure erudition, one which presents the fruits of research without constructing the story that should be its natural culmination, that it is "a contribution to knowledge." Is not this empty metaphor a relic of nineteenth-century positivism and of the theories of Auguste Comte who believed in *l'édifice de la science* to which every scientist contributed a stone? Langlois and Seignobos, the authors of an excellent, highly original, and oft-reprinted introduction to historical method, consider that text-criticism brings nothing new, and that, instead of putting us in possession of facts that were formerly unavailable, it merely burnishes up traces of the past that were already in being. They suggest that much effort is often wasted in providing texts with elaborate but altogether superfluous commentaries.[3]

---

[1] Bauer, *op. cit.*   [2] *Art. cit., Revue Historique* (1897), p. 50.
[3] Langlois, Ch-V, et Seignobos, Ch., *Introduction aux Etudes Historiques*, 5th ed., 1915, pp. 64–5. The English translation is of indifferent quality.

Erudites sometimes fail to pass beyond the research stage because they suffer from psychological deficiencies that inhibit them from performing the historian's proper task. This, according to Oman, explains what the French call "la fureur de l'inédit," and he observes: "In its extreme form this dislike for definite conclusions and dread of committing oneself to a theory sometimes drives students to shrinking from an attempt to write narrative history, and confining their activities to producing 'materials,' to collecting unpublished material and printing it with little or no comment on its general application, or to putting together statistics to fling at the head of the perplexed reader, or to compiling bibliographies of all sorts of authorities, good, bad, or indifferent, relating to a special subject."[1] I have already pointed out some of the reasons that make the task of erudition so attractive to certain people. Langlois and Seignobos, who also note that erudition satisfies a taste for collecting and for solving puzzles, consider that it will always appeal to those whom accident alone has thrown into historical studies, while they are deficient in powers of psychological perception and in stylistic ability.[2]

Should we, then, model ourselves upon Francis Bacon who wanted one group of men to observe nature while another group was to build theories based upon the results achieved by the first? Ought we to separate research workers from actual historians, and ask the latter to base their work entirely upon the material provided by the erudites? Langlois and Seignobos consider that the proposal has many virtues: the historian who finds that his documents are already correctly and completely edited should be free to write history without seeking for unpublished material.[3] They rejoice at the fact that men like Leibnitz and Renan did not heroically sacrifice their superior faculties for the sake of pure erudition. As for Bauer, the thought that anyone might be condemned to confine himself solely to erudition appears painful to him. "Nie soll die Kritik zum Selbstzweck werden!" he exclaims. If the research worker, he says, lacks the ability or the inclination to do the actual constructive

[1] Oman, Ch., *On the Writing of History* (1939), pp. 41–2.
[2] *Op. cit.*, pp. 99–100.   [3] *Ibid.*, p. 91.

53

work, he should at any rate endeavour to direct his work towards a constructive use.[1]

This much is certain: the man who has not communicated to his fellow human beings, by publication or by private circulation, a story of past events, whether a kinetic narrative or a static monograph, is not an historian. But the best historian is he who combines research with the telling of a story. As Pirenne put it: "Sans l'hypothèse et la synthèse, l'histoire reste un passe-temps d'antiquaires; sans la critique et l'érudition, elle perd pied dans le domaine de la fantaisie."[2]

§ 4

DIVISION

Life makes upon us one overwhelming impact. Is life one, or is it manifold? This is a question for the metaphysician. The part of life where the historian must seek the material for his story, the social human past, also impresses him as one. Could he cope with it, however, if he left it undivided? His existence is brief, his strength has limits. He must choose a field for himself, and without allowing himself to be imprisoned in it, he must dwell there for preference.

Writers on the method of history invariably present their readers with a list of headings under which they wish to divide the historian's subject matter. Some of these divisions are highly ingenious. Bauer bases his division upon various aspects of practical life. He distinguishes between narrative history; pragmatic history, which extracts from the past the lessons applicable to the present; genetic history, which considers the flow and change of all things; sociological history, which looks for the

---

[1] Bauer, *op. cit.*, p. 340.

[2] *Op. cit.*, p. 56. It will be noticed that I refer to the right-wing extremists, but not to their own statements. The reason is that their doctrines are rarely, if ever, stated in printed form. The identification of history and erudition is symptomatic of sterility. One meets it in common rooms, and on appointment boards, among academic politicians rather than among scholars. A consoling exception is the Cambridge Regius Professor V. H. Galbraith, who with his usual fearlessness defends both orthodoxy and right-wing deviationism in his inaugural lecture, *Historical Study and the State* (1948), (especially on p. 11).

laws that operate through the human past. Let us note in passing that the words "pragmatic history," which are used by other theorists as well, have no connection with the words "pragmatist" and "pragmatic" as used in the present study.[1] Those excellent methodologists Langlois and Seignobos forget their sceptical outlook when they draw up their own list with more than German thoroughness. They begin by establishing an all-embracing division in the past as we perceive it: 1, material conditions; 2, intellectual habits; 3, material customs; 4, economic customs; 5, social institutions; 6, public institutions. Each of these is given subdivisions. History is then divided and subdivided into subjects which correspond to each of these categories.[2]

Distinctions in the subject-matter of history are of the utmost importance. They influence the creation of new chairs in history, the appointment of scholars to these chairs, the curricula for students and the subject-matter of examinations. In certain parts of the historical world where general knowledge is looked upon as superficiality, a man's seriousness and scholarship may well be measured by his fidelity to the speciality which Fate has assigned to him. The severities of the professionals, like those of the methodologists, find their origin in a respectable and well-established intellectual approach, rooted in a pathetic thirst for certainty. Like the notion of definition which so frightens the honest scientific worker, distinction and division still labour under the disabilities imposed upon mental activity by the unrealities of Aristotelian logic. Its rules sound so reasonable. Here they are, formulated by an author guided at once by the lights of traditional wisdom and the doctrines of the Catholic Church. A division must, in the first place, be such that the parts exclude each other, both in reality and within rational intelligence. In the second place a division must be adequate; all the parts put together must equal the divided whole. Finally, a division must be into parts that have the same generic rank. One must not, therefore, divide mankind into Asiatics, Spaniards, etc.[3]

[1] *Op. cit.*, pp. 120–3, pp. 150 *sqq.*   [2] *Op. cit.*, pp. 202–3.
[3] Boyer, Ch., S. J., *Handboek der Wijsbegeerte* (1946), translated from the Latin original, Vol. I, p. 98. Even here the polished agnosticism of Rome reveals itself: "We should not lose sight of the fact," says the author, "that when carried too far division brings about confusion" (*ibid.*).

Let us now endeavour to do some clear thinking on the subject of division, even though in this instance clear thinking must lead to the advocacy of blurred outlines. Writing in the spacious days when Englishmen carried golden coins in their pockets, the logician Alfred Sidgwick declared that "the distinction between a sovereign and a sixpence, important enough in regard to their purchasing power, becomes unimportant for the purpose of 'tossing up'."[1] Distinctions and the divisions based upon them are not relevant from every point of view: they are not absolute or inherent in the nature of things. That is the first principle we must remember. They are inspired by the desire to achieve a practical purpose, and here is our second principle. Dewey makes this very clear when he says: "To classify is as useful as it is natural. The indefinite multitude of particular and changing events is met by the mind with acts of defining, inventorying, and listing, reducing to common heads and tying up in bunches. But these acts, like other acts, are performed for a purpose, and the accomplishment of the purpose is their only justification. Speaking generally, the purpose is to facilitate our dealings with unique and changing events. . . ."[2]

As soon as we look at the practical problems which arise in the performance of historical research, we see that it cannot make headway without a division of labour among historians. To write the history of the cloth industry in any part of Europe one requires a knowledge of the technique of spinning, weaving, carding, fulling and dyeing. Such a knowledge, however, would be of no use to the student who wishes to deal with a piece of diplomatic or political history. Yet, the more convinced we become of the practical utility of divisions, the more we shall dislike the classical rules that breed intolerance by their insistence upon the sacrosanct character of these divisions. We shall agree with F. C. S. Schiller that "exhaustive divisions are hardly obtainable" and reject the "adequate" divisions of the schools. Far from establishing divisions whose sum equals the totality of history, we shall emulate the scientist who, says Schiller, "habitu-

---

[1] *Distinction*, p. 265.

[2] *Human Nature and Conduct*, p. 131: "The primary purpose of distinctions is to facilitate our thinking," says Schiller, *Formal Logic*, p. 53.

ally operates with more than one principle of division at a time
... always subject to correction."[1] New questions are continually
put to the historian by society, past events hitherto unknown to
him are brought to light. The first rule of the schools must
disappear as well as the second; our subjects will forever inter-
penetrate and fertilize each other. Nor can we tolerate generic
hierarchies; at any time a subdivision may grow over the head
of its parent.

It is natural that Time should be asked to provide us with
the simplest and most obvious division of history. The division
into ancient, medieval and modern history gained currency as
a result of the advocacy of Christopher Cellarius or Keller
(1634–1701) of the University of Halle. He did not invent
these terms, which were first used by a scholar belonging to the
Low Countries, Rausin, of Liège, in his book *Leodium*, published in 1639.[2] This division reflected the mentality of the humanists, with their pride in their own epoch, on which the return to
ancient models had shed a brilliant light, their interest in the
ancient world, and their contempt for the uncouth ages in between,
the *medium aevum*. "Dix siècles au fond d'un trou noir," was
Taine's verdict on the Middle Ages two hundred years later.
Since then we have come to know them better and we take a
different view of the centuries of suspense. Nor are we so certain
that the difference between the ages is of paramount importance.
The classical age took centuries to die, and only examiners can
assign a precise date to the event.[3] There is more reason for
speaking of a new age when one passes from the Middle Ages
to modern history, although even in this case we should avoid
excessive insistence upon the difference.[4] Perhaps the best charac-

[1] *Formal Logic*, p. 76. See also Schiller, *Our Human Truths*, pp. 66 *sqq.*, on
division of labour and on disputed territory between the sciences, and G. N.
Clark on the possibility of new branches of learning arising (*Historical Scholarship*,
pp. 13–14). Also Halphen's useful discussion on division, in *Introduction à l'Histoire*,
pp. 66–8. [2] Bernheim, *op. cit.*, pp. 77–8.
[3] See Pirenne, *Mahomet et Charlemagne*, *passim*, esp. p. 143.
[4] In *Three Lectures* (1947) Powicke points out (pp. 39 *sqq.*) that the Renaissance
cannot possibly be called a sudden event. G. N. Clark warns us "not to apply a
mechanical criterion like that of date," and argues that chronological periods
ought not to be turned into mutually exclusive subjects (*Historical Scholarship*,
p. 13).

terization of the three periods is to be found in the distinction made by Pirenne and no doubt by others, that the classical period was lived round one sea, the Mediterranean, the medieval period round three seas, the Mediterranean, the North Sea, and the Baltic, and the modern period round all the oceans. The best reason for making the distinction remains the difference between the techniques of research needed for the story of each period. Meanwhile, it is certain that the division applies exclusively to our West European civilization.

The chronological division of history is horizontal, but vertical divisions according to subject are needed as well. This metaphor, by the way, should not be carried too far: the spirit-level and the plumb-line are as freely interchangeable in this case as the sovereign and the sixpence for the purpose of consulting the oracle. A good pragmatist division of history should present us with parts which, put together, cover more than the whole. Let us have as one division the story of human experiences undergone within, or about, or through, the state; let us call it political history. We may next distinguish the history which covers experiences where the state plays no part, or a subordinate, or secondary, or unimportant one, and call it social history. A third division may suggest itself, which can be said to belong to neither or to both: this will be the history of ideas. Such a system will provide a home for any kind of history known or, as far as can be foreseen at present, still to be born. No transcendental virtues can be claimed for it, and it can be abandoned the moment it proves unworkable. For the actual labels to be placed upon the subdivisions we shall look at the calendars of British and foreign universities, or at the catalogue of any library which, unlike the Library of Congress, has not allowed rationalism to run away with reasonableness.

Political history comes first by order of seniority and for no other reason. G. N. Clark thinks it still deserves its central position because "it is in public institutions that men express their will to control events, and therefore," he says, "it seems to me that historians will go wrong if they try to resolve political and constitutional history into other elements."[1] Pirenne's attitude

[1] *Op. cit.*, p. 18.

is more that of a pragmatist; things still work best that way, in his opinion. Voltaire, Guizot, Augustin Thierry, Macaulay, Droysen, Ranke, were all primarily interested in political history, and all of them place the state in the first rank, he points out, although it is a relatively artificial phenomenon. But, he reflects, the state is the most apparent and visible link that unites men, while its very artificiality makes necessary a constant endeavour to keep it going—a very good reason for paying special attention to it.[1] In practice the Provost of Oriel and my late teacher are in agreement. Both have shown their respect for the established rights of political history, both have shown the importance they attach to other facets of the story of the past.

Political history was once the history of kings, treaties and battles. The interest taken in the experiences of the common people has brought about a revulsion among those who tell the story of the past. But there were times when the deeds of kings did matter supremely, and when conquests shaped the destinies of ordinary men. Conquest is unhappily still a vital factor in world affairs, and society has still to ask its expert story-tellers for particulars concerning the rise and fall of empires. The internal history of states is as important as ever. No matter what reasons make men struggle for the control of the state machine, politics still influence the life and the human dignity of the individuals who owe allegiance to the state. It is still highly necessary for statesmen to know precedents good, bad and indifferent, for the purpose of comparison and subsequent action. The story of party life has to be known by the politician and the citizen.

Constitutional history is an important aspect of political history. Like the story of the struggle for mastery in the state, otherwise the history of politics, it deals with government. But it places less emphasis upon actions, and the events of which, before all else, it takes cognizance are, as a rule, less clear-cut and less individualized. Its interest goes principally to institutions, which I have called the habits of societies. Constitutions are habits made concrete; they are the methods, the conventions, the body of practice adopted by men in governing the state. Written consti-

---

[1] *Revue Historique, ut supra,* p. 52.

tutions are the most tenuous part of the subject-matter of constitutional history. Constitutional history is particularly lacking in self-sufficiency. The history of the state is but one aspect of it. It would be impossible to think of medieval institutions like the manor as being merely aspects of medieval constitutions: they are also social and economic phenomena. The constitutional historian has to go beyond political history for his events, for his arguments, for his sphere of interest, if he is to provide the community with an accurate and satisfying story.

Parliamentary history is a subdivision of constitutional history; it deals with one particular institution which occupies a position of the greatest importance among the experiences of men in certain countries. Without paying considerable attention to the story of the English Parliament it would be impossible to tell the political story of the British people. Present-day preoccupations, and the attempts of enemies of human freedom and dignity to pour ridicule upon the "talking shops" that still exist in a number of countries, give a poignant relevance to parliamentary history and place upon those who write it a particular responsibility for keeping alive a most valuable series of human experiences.

Dr. Arnold J. Toynbee, Research Professor of International History in the University of London, rebukes historians right at the beginning of his *Study of History*, for having given their allegiance to the sovereign state which is inspired by the spirit of nationality.[1] It is easy to regret the existence of national sovereignty, and to dream of peace in a United States of Europe or of the World. Meanwhile, most people's experiences have been acquired within the framework of a sovereign national state. Poised precariously between the two ambivalent psychopathological deviations known as fascism and communism, which cause patients to dream of modelling human societies upon those of the termites, western civilization finds its supreme values embodied in parliamentary institutions acquired and developed by the sovereign national units of which it consists. If we were to abolish national sovereignties tomorrow, the story of the struggles between kings and nobility, between kings and parlia-

[1] Vol. I, p. 9.

merits, between burghers and their feudal masters, would continue to form a body of past experience to which western society would have to refer again and again while fixing its standards and its practice. National histories are a precious aspect of the history of mankind.

Legal history is obviously connected with constitutional history, though it differs from it in many respects. The legal historian must be a lawyer. The utilitarian connection between his subject and the law is patent. Precedent plays in the courts of law of most countries a part to which it is entitled nowhere else, that of a norm that stands almost above discussion. In Great Britain, where the memory of the law goes back further than in any other country, the story of the enactments of Parliament and of their application by the Courts of the Realm is a matter of considerable practical importance as well as a subject asking for the most radical specialization. Yet the legal historian must not exclusively dwell in a world of his own: he cannot remain indifferent to the advance made by certain other branches such as political and economic history.

The external relations of states are in the hands of groups of experts, diplomats and dwellers in foreign offices, who collaborate, not always in perfect harmony or loyalty, with the politicians. Previous experience is almost invariably considered by them as a norm, and for this reason a knowledge of the past belongs to their professional equipment; indeed, although the breaking of fresh ground would be most fruitful for smooth relations between states, historical awareness is as necessary in these matters to the innovator as to the traditionalist. The history of relations between states is usually known as *diplomatic history*. It is sometimes called international history, and there is a tendency to establish a distinction between the first, which is assumed to be strictly limited to the actions of diplomatic and court circles, and the second, which takes into account factors of a more general nature by which the course and the issue of negotiations is affected. In practice the distinction is hard to maintain.

Diplomatic history, from which, for methodological reasons, the various kinds of military history are excluded, is more concerned with the lives and idiosyncrasies of individuals than any

other department of history. The research work that precedes
it is circumscribed, and at first sight rather uninspiring. As is
the case with every kind of history, this description ceases to be
true the moment the student penetrates more deeply into his
subject. No sooner has it become better known, than the most
intricate negotiation acquires the glow and tactile values of life.
Moreover, the diplomatic historian must always keep an eye
upon the world at large, for the actions of statesmen and diplomats can be influenced by events outside the chancelleries and
embassies. During the Seven Years' War, in 1762, both England
and France had good reasons for wanting to make peace, but
neither Bute nor Choiseul was able to do anything useful towards
it. Then, on June 6th, an English fleet appeared before Havana,
which belonged to France's ally, Spain. The town capitulated
a week later, on the 13th. On September 29th the news became
known in London where it caused a wave of enthusiasm. All
war-weariness was gone, and there was a general desire to
continue the struggle. Bute thereupon informed Choiseul that
unless peace were concluded at once, and before the impending
meeting of Parliament, George III would have no alternative
but to tell both Houses that the war would continue. The French
now brought pressure to bear upon their Spanish ally, and pre-
liminaries of peace were signed. Military history and the history
of public opinion have, in this case, a contribution to make to
the story, which could not be complete if it were limited entirely
to the activities of diplomatic circles.[1] Let us also remember
that every negotiation deals with one or more concrete issues
which are not themselve diplomatic in nature, but economic,
legal or cultural. Diplomatic history can therefore not be
isolated from other kinds of history.

There is no need to define *military history*, although it may be
observed that the term can be used to indicate the story of warfare
in every form, or can be applied more particularly to warfare
on land. The fact that naval history and the history of aerial
warfare presuppose the knowledge of special techniques makes

[1] A particularly valuable discussion of the methods and problems of diplomatic history in Sir Charles Webster's inaugural lecture on *The Study of International History*, in *History*, July, 1933.

it preferable to use the name "military history" in its specific connotation. It will, of course, deal with tactical as well as with the strategic aspects of land-fighting. It must also take cognizance of military engineering, ballistics, and of the developments in military transport and of large-scale provisioning which nowadays goes by the name of logistics. Older people still with us have not forgotten that where "kings-and-queens" history used to be taught battles took place of honour, and taxed the pupils' powers of attention even more than their memory. Nevertheless, one need not be a militarist or a war-monger to find entertainment in the story of military operations. It gives rise to stimulating questions. To what extent, one may ask, do military operations depend for their success on planning, to what extent is their outcome the result of accident? One can also ask whether the outcome of battles ever affects the fate of nations whose armies win them or lose them, or whether, in the perspective of time, a war was necessary or unnecessary. Men of the twentieth century who seem to live in the permanent din of battle look upon such matters as live issues; they will expect to be told their military history by people who are alive to issues such as these. The mentality, the psychology, of the captain, the war leader, present the story teller with opportunities for the exercise of acumen and judgment.

A fundamental problem for the military historian is, or should be, morale. Persian slaves were driven to battle by whips, warriors of the middle of the twentieth century by means of conditioned reflexes. Both were made to do something alien to human nature: to hurt and kill, to be hurt and killed. Wholesome normal human individuals are those we meet in peace-time, at work and at play. How are they to be turned into soldiers and made to behave unnaturally? Civilized societies are faced with this increasingly difficult problem, since in peace-time life becomes more and more agreeable, thanks to technical and economic improvements; they are bound, therefore, to ask their military historians to tell them the story of the experiences of men who have had to cope with this problem of morale. I cannot forget how that great Persian scholar and enlightened *bon vivant* Sir Denison Ross[1]

[1] See *Both Ends of the Candle, the Autobiography of Sir E. Denison Ross*, 1943.

said to me in the spring of 1939: "They are going to fight another great war. They are going to ask millions of young men to lay down their lives and the young men are going to do it. How can they? And how can the old ones ask? Life is so sweet!"

Battle is not, of course, the soldier's normal experience. It is the culmination of a long preparation. Military theorists might even observe that a soldier exists less for the purpose of fighting, than for the purpose of being available for battle. Power is force held in reserve, potential force. They will add that the soldier's behaviour in battle is determined by what happens to him during the long period—months, nowadays, but once it was years—when he is being trained in the arts of obeying and of merging his personality into a larger whole. The modern theorist will talk of conditioning.[1] Undoubtedly, the story of training will occupy an increasing place in the contributions of military historians who lend an ear to the questions they are asked by society. Facts that were by no means unknown will acquire more significance, and it will be noted, for instance, that during the Middle Ages many of the discoveries of soldier psychologists belonging to the classical ages were lost. It would appear that the habit of marching in step with the resulting benefit of merging the soldier's individuality into a corporate unit was forgotten by medieval armies. Classical drill was reintroduced at the end of the sixteenth and early in the seventeenth century, and among those who were most active in bringing this about were the Princes Maurice and Frederic Henry, sons of William the Silent. They founded a school of military art in Holland, and among their students were Swedish noblemen, who carried this by-product of the revival of learning to their country. Without it Gustavus Adolphus could not have brought about the revolution in military art which carried him triumphantly into the heart of Germany during the Thirty Years' War. He applied to cavalry, which since the invention of gunpowder had ceased to be a fighting weapon and had degenerated into a means of rapid transport for infantrymen, the drill and concerted movement restored to the infantry by the Princes of Orange. At the same

---

[1] See the readable and instructive little book by Norman Copeland, *Psychology and the Soldier, the Art of Leadership* (Allen & Unwin, 1944).

time, by the way, but thinking still in terms of the mobility to which the Mauritian discoveries had given rise, he invented field artillery, a development which was made possible thanks to the assistance of the Dutch financier and metallurgist De Geer. Even so we cannot look upon training as providing the final answer to our questions about morale. For the French defeated the Prussian and Austrian veterans by throwing raw levies into battle in 1792![1]

At one time the life from which the soldier was dragged to camp or barrack square might have seemed unlikely to inspire him with nostalgic feelings such as would have interfered with the performance of his duty. The men who took the king's shilling or were gathered in by the press-gang lost little in the change, and if Corporal Trim almost persuades us that a soldier's life in the days of Marlborough was romantic, the existence of sailors, as described in *The Floating Republic* of Mainwaring and Dobrée, seemed hardly preferable to death in battle. However, in wanting to stay alive men pass no judgment upon the quality of life, except to pronounce it better than death. The acceptance of death in battle cannot be explained by a desire to escape from an intolerable existence.

Devotion to an ideal, the glory of laying down one's life for one's country, or for the happiness of future generations—here is another explanation offered for the weird act that consists in the acceptance of death. But did not mercenaries die for a cause that was not theirs as readily as the soldiers of democratic armies? This undeniable fact is the more surprising since, except on the battlefield, mercenaries were such a difficult problem that their use shaped the strategy of wars during the seventeenth and eighteenth centuries. A general's main preoccupation was to prevent the desertion of those expensive specialists who sold their services to the highest bidder, and to provoke the desertion of the specialists employed by the enemy. He tried to cut the enemy's communications with his magazines, so that the enemy found it difficult to feed his troops, whereupon the soldiers

[1] See bibliographical data in J. W. Wijn's introduction to his edition of *Krijgskundige Aanteekeningen van Johan den Middelste van Nassau*, Werken "Utrechts Historisch Genootschap," 3rd series, nr. 76, 1947.

became dissatisfied and deserted, if they had a chance. The role of gendarmes and maréchaussées was to prevent the working of economic factors in circumstances such as these. Once or at most twice a season a battle was fought, mainly for the sake of humouring the generals. The death of these mercenaries was more embarrassing to their employers than objectionable to themselves. For one day, and without being surrounded by gendarmes, they were pitted against the enemy, and invited to do their worst. They had to break the cohesion of the opposing army, since in those days without aviation and wireless telephony, co-ordination consisted in being within galloping distance of the Commander-in-Chief. Once more, why did the mercenaries allow themselves to be slaughtered on such occasions? Was it the individual's superstitious belief in his own invulnerability? I doubt it. It is more likely that the mercenary, like the soldier of the national levies of Germany in the nineteenth century, went into battle in the full expectation of death.

> Morgenrot, Morgenrot,
> Leuchtest mir zum frühen Tod?

No, the readiness to lay down one's life is not invariably connected with idealism or with the notion of sacrifice. It occurs among those whose existence is rich and worth-while, and among those who have little to lose. Similarly, the fear of death is found among old people who cannot expect much more happiness or even contentment at least as frequently as among those who are still entitled to expect good things for themselves.

Like every kind of historian, the military historian will find that to prepare himself for his task it is not enough to collect past events through research. He will have to consult auxiliary disciplines from which he can learn to ask relevant and significant questions and to connect events into a coherent and convincing story. One of these auxiliaries is psychology; the modern military historian will have to go to it for the guidance needed to answer questions concerning morale. Let me present my own solution and let it be understood that I do this in no dogmatic way. I have made it clear that explanations are not of the essence of historical narrative, but form its unavoidable concomitant. About

the facts there need by no divergence of verdict among honest
people who know the rules of historical criticism. The facts,
expressed in general terms, are simple; men have died in battle,
whether they were driven slaves, valuable mercenaries, or democratic or totalitarian cannon-fodder. Is there a way of explaining
this universal acceptance of unnatural death? What made them
forget the principle of Denison Ross, that "life is sweet"?

Normal behaviour on the field of battle would consist in
running away. When a chimney stack threatens to fall down
on us we run away without loss of face. The coward is sane, but
he is stupid. He overlooks the existence of the red-cap, he forgets
the court-martial and the firing-squad. As for the normal soldier,
the good soldier, the unheroic fighting man, he is, like the
hero and winner of the V.C., temporarily insane. The coward
has struck a bargain with his fear and tries to humour it; the
fighter surrenders to it. For what is fear? Physiologically, it is
a defence mechanism against danger: it enables us to run away
faster, it changes our appearance by making us look fearsome
to our enemy. The busby is an instrument of mimicry; it makes
the soldier look like one whose hair is raised by awe-provoking
fear. What happens to the souls of men subject to fear? Let us
ignore as irrelevant in practice the question whether these psychological phenomena are the cause or the effect of the glandular
secretions that take place in the fear-stricken individual. "All fear
is fear of the approach of death," says Janet, quoted by the Dutch
psychologist A. M. Meerloo, who adds that the hero's attitude
is "an apathetic and fatalistic acceptance of fear and death."[1]
This is how Meerloo explains his dictum: "As one of the primitive and passive reactions to fear I have already mentioned
unconditional surrender to the things feared. Many a human
being cannot bear the tension of the indefinite fear-sensation.
He would rather rush into danger than continue enduring the
suspense. Fear even entices him, danger hypnotizes him, just as
an inexperienced mountaineer might feel a compulsion to cast
himself over a precipice. Some people who are continually
oppressed by the fear of death finally commit suicide. A criminal

[1] *Aftermath of Peace*, New York, 1946, essay on "Aspects of Fear," pp. 59–110.
See also the same author's *Total War and the Human Mind* (1944), *passim*.

67

who lives in fear of being arrested may end by giving himself up with a sigh of relief. Passive anticipation has unnerved him and greatly increased his fear. The certainty of being jailed at last has freed him from fear."

Fear, then, is surrender to the thing feared. But death, the thing that is feared, is at the same time the thing that beckons. I have mentioned in an earlier connection the Freudian theory of the death-wish, which has also been described by an intelligent thinker of the pre-psycho-analytical period, Samuel Butler. The human being is forever possessed by an unconscious desire to cancel the result of the painful experience that was birth. In ordinary life this longing manifests itself in the form of fugues, retreats into bed or into a bath, or the incongruous adoption of a foetal attitude. In circumstances of exceptional stress it becomes a death-wish, or at least a paralysis of death-escaping mechanisms: cataleptic conditions often form a syndrome of intense fear. The unusual occasion of battle liberates man's deepest longing for the annihilation of his post-natal personality. He experiences fear, which, like all emotions, operates in an ambivalent way;[1] he fears death and longs for it as the only complete escape from fear. He has a deadly fear of fear. This makes him behave like a good soldier and run into the face of death. I have conversed with an eminently sane senior officer of the Dutch army who was not usually given to flights of fancy, and who grew lyrical in his praise of the act of dying in battle. Dying, the supremely bitter-sweet acceptance of the end of all things, appeared to him as an act that possessed value in itself. Many civilians have experienced this craving for Nirvana in the course of aerial bombardments.

What is the conclusion of this excursion? It is, no doubt, that the world holds out mighty promises to the future military historian, and that the pacifist and the agitator for world federation do not threaten his career any more than that of the professional soldier.

Military history is not only the story of the military experiences of human societies. It also tells the experiences of military societies, e.g. in regimental histories. In this connection loyalty to the unit, which regimental histories help to foster, should be

[1] See below, III: iii: § 2.

68

mentioned as a maker of military morale. It cannot, however, take the place of the explanation I have just offered. No doubt the unit may be looked upon as a mother, and the regimental commander will be endowed with certain paternal properties. The unconscious mind revels in analogies. But in so far as the unit is a mother-substitute it will merely strengthen the effect of the death-wish that is so intimately connected with the mother-child relation. Meanwhile, it ought to be clear by now that to perform his task adequately the military historian must be acquainted with psychology. He needs knowledge of many different kinds as well, e.g. of topography. What he requires most of all, although he is, often enough, disarmingly unaware of the need, is an understanding of plain everyday general political history. The official history of the army of the Dutch Republic written by Colonel F. J. G. ten Raa and Lieut.-General F. de Bas,[1] is really a series of excellent regimental histories and a mine of miscellaneous information. But the historical knowledge displayed by these gallant soldiers is painfully inadequate; their treatment of the policy of John de Witt, to take but one example, is ludicrous.

Apart from the history of armies and land operations, military history in the broader sense includes *naval history*, which cannot be separated from questions of political power and of trade, and the *history of aerial warfare*, which may one day become the most important of the three, and cannot be written without a knowledge of engineering and physical science.

Colonial history belongs to political history, but not entirely. It is not only the story of the expansion of European nations overseas, but also overland, since it includes the Russian penetration of Asia. As long as Europeans continued to gather the fruit of their colonizing operations, which were often a display of energy rather than of ethical sense, it is natural that the accurate story of these operations should have been in demand. Now, slowly in some cases, rapidly in others, colonies are acquiring autonomy or independence. This brings about a refocusing of the story, not a cessation of the interest it inspires. We shall want to know, more and more, what came to us from those colonies—what in

---

[1] *Het Staatsche Leger*, 1568–1795, many volumes, Breda, since 1911.

the way of wealth, culture, customs, diseases—and what was our gift to them. While it loses its grip on these territories, and suffers economically as a result, Europe stands in need of the palliative its pride can receive from the realization that it has given birth to these mighty communities. The answer to these questions comes partly from political history, in particular from constitutional history, but partly also from social and economic history, which we must now describe.

Social history is the story which leaves out the state. It has been excellently defined by the Dutch historian P. J. Blok, who also called it the history of the people—*volksgeschiedenis*—and said that it deals with "the thought and the work, the daily life, the belief, the needs, the habits, of our ancestors."[1] In the hierarchy of division, it ranks with political history. As Blok rightly points out, social history includes *economic history*. The Dutch economic historian Van Dillen goes farther; he identifies the two and calls the composite discipline social-economic history.[2] This is something more than a mere difference in nomenclature. Let us agree that economic history is a branch of social history which has grown into an autonomous section of history because of the wealth of material at its disposal and the amount of attention it commands. But it will also have to be admitted that social history is the kind of non-political history that cannot be claimed as belonging to economic history. This much is clear: the territory of economic history is more precisely defined. We shall therefore deal with it first.

Economic history has a longer pedigree than social history; it made its first appearance as the history of commerce, and widened its scope as historians perceived that trade was only one aspect of the economic activities of men. For the relation between economic theory and economic history has always been intimate, and one might describe economic history as the story of the experiences of men in so far as they were concerned with matters of which

[1] *Afscheidsrede* (1925), p. 8.
[2] *De Sociaal-Economische Geschiedenis in haar Verhouding tot Economie, Sociologie, en politieke Geschiedenis* (1934), *passim*. This is a view which finds much favour in certain historical circles in London. It is, however, not free from "academic politics." In practice it amounts to a reluctance to recognize the utility or the necessity of chairs in social history.

70

economists take cognizance.[1] A definition of economics would therefore be useful for an understanding of the scope of economic history, but economics is a discipline whose servants find objectiveness extraordinarily difficult, which is not surprising since its subject matter is more sacred to men than religion, country, or love. Economists will be wise if they wait yet awhile before they plant their frontier posts into the ground, and economic historians must of necessity wait till the economists are ready to speak, if not in unison, at least without disharmony. Economic historians will serve the dignity and utility of their own speciality best by realizing that divisions are methodological and not essential. Meanwhile, their concern with theory places them in a separate category among historians. They must acquaint themselves with some economic theory to know which questions society is asking them. They know that, as Sir William Ashley said, "economic thoughts are themselves economic facts."

The history of economic thought belongs partly to economics and partly to economic history.[2] In so far as it deals with theories as they appeared in the writings of economists, under the influence of previous theories, and influencing in their turn the theories of later economists, it belongs to economics. Every discipline, every science, has an historical aspect which is part of its patrimony, and which its votaries can ignore at their peril only. Once, however, ideas influence the acts of statesmen, shape the prejudices or purposes of societies, or serve as pretext or justification for the behaviour of classes or societies, they belong to history. Is there a way of distinguishing between these two categories? I think that, provided one never forgets that there are no final lines of demarcation in the world of the mind, one can indeed establish

[1] Sir William Ashley defined economic history as "the history of actual human practice with respect to the material basis of life" ("The Place of Economic History in University Studies," *Economic History Review*, January 1927, p. 1). Ashley also says that economic theory and economic history cannot be separated (p. 4). N. S. B. Gras says that "economic history is the story of the various ways in which man has obtained a living" ("The Rise and Development of Economic History," in *Economic History Review*, January 1927, p. 12). See also T. S. Ashton, "The Relation of Economic History to Economic Theory," in *Economica*, May 1946, and G. N. Clark, "The Study of Economic History," in *History*, July 1932.

[2] Cf. Stark, W., *The History of Economics in its Relation to Social Development* (1945).

a principle of distinction. It would be provided by the interest of an historian who does not specialize in economic history but takes his work sufficiently seriously to be curious about the result of the work of economic historians. Economic theories that can inspire an interest in such a reader belong to history: those that do not, belong more properly to economics. The economic historian will certainly wish to know to what extent economic ideas have arisen out of economic conditions. We can expect that he will take up a position between the sovereign rule of the idea and the dictatorship of the event.

As a result of its close connection with economic theory economic history is exposed to one danger. Those who write it are sometimes inclined to forget the kinetic requirements of a good story, and will tend to present the result of their investigations in the form of a series of monographs. The danger does of course exist in other branches of history as well: constitutional history also tends to become a set of isolated chapters dealing with various institutions, in which the requirements of chronology are ignored. The Dutch Republic, which was so rich in economic experiences, has not been lucky in those who undertook to tell the story of these experiences. The best book on the subject, Baasch's *Holländische Wirtschaftsgeschichte* (1927), contains much excellent material and is written with considerable insight into the subject. But it has a number of drawbacks. Perhaps the most irritating is the continual jumping from one period to another in order to deal systematically with trade, industry, fisheries, etc. It is almost impossible for the reader of this book to form an idea of the economic condition of the country at any particular moment. We should not forget that, like all history, economic history is a story.

We can now return to social history, which is history without politics, almost without the state, but also without economics. As I pointed out, this last restriction is exclusively methodological. The social historian will certainly wish to take cognizance of the story told by the economic historian, and will include its main outlines in his own story. But he will not push his research deeply into economic matters, just as his interest in disease, the importance he attaches, for instance, to the spread of syphilis in Europe at the end of the fifteenth century, will not persuade him to study the details of medical history. He will leave this subject to historians who specialize in medical history, and will merely incorporate in his own story the generalizations made by them. Let it be stated once more: social history is not finally and in the nature of things distinct from economic history, nor can the two be identified. No one who is conversant with the pragmatist conception of division will find this an unsettling statement.

One important difference between the two divisions of history with which we are dealing is that unlike economic history, social history is not the historical counterpart of a science or department of human knowledge. Sociology, like economics, is still vague in outline, but it can fight its own battle, and knows the nature of its problems and the fields in which it is expected to work. Social history is confessedly amorphous; the only way of defining it is by elimination. This means that the relationship between social historians and sociologists is neither intimate nor compelling. Social history goes its own way without having perpetually to look over its shoulder at its distant relative in the faculty of social sciences. No doubt sociology has questions to ask from social history, and can make suggestions to the historian about the direction in which he might carry out his preliminary research. But sociology has too many good acquaintances like anthropology, ethnography, social psychology, geography, ever to form intimate friendships. It will not jeopardize its popularity at the club by hobnobbing in one corner with social history alone.

The methodical exclusion of politics and the state from the field of social history does not mean the emancipation of social history from old-fashioned political history. The chronological framework of political history is indispensable to social history. Government interference and planning affects the life of ordinary men, and causes it to differ from country to country. This is an aspect of human existence which cannot be ignored by the social historian. His story is an answer to the question: how did people live in the past? Nothing can therefore be finally excluded from his field. Nothing is too large, neither is anything too small for him. This is why he should also pay attention to limited fields like the story of nutrition, which has other than economic

73

aspects, the history of manners or of costume and, in general, that which the French call *la petite histoire*. Excursions into the by-ways of the past offer possibilities of recreation to the serious historian who does not wish to play patience or solitaire when he needs a rest from his main task. The French are brilliant and often sound at this kind of work, because they do not despise it, but most English historians are as loath to venture into By-path Meadow as Christian's companion Hopeful. In Holland, too, social history on the smaller scale has been neglected by those who enjoyed a professional training, and the history of manners has been told by self-taught men like Schotel, whose valuable work suffers from lack of clarity and from an astounding inno-cence of chronological sense. What the French call *histoire des moeurs* and the Germans *Sittengeschichte* can, when undertaken in a serious frame of mind, provide the psychologist with valuable material.[1] Who is prepared to deny that information about the rise and fall of honesty or of sexual morality in relation to the fortunes of religious beliefs and institutions is of value to society? The sociologist and the philosopher of history will gladly accept data of this kind conveyed to them in the story told by the social historian.

Does the *history of ideas* form a vast autonomous territory within the circle of history? Does it require its own specialists? Or is it an aspect of the study of politics, in the way in which the history of philosophy is an aspect of a properly conceived study of philosophy? We have seen that the history of economic doctrines resorts in part under economic theory, in part under economic history. Can the history of ideas be distributed entirely among disciplines with a past? As we said in the case of the history of economic doctrines, part of the history of ideas will

---

[1] Typical of the genre at its best is the *Sittengeschichte Griechenlands*, by Hans Licht (Zurich, 3 vols., 1925–8), which is a work of erudition. The other kind, represented by the well-known *Illustrierte Sittengeschichte* of Eduard Fuchs (Munich, 6 vols., 1909–12), is an unsystematic medley of valuable information and irrel-evant material. *Sittengeschichte* is an extremely difficult subject to handle. Gaiffe's *L'Envers du Grand Siècle* is an ill-tempered compilation of obvious data, presented without any understanding of the past. *La Femme au 18e Siècle*, by the brothers de Goncourt (1862) is deservedly famous. Its quiet self-assurance and its perfect style mark it as a masterpiece. But it is boring.

interest the ordinary historian, and belongs to history, while the remaining part interests the specialist who is not an historian. The pronunciation of the consonant "g" in France through the ages interests the philologist rather than the historian. At any time, however, questions may arise which put an end to the indifference of the historian: a pronunciation may acquire importance because it indicates a class distinction. Similarly the historian may become interested in the adventures of an idea which left him indifferent while it appeared to have influenced nothing but other ideas. One might study Dutch political and religious pamphlets of the seventeenth century from the point of view of the repetition of themes and the influence exercised by one writer upon another. This would not be history. But the study of the interests and groups that inspired pamphlet-writers, and of the effect of pamphleteers upon political events, provides a story that belongs most certainly to history. The historian will wish to take up an intermediary position between the pan-idealism of Croce-Collingwood and the Marxist denial of the right of any idea to a a life of its own. As Dewey has pointed out, "ideas belong to human beings who have bodies, and there is no separation between the structures and processes of the part of the body that entertains the idea and the part that performs acts."[1]

Two and perhaps three main divisions of history have been discussed and have revealed themselves in their importance and their indistinctness. A number of other branches of history occur to the mind, subdivisions rather than divisions, though it would be difficult to decide where they must be placed. *Biography* is one of them. We have already seen that however much the social function of history is insisted upon, biography cannot be excluded from it. In actual fact every human individual belongs to society, and the story of his life belongs to history. Certain aspects of a life, however, will interest the psychologist more than the historian, although Masson, the biographer of Napoleon and of his family, pleads with considerable plausibility that every aspect of the man who has played an historic part, even the most private corners of his personality, are historically important.[2] The historian cannot help being more particularly attracted by the

[1] *The Public and its Problems*, p. 8.   [2] See Geyl, P., *Napoleon*, pp. 180–1.

possibilities for illustrating the character of a period or a moment of the past of society which he finds in every life-story. Bauer considers that a biography should place the experiences and characteristics of a person in their right relationship with those economic, political, social and artistic conditions of the period to which he owes his rise. The biographer should not only give the subject's physical, but also his moral genealogy.[1] We must beware, however, of the "Life and Times" method so often adopted by English biographers. It entices all but the most level-headed authors into exaggerating the part played by their hero. Many a "Life and Times" biography presents a lop-sided picture of the times it sets out to recount. As usual, wisdom counsels a middle course. The biographer must endeavour to give as much background as is needed to make the life of his subject intelligible, and no more. A moderate partiality is more pardonable in biography than in any other historical genre, provided the bias is in favour of the subject. A denigrating or patronizing biography is nauseating; the only question to which it gives rise is: what made the writer choose this particular subject? As long as partiality is kept within bounds, it is justified. At bottom every human being is good, pathetic, and endearing. The biographer who can detect no virtue in his hero is a poor psychologist and a worse historian.

Provided it does not sail under a false flag, the biography which permits itself to make use of invention may still be worthy of the historian's respect.[2] Under the name of *biographie romancée* it has reached high standards in the hands of French writers. Maurois has revealed much that was unknown to his compatriots about the mind of the English in his lives of Disraeli and of Shelley. *La Prodigieuse Vie d'Honoré de Balzac* (1923) by René Benjamin gives a convincing impression of the gigantic dimensions of the great French novelist, even though it contains invented

---

[1] *Op. cit.*, pp. 129–30.

[2] I insist very much upon this proviso, and do not wish to go beyond the statement that the *biographie romancée* may, like the historical novel, deserve the historian's respect. Or it may not. It entirely depends on the professional historians. If J. E. Neale's *Queen Elizabeth* has fulfilled its function, it will have done away with the need for Strachey's *Elizabeth and Essex*. Huizinga, in *De Wetenschap der Geschiedenis* (1937), shows strong objections to the romanced biography. Huizinga's book is important, but it often fails to draw the ultimate conclusions implied in its premises.

dialogue and details for which there is no historical justification. The reader of Strachey's *Elizabeth and Essex* learns something about the history of manners of the Elizabethan period, while *Eminent Victorians*, by the same author, though similarly a caricature of the personages whose lives are described, is apt to create an absorbing interest in the period to which they belong, an interest that will send many a reader to sounder authorities for the satisfaction of his newly kindled curiosity. The "romanced biography" must, of course, not masquerade as history. If honestly presented as being no more than it is, this genre deserves, like the historical novel, to be recognized as first-rate propaganda material for the promotion of historical studies. It would be churlish to grudge the intense pleasure of reading and thinking about the past to those who cannot take in what historians have written. If historians were less inclined to despise popularization and to leave it to the non-professional they would be better able to face the competition of science for the goodwill and the support of peoples and governments.

Historical geography belongs to geography as much as to history. *Local history* is an important division of history; it has great possibilities as a means for interesting young people and those who cannot become professional historians in the methods of research, and of revealing to them the joys to be derived from a knowledge of the past. It is supremely flexible, can be approached from a number of angles, and can be practised by the scholar as well as by the honest amateur. In the latter case it is exposed to one danger, that of degenerating into sterile antiquarianism. This will happen only when it is pursued without any reference to general history and to larger issues. The professional historian can do much to protect local history from this danger by encouraging those who practise it, by taking an interest in the results they achieve, and by making use of these results in the telling of his own story. The study of local history has rejuvenated the history of the French Revolution and liberated it from much irresponsible theorizing. The peculiar constitution of the Dutch Republic which gave so much power to the administrators of small towns makes local history of the utmost importance for the understanding of the foreign policy of the Republic.

Ecclesiastical History is not the same subject as the history of religion. It belongs to political more than to social history. The story of the Church of Rome cannot be separated from diplomatic history, nor, indeed, from military history. It would be difficult, however, to tell the story of monasteries or of the secular clergy without taking into account the findings of economic and social history.

Clearly, then, distinction and division in history has no absolute or final character. Its relative and provisional nature is a warning against exaggerated specialization. The division of history into periods is methodological and little else, and historians cannot be asked to imprison themselves within one of its divisions or subdivisions. It is good, perhaps, to become particularly proficient in the history of one century, but the man who refuses to look over the wall of his period is guilty of what Bussemaker once called "a foolishly exaggerated specialization, brought about by the terror of appearing unscientific and dilettante."[1] Bussemaker tells the story of a German historian who, on being invited to deliver a lecture on the sixteenth century, indignantly replied: "My life-task is the history of Germany from 1525 to 1530!"

It is also dangerous to attach too much importance to the division of history into subjects and to allow oneself to become exclusively absorbed by one of them. Over-specialization in economic history, for instance, may induce an historian to share the fallacy of those who imagine that even the simplest occurrence invariably finds a place in a causal chain beginning and ending with economic events. As G. N. Clark remarks: "There is still scope for general historians who bring together the conclusions of specialists and supply all of them alike with a comprehensive view of the interrelated diversity of past times."[2] If professional historians refuse to write general history, their duty will be carried out by amateurs.[3]

---

[1] *Op. cit.*, p. 7.   [2] *Historical Scholarship*, p. 18.

[3] The indignation of professional historians against H. G. Wells was therefore curiously illogical. Toynbee is a generous exception to the fashion of crying haro at H. G. Wells (*cf. The Study of History*, Vol. I, pp. 4–5). I remember in what horrified tones a British colleague once told me that a German scholar who had made a reputation for himself with his studies on nineteenth-century German history was now engaged in writing a *Weltgeschichte*.

Chapter III

THE PAST ITSELF?

§ 1

A MATTER OF LANGUAGE

HISTORY is the story of the experiences of men living in civilized societies. Are these experiences the result of the jerks of infinitesimally small packets of energy that go by the name of matter, are they the *Gesta Dei per nucleos*, trials inflicted by God upon created souls for their good and for His glory? This is no more the concern of the student of the methods of history than it is the concern of the historian as historian. Our definition takes hold of history in action, not in its essence; as an operation, not as a thing. It excludes the interpretation of those who would make history a universal philosophy of life, just as it rejects, and with equal emphasis, the views of those who would limit history to the preliminary search for events. Can it be claimed, after so radical a limitation, that our approach is tolerant and liberal, that it leaves room for the utmost variety of treatment and interpretation?

To begin with, if the historian is represented here as the servant of society, emphasis is laid upon the fact that his service is free and respects the dignity of the human individual. Moreover, no doctrinaire exclusions are advocated: our criterion is strictly methodological. The extremists on the right and on the left are not sent into the wilderness. Provided they leave history undisturbed in the possession of the ground to which it is entitled, the antiquarians and the Croce-ites may write and teach to their hearts' content. Meanwhile, freedom is safe also within the region which genuine historians intend to keep as their own. Since comment, inessential and unavoidable, does not affect the factual character of the story, it is allowed to blossom and to bear its varied crop.

One issue remains to be dealt with if we are to give a complete answer to the question "what is history?" For it cannot be denied that, in every language, the word "history" or its equivalent has a legitimate acceptation apart from that represented by our definition, and which tallies in no way with it. When we say: "history repeats itself," or, more wisely, "history does not repeat itself"; when we assert that "history is one big stream in which there can be no divisions," we are, surely, not referring to a story. Nor can the statement that "history is pitiless, and respects those only who are tough" be true, or false, about a story. The word "history" is often used as the name of the content of the story, as synonymous with "past experiences of human beings living in civilized societies," or simply with "the past." The philosopher Schiller uses it in this way when he says "history has never crushed the faith of the optimist, even though it has never realized his dreams," and "we can, to some extent, steer our course and that of history."[1] The *Oxford English Dictionary*, which gives as first acceptation of the word that of a written narrative of important public events and the branch of knowledge which deals with them, gives as a sense acquired later by the word: "The whole train of events connected with a particular country, society, person, thing, etc., and forming the subject of his or its history," and also "the aggregate of past events in general, the course of events or human affairs." In his *Barnevelt* Motley mentioned, says the *O.E.D.*, "the tragi-comedy which we call human history" (1874). This new acceptation of the word is sometimes called "objective history," while the older sense, which we have defined in the previous chapter, is then called "subjective history."

Some authors limit their use of the word history to the "objective" sense. For Powicke history is "the events themselves," and he sees history as a lofty mountain, cold and stark, upon which the historian's mind plays like a gleam. When the gleam has gone history is still there, and so, naturally, the historian "will know that his work is imperfect, his vision transient, and his goal still far away."[2] One can heartily agree with this realism without admitting its lexicological foundation. Sir Maurice Powicke

---

[1] *Must Philosophers Disagree?* p. 277. On history subjective and objective, *cf.* Bauer, *op. cit.*, pp. 11–12.

[2] *History, Freedom and Religion*, pp. 8, 13–14. The precise opposite of the doctrine of Oakeshott, and, through him, of Collingwood.

favours the "objective" interpretation of the word history as a preliminary to his agreement with the mysticism of Collingwood, an agreement which, as we have noticed before, is not thoroughgoing. Most adherents of the school of historical clairvoyance, however, welcome the fact that the word history is used in two different ways.

For Hegel the union of an objective and a subjective aspect in the one word "history" is a source of delight. One word for the *historia rerum gestarum* and for the *res gestae* themselves! This is no accident: "es ist eine innerliche gemeinsame Grundlage, welche sie zusammen hervortreibt."[1] Hegel then explains how important is the historical narrative for the preservation of the finer elements of the civilization and culture of a people, in pages that are pleasant to read. He shows that the Chinese had a history, but the Persians and the Indians had not, and what an immense difference it made to all of them. But all this would be equally true if the subject matter of history were called "the human past" instead of "history." Nothing Hegel says really proves the advantage or the significance of the fact that the word "history" has two different meanings. Dardel, whom I have already mentioned, is aware of the *double entente* to such an extent that he distinguishes between *l'Histoire* in the objective sense and *l'histoire* in the subjective sense. This play with capital and lower case cannot be adopted in English, where "history" can easily be the first word in a sentence, while ordinarily *histoire* does not appear without its article. Dardel makes no secret of his preference for *l'Histoire*; he speaks of "la discordance qui sépare la réalité historique et vivante de la pâle image qu'en propose une science historique anonyme."[2]

Not every writer who uses the word "history" in its two acceptations is as frank about it as Hegel or Dardel. In *The Meaning of Meaning* Ogden and Richards mention a device used by controversialists which they call "the Utraquistic subterfuge," which, they say, "has probably made more bad argument plausible than any other controversial device which can be practised upon trustful humanity. It has long been recognized," they add, "that the term 'perception' may have either a physical or a mental

---

[1] *Vorlesungen ueber die Philosophie der Geschichte* (2nd ed., 1837), p. 75.
[2] *Op. cit.*, p. 2. Let he who can reconcile this statement with Dardel's idealism.

referent. Does it refer to what is perceived, or to the perceiving of this? Similarly, 'knowledge' may refer to what is known or to the knowing of it. The Utraquistic subterfuge consists in the use of such terms for both at once of the diverse referents in question" (p. 239). It is, if I may allow myself a very brief excusion, rather regrettable that these two scrupulous students of "meaning" should have chosen such an unfortunate name for this controversial device. Indeed, the Utraquists whose story is told by ecclesiastical historians were such sticklers for precision that they insisted upon distinguishing between the flesh and the blood of Christ to the extent of demanding that the sacrament be administered to laymen under both species. Those who were really guilty of what our authors so wrongly call "the Utraquistic subterfuge" were the enemies of the Utraquists, the orthodox, who contended that the flesh and the blood were present under either species:

> Caro cibus, sanguis potus,
> Manet tamen Christus totus
> Sub utraque specie.

Those who have recourse to the subterfuge exposed by Ogden and Richards do not, as these authors allege, use certain terms in both their acceptations at once. They use the term now in the one acceptation, then in the other, without giving notice of the fact. There is an old name, regularly used by traditional logic to indicate this sin against good sense. The term is "equivocation."[1] But it sounds less forbidding than Utraquism, which we might therefore adopt as a useful deterrent. For it is not only the Croces and the Collingwoods who revel in "Utraquistic" play upon the word "history." What, indeed, are we to make of the statement by Professor Galbraith that "history, I suppose, is the Past—so far as we know it," followed, in the same paragraph, by the words "history, then, is made by the historian"?[2] Historians cannot make the past. To be the *sempiternum nunc* is the prerogative of Divinity, "I am that I am—Ego sum qui sum" (Exod. iii. 14).

The trouble is that though there are less ideas in our world

---

[1] Schiller, *Formal Logic*, p. 365.
[2] In *Why we Study History*, Historical Association publications, nr. 131 (1944).

than heads to house them in,[1] words are scarcer still. It is by no
means improbable that men learned to think while they were
learning to talk. But possibly because the brains of men are more
complicated than their vocal organs, the growth of thought was
less backward than that of speech. Our restricted mental patrimony notwithstanding, we must allow many ideas to go name-
less, or let them share a name with others. The same word has to
serve as a symbol for more than one idea. Lexicological meta-
morphoses were not guided by an Enlightened Logician; they
were the result of naïve imaginings, feeble puns, obscure allu-
sions, vague, unconscious associations, in short, of processes that
are studied by the followers of a relatively recent discipline called
semantic.[2] It is by chance, or, more precisely, as a result of causes
which have nothing to do with the nature of history that its
name acquired a second acceptation. Let us resignedly accept this
complication of our vocabulary.

Efforts have been made to escape from equivocation and
"Utraquism" by using the word "historiography" instead of
"history" as the name of the discipline we have defined in the
previous chapter. Oman, who was not a devout servant of
language, and was an unstable master of definition, once said, in
referring to history: "I mean the record of actual past events and
not historiography, the art of dealing on paper with past events."[3]
There is much to be said for the policy of avoiding homonyms,
but it should not be done in defiance of language. Language may
be a poor tool, but it is the collective property of a nation, and
transcends the fads of individuals. "Historiography" is an ill-
starred word. It commands the affection of the extremists on the
right, of the people who wish to identify research and history,
and who, apart from calling the story of the past "historiography,"
would readily call the study of the past "historiology." They
would reserve the name "history" for research, on the ground

[1] "Tout est dit, et l'on vient trop tard, depuis plus de sept mille ans qu'il y a
des hommes et qui pensent," La Bruyère, Les Caractères, "Des Ouvrages de
l'Esprit," I.

[2] Michel Bréal, inventor of semantic, whom I learned to know in my youth
by his Essai de Sémantique (1897) and his Pour mieux connaître Homère (1906) is, I
suppose, no longer à la page. But he opened a new field to philologists, and his
work is a milestone.   [3] The Writing of History, p. 187.

83

that the Greek word *historia* meant investigation. Etymology is a poor guide for the correct use of language.

§ 2

PHILOSOPHY OF HISTORY

The dual acceptation of the word "history" is most aptly illustrated in the expression "philosophy of history." We cannot yet profitably define the term "philosophy," but we might reach a provisional agreement about it, as we did about the word "history" at an earlier stage in this book, and say that we intend to use it for any investigation which is more thorough and more leisurely than would be warranted in the ordinary practice of life. The philosophy of history is, then, the thorough and leisurely investigation of history and of its problems, and since history must now be taken to signify both the story and its contents, the philosophic investigation also falls into two parts. The distinction is clearly made by Bauer, who says that there are two kinds of philosophy of history.[1] There is a formal *Geschichtsphilosophie* which investigates the logic and the epistemology of history. This, of course, is the systematic study of history as a story. The present book can be called a philosophy of history in this sense of the word; it is almost invariably in this acceptation that the Germans speak of *Geschichtsphilosophie*. Bauer's second division is a philosophy of history "in the narrower sense," as he puts it; it tries to understand the course of historical events. It takes history in the sense of the civilized human past. This is the sense which the French attach to the words *philosophie de l'histoire*.

We can easily avoid confusion and equivocation by using the expression "philosophy of history" in the French sense exclusively, and it will not appear in any other sense in the following parts of this book.[2] To indicate the formal philosophy of history we shall use the name "methodology," which means the systematic or philosophical investigation of method. This word has the sanction of usage, is precise, and belongs to the common vocabulary which the different departments of human knowledge are slowly evolving to their common advantage.

---

[1] *Op. cit.*, p. 40; *cf.* Bernheim, *op. cit.*, pp. 685 *sqq.*   [2] Below, III: iv.

Part Two

THE DETECTION OF EVENTS

Chapter I

EVENTS AND THEIR TRACES

THE historian has to tell, as accurately as possible, the story required by society. Let us now observe him while he carries out his task.

Too often methodologists think of history merely as a department of human knowledge; their concern is solely with knowledge and how it can be increased. They deal with their subject systematically, divide it formally, and allot to their views about the actual narrative a modest place at the end of their survey. The divorce between methodology and practice can be observed in postgraduate students who undertake their first independent work. They rush at texts and documents, copy and summarize indiscriminately, and acquire more notes than critical sense. They see no clear purpose before them, because they have not been taught that history is the performance of a function, that it is an operation, an activity, that method must be practical before being methodical, that it must look forward instead of looking back anxiously at precept and precedent.

The blacksmith who must shoe a horse begins by placing an iron bar in the fire. He prises off the horse's old shoe, blows the bellows, does some hammering at the anvil, files and evens the horse's hoof, goes back to the anvil for more hammering and shaping. If he carried out each operation in strict rotation, the job would take him twice as long. The practical purpose dictates his method, not an intellectual concern with the theory of horse-shoeing. The task of the historian must, of course, be divided into different activities, most of all if he is a beginner. We have clarified our views about distinction and division when we surveyed the field of history.[1] We know that divisions must be unambitious, rough-and-ready. Let us say, then, that the historian has in the first place to collect the material out of which his story will be composed, and in the second place to tell the story. We must, however, note at once that the first operation may well continue

[1] Above, I: ii: § 3.

87

while the second has already begun, and also, that throughout the first operation the coming task of story-telling influences his mind. The blacksmith buys his iron bar from the right manufacturer, he further makes sure of its quality by testing it while he handles it with his pincers, and hammers it. In days to come he will also learn what the owner of the horse thinks of the quality of the shoe that is now being made. Throughout, then, the finished article in use is not only the purpose, but the norm of the blacksmith's operations. We shall discover at a later date to what an extent the telling of the story must provide the final test of the value of the material collected by the historian.

§ 1

ACCEPTED HISTORY

Leaving the story till we reach Part Three of this book, we shall now examine the problems that arise while the historian collects his material. We shall note first of all that he does not begin with a clean slate. If he did, he would be unique among intellectual workers. Every enquiry goes from the known to the unknown, from the discovered to the undiscovered. William James speaks of those "previous truths of which every new enquiry takes account."[1] Dewey says: "What is already known . . . is of immense importance; inquiry could not proceed a step without it."[2] The methodologist Bauer takes the same view: "Alles wissenschaftliche Forschen ist im Grunde ein Weiterforschen."[3]

A relay race of indefinite duration: Galbraith sees it as "handing on the living tradition of historical knowledge."[4] If we look at it from right to left, as it were, we see the new historian taking over

---

[1] *Pragmatism* (1907), pp. 245-8.

[2] *Experience and Nature*, p. 154. *Cf.* also *ibid.*, pp. 428-9. Alfred Sidgwick points out that in acquiring the facts of any recognized science or profession, a period of studentship has to be gone through, "a period of acquiring *accepted* notions and formulas" (*The Process of Argument*, p. 191).

[3] *Op. cit.*, p. 82. *Wissenschaft*, of course, to be read as "learning" not "science"! G. N. Clark says: "Historical knowledge . . . is built up by specialists who perpetually revise and correct the details of accepted conclusions" (*Historical Scholarship*, p. 9).   [4] In *Why we Study History*, p. 7.

the torch, accepting the story told by his predecessors. It seems so elementary, but I have found out, in the course of postgraduate teaching, that it was the most difficult part of my task to make this clear to beginners. Many who have long passed the learner's stage are unaware of the need to apply this process. A vast body of narrative, the quality of which no one disputes, is available to the historian. He finds it in up-to-date textbooks and in the monographs written by his predecessors. He finds it in the works of recognized historians. Of course, he must not look upon this material as immutably valid, as forever worthy of being believed and repeated. As Dewey observes in the passage from which I have just quoted, this material "is held subject to use, and is at the mercy of the discoveries which it makes possible. It has to be adjusted to the latter, and not the latter to it."

However conscious he may be of this important proviso, the historian will have to accept much knowledge on trust. He must specialize, as we know, for practical reasons. What is outside his special area will have to be accepted by him, not only at the beginning of his task, but throughout! The social historian, as we saw, constantly uses the results of the research carried out by economic historians. The historian who specializes in the story of social and class relations in the Dutch Republic will be well advised to acquaint himself with the story of similar relations in other commonwealths of merchants like the Venetian Republic and the bourgeois cities of Switzerland. It would be inadvisable to tell the story of the cloth industry at Leyden at the time of the Dutch Republic without a knowledge of the story of that industry in the towns of medieval Flanders or in Florence. But if the historian of the Leyden industry were obliged to break fresh ground before he can satisfy his curiosity about Ghent, Bruges, Ypres, or Florence, the town of Leyden would be kept waiting indefinitely. Its historian must therefore go to the body of writings to which, with Oman, I give the name of "accepted history."

No blind surrender to his predecessors is demanded from the historian. In the course of his training he has acquired critical acumen; he has increased it each time he prepared a new work. The books he reads will have been recommended in their bibliographies by specialists whom he has reason to trust.[1] Even though he knows no details about the research that went into their preparation, he can assess the way in which their authors have applied the historical method. A specialist historian who will not venture an opinion on the work of a specialist in another field betrays his inner uncertainties and casts doubt upon his knowledge of historical method. Halphen points out that there is a *petitio principii* in the fact that, with the purpose of extracting the lesson contained in a document, one has to read much second-hand literature. To learn, one has to know a good deal already. Halphen says that there is a begging of principles on the threshold of every discipline, and that it is better to admit this than to imagine that one's own fantasy suffices for the interpretation of a document.[2] Haphen's little introduction to history is excellent, but what he says here illustrates the disadvantage of treating the matter too theoretically. What does happen in this case is, amusingly enough, that the theoretical approach proves self-contradictory, and that to escape from the difficulty Halphen has to admit that theory is unnecessary, since practice is self-explanatory and self-sufficient. A further, and somewhat pathetic example of the way in which theorists find themselves betrayed by their theory occurs a few pages further on; we are warned by Halphen that, when consulting a witness, we must make sure that he is a real witness, not one who repeats the testimony of others. But here the author feels constrained to make an admission—"un aveu s'impose." We may find, he says, that an event is known to us solely through an authority based entirely upon the statements of witnesses who are no longer available. Most of the works of Livy, the first books of the history of the Franks by Gregory of Tours, belong to this category. Since there is no other way of

---

[1] This trust is the result of complicated mental operations. Historian A is said by historian B, who reviews his work, to be trustworthy. We accept the verdict of B because C, whose work we can test from our own knowledge, thinks highly of B. Reality is even more involved, but unless we believe in a vast conspiracy we shall act upon the assumption that the scaffolding consisting of these intricately crossed pieces is solid enough to carry us. No certitude, but practical *efficacy*. Bussemaker (*Over de Waardeering der Feiten*, pp. 9–11) and Langlois and Seignobos (*op. cit.*, pp. 198–9) point to the necessity of accepting the work of one's predecessors, subject to the exercise of the critical faculty acquired through one's previous work.   [2] *Introduction à l'Histoire*, p. 22.

knowing the story they tell us, we must provisionally accept their version. This brings us back full sail to accepted history as the starting point of all historical investigation.

Accepted history, then, is the story of civilized human societies down to the present day as told by historians. No historian can be expected to acquaint himself with the whole of it, but he cannot know too much of it, in his own field, around it, and away from it. It is in accepted history that society has to seek the points of comparison that will guide its action in difficult situations. But accepted history, point of departure and point of arrival of all historical work, must be subjected to constant emendation in two respects. Since the story must be as accurate as possible, the historian will, whenever he has the opportunity to do so, correct its details by rejecting from it elements, and most of all generalizations, that clash with events unearthed and duly established by his own research. Workers who use the Institute of Historical Research in London collect factual improvements to the stories told in the *Dictionary of National Biography*. Such work of pure correction, inspired by the accidental emergence of new events, is of real, but subsidiary, importance. Only the right-wing extremism which identifies history with research could give rise to the mistaken view that the corrective aspect of research is the more important. There is another kind of revision at once more thoroughgoing and more significant. I have dealt already with the need for refocusing the narrative as a result of questions asked by the historian himself acting as a representative member of society,[1] and I gave some examples of the way in which this operation is carried out. In the light of what has now been added it will be seen that this refocusing is the principal duty of the historian.

In normal circumstances the refocusing of the story takes place unselfconsciously. Only occasionally can the retelling of the story be called sensational. The revolutionary refocusing of the story of the Revolt of the Netherlands by Geyl is an example. It demolished all that remained of John Lothrop Motley except his immortal style. Yet, years after the publication of the first volume of Geyl's *Geschiedenis van de Nederlandse Stam*, and of the

[1] Above, I: i: § 2.

91

appearance of an English translation of the relevant part under the title of *The Revolt of the Netherlands*, Mr. Cadoux thought it right to publish a book based upon the story told by Motley.[1] Clearly, in using accepted history we must make sure that it still deserves to be accepted. It is a gift horse that cannot be looked too often in the mouth. Like all precedent, it must bear credentials of quality.

The posthumous story of Mazarin is another illustration of this precept. For many years Luigi Mazzarini has been looked upon as one of those foreigners who rode the country they administered with ruthless disregard of its interests, like Buonaparte or Alberoni. The generalization is dangerous in any case: Alberoni was probably as good for Spain as Napoleon was bad for France, and Bernard Shaw was wise in giving twenty-first century England a Chinese Prime Minister in *Back to Methuselah*. The responsibility for Mazarin's evil reputation lies with Voltaire, who drew a most unflattering portrait of this minister in his *Siècle de Louis XIV*. It happens that Voltaire took his portrait from the *Mémoires* of Saint-Simon. ". . . Tel fut l'ouvrage du détestable Mazarin, dont la ruse et la perfidie fut la vertu, et la frayeur la prudence." Voltaire read the *Mémoires* in manuscript form. Now although Saint-Simon was born after the cardinal's death, he hated the memory of this builder of absolutism who had contributed so much to make the high nobility subservient to the monarchy. For the Duke of Saint-Simon was a reactionary who wanted to restore the traditional power of his caste. Voltaire implicitly believed Saint-Simon, and his story had a long run. It was accepted from 1751 to 1879, when another French historian began the publication of his voluminous life of Mazarin.[2] André Chéruel also edited the correspondence of the cardinal and studied the note-books in which Mazarin jotted down from day to day his views on political affairs, not for the eyes of posterity, but solely to clarify his own mind before taking action. Chéruel

---

[1] I drew the attention of the late Mr. Cadoux to the danger he was running while his book was still in manuscript. There is no need to revert to this painful subject after his death. Cadoux's work proves that our distrust of specialization should not be carried to extremes.

[2] Chéruel, A., *Histoire de France pendant la Minorité de Louis XIV*, 4 vols., 1879, and *Histoire de France sous le Ministère de Mazarin*, 1651–61, 3 vols., 1882.

gives of Mazarin a picture that differs considerably from what was then the accepted story. While admitting his faults, he praises his virtues, which were many, and shows what great services he rendered to the monarchy and to France. Yet, more often than not, historians continue to treat Voltaire's interpretation of Mazarin as though it were still accepted history. Chéruel wrote at a time when the French, smarting under their recent defeat, consoled themselves with thoughts of the power and glory of past centuries. The Sun-King was to them an object of pride—they still find it difficult to judge him objectively—and the roots of his greatness, with Mazarin among them, became a matter of immediate national importance. Chéruel refocused the story in answer to questions dictated by the preoccupations of the French community of his day.[1]

The process of constant revision to which accepted history is subjected is nowhere more patent than in the judgment passed upon periods of history by successive generations. The Renaissance saw antiquity as an age incomparably superior to itself. We can equal the ancients neither in their vices nor in their virtues, says Montaigne, for both were greater.[2] A remarkable confession of decadence, which the greatest admirer of classical antiquity would not care to repeat nowadays. All our backsliding notwithstanding, progress in some form or other has become an article of faith with the majority of civilized men, and accepted history has ceased to look upon antiquity as a period of human perfection.

§ 2

EVENTS

Like the finished story which the historian hopes one day to produce, accepted history consists of two elements: "a hard core of facts,"[3] and the expression of personal views which previous

---

[1] See the varying views taken by English writers of Cardinal Wolsey, as analysed by F. Pollard in *Wolsey*, pp. 2–4.

[2] "Nos forces ne sont non plus capables de les joindre en ces parties là vitieuses, qu'aux vertueuses; car les unes et les autres partent d'une vigueur d'esprit qui estoit sans comparaison plus grande en eux qu'en nous," *Essais*, I, xlix.

[3] "We must not forget that there are such things as facts. . . . All our interpretation of the past has a hard core of facts, however much it may be concealed by

historians were unable to omit. With this second element the new historian will do what he likes. He will take it, reject it, or adopt it in part. It is the factual core that matters. The historian accepts it, adds to it, may modify some of its detail. We must, in this section, examine its nature more closely.

The human past consists of things that happened. There is no hierarchy among these occurrences. Each of them is a sequence of occurrences of a lower and more elementary order, and part of a sequence of occurrences of a higher and more complex order. It is conceivable that all occurrences are physical, and that the day will come when they can be described in their physical details by minds better informed than those of the best informed physicists of our day. Meanwhile, an occurrence remains an elusive phenomenon. It is never single, as I have pointed out, and cannot be isolated. The apprehension of the occurrence by the human mind is in itself a mystery that has baffled and still baffles metaphysicians. The historian, who is a pragmatist even if he does not know it, asks no more than to be allowed to behave as though his mind can get hold of occurrences which, by means of the linguistic symbols that stand for them, can be put into his story.[1]

Now among the occurrences which must have taken place in the past a vast majority cannot possibly interest the historian. They have never earned a place in accepted history; the historian will never need them for his story. Some occurrences on the other hand appear suitable for insertion in the story, because they possess a significance. Mr. Lloyd George had breakfast every day; a long, a lengthy sequence of occurrences. But sometimes he collected a number of persons, most of them, in all probability, endowed with the ordinary mortal's reluctance to things matutinal. He wearied them at the breakfast table with his exceptional vitality, and, in their defenceless condition, extracted concessions from them. Such a Lloyd Georgian breakfast was more than an occurrence, it was an event. The Dutch writer on

the surrounding pulp of disputable interpretation," Clark, G. N., *Historical Scholarship*, p. 20. I noted before that, although this author does not admit that history is a story, his interpretation does not *in actual practice* differ from that which I offer. [1] See, however, below, II: iii: § 2.

the philosophy of history Van Schilfgaarde makes a distinction between occurrence and event (*gebeurlijkheid* and *feit*), but for him the difference is one of essence. Anatole France, whose important contribution to historical thought will be examined at a later stage,[1] makes a distinction between historical and non-historical occurrences which amounts to the same thing. He does not believe the difference to be essential. He looks upon it as arbitrary.

Actually, as an unprejudiced analysis of the historian's practice will show, the difference is neither essential nor arbitrary. Certain occurrences are important from the point of view of *my* story. I look upon them as significant, because I shall want to include them, or may want to include them in it. For me they are events. The noting down of a name in a baptismal register is an occurrence. For a biographer such an entry may be an event. One historian's occurrence is another's event. The distinction does not depend upon the historian's personality or preferences. It depends upon the use to which the occurrence or event can be put: it is pragmatical. We have to note another aspect of the event. It is, and remains, an occurrence, if considered by itself, and is therefore, like every occurrence, reducible to a sequence of occurrences of a lower degree,[2] or it can be linked with a sequence of other events to form one event of a higher degree or order. On such a day, Field-Marshal Montgomery drank no wine: occurrence. Field-Marshal Montgomery never drank wine: event, consisting of a sequence of occurrences. It can be stated in the form of a description: "Field-Marshal Montgomery was a teetotaller," but this noun still indicates an event or a sequence of occurrences. Mr. Churchill made a speech: event. Mr. Churchill's speeches at one time gave expression to the determination of the British people: sequence of events, forming an event of a higher order.

As a result of these observations the task of the historian lends itself to description in two different ways. We can say that he must collect a number of occurrences, and determine afterwards which of them rank as events from the point of view of the story

[1] Below, II: iv: § 2.
[2] "... wie jede einzelne geschichtliche Tatsache eine Verflechtung von Erscheinungen verschiedenartigster Herkunft darstellt ..." (Bauer, *op. cit.*, p. 29).

he wishes to tell. Or we can say that, ignoring mere occurrences, the historian will collect events likely to interest him from the point of view of his story, and will determine at a later stage which of these events will be retained finally as useful in the telling of the story. The difference between the two statements is verbal. In practice they are equivalent. I shall use the second version, but the first version can be substituted by anyone who finds it more satisfactory. Let us, then, agree to call "event" any occurrence that is, or may become, of interest to the historian.

We must also observe, for future reference, the fact that events can be grouped together, not only in sequences, i.e. chronologically, but in series. Series are logical: they are connected by links that may be real, but that are, in any case, determined by the human mind. A short-circuit may figure in a series of events that interests the electrical engineer and in another series that interests a fire insurance office. It may, at the same time, belong to a series or to a sequence that interests the newspaper reporter and even the social historian.

§ 3

TRACES

The material out of which the historian must compose his story consists of events. How, where, is he to find them? They happened in the past, they have disappeared with it. No profound philosophy is needed to justify the assertion that the historian cannot have a direct knowledge of past events. But he may assume that they have had some effect, that they have left "relics" behind them, as Collingwood says,[1] or "traces," to adopt the word used by those wise methodologists Langlois and Seignobos.[2] We shall endeavour, at a later stage, to examine the deeper implications of the relation between trace and event, and the difference, if there be any, between the manner in which we know the one and know the other.[3] Meanwhile we are given a hint by the

[1] *The Idea of History*, p. 282.
[2] They make repeated use of the word "traces": "les traces qu'ont laisées les pensées et les actes des hommes," *op. cit.*, p. 1. Also pp. 2 and 44.
[3] Below, II: v: § 1.

Latin language which uses the word *vestigium* for the trace left by the sole of the foot and also the sole of the foot itself, with the implication that an intimate relation exists between a trace and that by which it was left.

To be acquainted with a trace brings us nearer to the event by which it was left: the historian in search of events that have gone will look for traces that are still there. Of what nature are these traces; where are they to be found; are there ways of estimating their value as traces? Invigorating questions that should prompt men to action. But methodologists do not ask them; historians put them to themselves unconsciously. With a unanimity that is rare in the historical world, the orthodox, the deviationists to the right and to the left, the pure theorists, all chant: we obtain our knowledge from historical sources! Huizinga has advanced the view that there is a play-element in all modern scholarship. The tendency to carry system to extremes that are detrimental to observation and inference is play. The specialist plays with his technical terms. Much of the competition between the practitioners of learning is unnecessary; it is "ludic."[1] Historians kneeling at their sources, dipping the ladle of research into the waters of knowledge, and preparing to decant its contents into the amphora of publication with a view to making "a contribution to knowledge" (otherwise, to close a perpetual circle of futility) are men playing with a metaphor. It is a dangerous game. It encourages the superstition "that knowledge is valid in the degree in which it is a revelation of antecedent existences or Being."[2] Here is the past distilled into knowledge, dripping down to us from a source: let us catch some of it!

Unfortunately there is no Past, available for distillation, capture, manipulation, observation and description. There have been, and there are, events in complex and innumerable combinations, and no magic formula will give us mastery over them. "La science historique ne gagne rien à s'envelopper de mystère," says Louis Halphen.[3] There are, instead, some rather humdrum operations to be performed. We suspect or surmise that an event,

---

[1] *Homo ludens* (1938), pp. 292–4. There is an English translation.
[2] As Dewey summarizes the aberration in *The Quest for Certainty*, p. 45.
[3] *Initiation aux Etudes d'Histoire du Moyen-Age*, 2nd ed., 1946, p. 159.

a set of events, has taken place: where can we find the traces they must have left behind them? Or we have come across some traces: what are they worth, as traces, and to what events do they point? Later on we shall find out which events we can, from our own knowledge of their traces, safely believe to have taken place. It remains a fact, nevertheless, that the whole historical world uses the word "sources," and will continue to do so. By refusing to follow its example we shall at any rate draw attention to the fact that history is not a deductive science, but an activity and a craft. And when we come to the question what knowledge of past events the historian can actually reach, we shall find that the trace-event relation provides us with an answer that could hardly be found in the theoretical knowledge-source relation which, in any case, begs the question instead of answering it.

The methodologists establish distinctions among their sources and divide them. We shall follow their example and attempt to classify our traces, although we shall avoid complicated divisions and subdivisions, as they are merely an intellectual game.[1] A first distinction that occurs to the mind is that between traces left unintentionally by men in the course of their activities, and traces intended by men to inform posterity of their deeds. The distinction lacks classical beauty: it does not provide a sharp boundary line. Must we call a Pyramid a tomb or a boast uttered in the face of eternity? Is a diary the trace of a man's wish to live in the mind of posterity, or of his need for self-expression, or of his desire to note his experiences for the sake of refreshing his memory when necessary? Is it written for the diarist himself, like that of Pepys, or for his children and descendants, or for posterity in general? Is it a trace of the diarist's desire to achieve all these purposes at once?

A few minutes spent in meditating upon the answer to these questions will give us a deeper insight into the nature of traces. It will reveal two things about them. The first is that they seldom, if ever, occur singly. They appear in bundles. A diary can be at the same time a trace of self-absorption, of efficiency, of loneliness, of the desire for immortality, or to put it differently, of the fear of death. The same diary can be a trace of a writer's using a

[1] Bauer gives an impressive classification, op. cit., pp. 161–2.

goose-quill, of his being a connoisseur of paper, a faddist about ink. It can be a trace of the fact that he was a good business man as well as a stylist, it can be a trace of his patriotism or his lubricity; it is, in any case, a trace of the impression made upon him by a number of events.

Even though, as I suggested, we may postpone for a while the consideration of the deeper implication of the relation between trace and event, we have found out enough by now about the act of trace-producing to venture into a definition of a trace. Surely, a trace is nothing but the still perceptible termination or culmination of a sequence of events or of several sequences of events. The method which uses traces produces more immediate results than the orthodox method which thinks in terms of sources.[1] The source gives us knowlege, which is a reflection and an abstraction. The trace is itself an event, and by looking at it we begin to perceive events that stand behind it, but are of the same nature. We sample the past itself without intermediary. We are, from the outset, constructing our story and carrying out our social task. And it is from the practical point of view, with an eye to the manner in which they must be handled, that we shall most profitably divide our traces. This is why we shall first distinguish between historical and non-historical traces. Everything around us is a trace of past events. The table, the books, the pictures and all the furniture in my study are traces of human activities, but they are not all of interest to the historian, though any of them may become historical traces if they can lead the historian to find out through them sequences of past events that would be of value for the composition of his story. Among historical traces we shall distinguish between immaterial and material traces, and we shall divide material traces into those that are written and those that are not. Since the hierarchy of divisions has no practical importance we shall therefore simply establish

[1] Unconscious "undinism"? (Havelock Ellis, *My Life*, 1940, pp. 68–70). I referred to the ludic element in the use of technical terms. Karl Menninger observes that "the function of play is to furnish an outlet for those impulses which are denied by reality" (*Love Against Hate*, 1942, p. 180). The highly artificial distinction between "primary" and "secondary" sources, a further complication of the running water metaphor, can be discarded by the methodologist who thinks in terms of traces.

three categories of traces: immaterial, material, and written traces.

Immaterial traces are those subtler traces that still live in societies, such as their institutions, the customs of the people, religious cults and doctrines, current ethical principles, traditions, legends, superstitions. Frontiers and languages are also immaterial traces. The word immaterial is not used here with any particular implication. It is intended to convey the idea of intangibility, of knowledge through reasoning rather than of perception through the senses. Accepted history is such a trace: it is the termination or culmination of the process by which previous research and older accepted history have been filtered through the minds of past historians. The question whether these immaterial traces are authentic does not arise. They exist around us, they still live. Not only do we perceive them, but we feel their effect upon our life. Unlike the metaphysian, the historian need not ask whether Parliament, the Roman Catholic Church, the English language, the frontier between Belgium and Holland, are what we are told they are. He can, even today, be imprisoned by order of the Speaker of the House of Commons; the Roman Catholic Church can prevent the publication of his advertisement by a paper; he can mishandle the English language or be impressed by its adequacy and its beauty; he can be asked to show his papers when crossing from Belgium into Holland. But each of these traces is what it is because a long sequence of events has taken place in the past; it reveals the existence of that sequence, and may lead, together with other traces, to our acquiring sufficient knowledge to include that sequence in a story.

The whole present, one might say, is a trace of the past. No doubt the question might be raised: what is the present? Is it not merely the meeting point between the past and the future as, according to Montaigne, the Stoics proclaimed? Is it a line without thickness, a pure abstraction? Not entirely. The present is that portion of experienced time about which we have a feeling that it has not yet been absorbed into the past. People meet in a room for a lecture or a conference. All the minutes they spend together form the present, for them. Just before they disperse the moment when they met is still the present. The present Parliament may be four years old. The present reign may have lasted much longer. The present is the provisional termination of sequences of events. It is their immaterial trace. No Crocean doctrine is required, therefore, to set into motion a search for the roots of the present. There is no need to insist upon all history being contemporary history on the ground that it is born of present-day interest. What happens is that society asks for the story of its past experiences: we know why; the historian satisfies the request. He collects events for his story. He knows them through their traces. The present is a rich mine full of traces. He will use it as he uses other traces that come to his attention. The historian of Parliament in the eighteenth century will look at Parliament as he finds it today, and ask whether it is a trace left by parliaments of older days. The answer will be that it is. The historian of the States General of the Dutch Republic will look at the Parliament of the Kingdom of the Netherlands, and ask himself whether it is a trace left by the former States General. He will answer that the name is, but that the thing itself is more truly a trace of the Legislative Assembly of the French Revolution or of the Parliament of Westminster than of the States General.

Material traces of the past are objects that result from the activities of men who lived in the past. They may still be in use: Westminster Abbey. The most striking, though not necessarily the most useful to the historian, are buildings, or, as they are generally called, monuments. But the word monument is also used for other material traces including written traces: the *Monumenta Germaniae historica*. It is too imprecise a word for use by the methodologist. Other material traces are furniture, pictures and portraits, tools and utensils, weapons, and all the objects that are brought to light through excavations. Coins are material traces, but, like inscriptions, they are written traces as well. The archaeologist is a craftsman who deals with ancient objects, but there is no complete separation between his work and the preliminary work of the historian.

Provided it is clearly understood that the historian is at liberty to make as much use as he wishes of traces belonging to the first or the second category, we may say that he is mainly concerned with written traces. Immaterial traces will often "deliver their message" without formal consultation; material non-written traces can be handled only by those who have mastered the appropriate technique. Written traces, however, result from the use of he medium most familiar to the historian: language. They can be reproduced in print, so that the historian may consult them at convenient places. It is agreed that a piece of writing carefully edited and printed may be looked upon as an original trace: a specialist has intervened to facilitate its use. Improved methods for observing written traces and for finding out the events which culminated in their production enable the historian to attain, in many cases, that provisionally guaranteed knowledge of the past which is indeed not certainty, but which will allow him to tell his story with a clear conscience.

A general appellation for written traces, suggested by the fact that they teach us something, is "documents." One might, perhaps, divide documents into those that were self-consciously produced and those that were not; but this could easily lead to systematization for its own sake. There is a practical difference, however, between documents that were produced with the intention of putting a point of view before later readers and those that were actually produced in the course of transacting business. The business may be of an official nature; the document may have been written in the course of business by a servant of the state, of a municipality, of a public corporation like the Dutch East India Company or the Metropolitan Water Board. Especially if still in the keeping of the body in whose service it was produced, such a "record" presents itself as a trace of greater trustworthiness than a letter written by a schoolgirl to her friend. That there may be more lies in a state document than in a love letter or a ship's log is an obvious statement, which raises questions that will have to be envisaged by us in due course.

Among the documents that are not records are those of a personal nature like diaries, memoirs and letters. A diary is the trace of a man's wish to put down on paper experiences that befell him, and of the fact that he fulfilled his wish. It is also the trace of the impression made upon him by his experiences, and therefore, at second remove, of these experiences themselves. It may also be a trace of a man's desire to be seen in a certain light by later readers of his diary. Memoirs are, as a rule, the trace of such a wish, although they may also be the trace of an intention to recapture past events and to save them from being forgotten by oneself. Letters are the trace of the desire experienced by someone to convey information to someone else, and therefore, indirectly, a trace of the events mentioned in the letter, or of the desire experienced by the letter-writer to achieve an end, to carry persuasion, etc. Some letters are official and if in official custody they are official or public records.

Certain documents are narrative, and might be looked upon as part of the accepted history of ages that have gone. Medieval annals and chronicles are of this nature. The annal enters events as they have come to the notice of its compiler. It has some resemblance, therefore, with diaries. The diary, however, is a more immediate trace than the annal. For the diary gives us, in an ascending sequence, traces of a desire to write, and of experiences undergone. In the annal the time-sequence would be the desire to write, preceded by the reception of information, which in its turn was preceded by the event perceived by the informer or by the informer's informers. Like the memoir, the chronicle stands at a distance from the event that is still greater. Unhappily, it is sometimes the only perceptible trace left by certain events.

Records give to the investigator a sense of immediacy which a narrative document can never produce. If we handle a bill, which is a private record, or a ledger, an order for the delivery of goods, we are in touch with traces of a commercial transaction that are more direct than the traces of the same event which we might find in the diary or the memoirs of the merchant who carried out this transaction. On the other hand narrative documents often contain traces—but at one remove—of the atmosphere that accompanied these transactions. They are, therefore, less safe starting points than are record-traces.

While reading a document the historian has to ask himself all the time: of what events is this the trace? This is a much more fruitful approach than if he says: of what knowledge is this the source? His answer to the second question is grey and abstract. But the first question leads to an answer that puts him already in possession of fragments of the story, because when traces present themselves to him each one has behind it a whole array of events. Contact is made with the past, and the whole machine of history-writing is set in motion. Let me give a familiar example. The lecture notes of a professor were produced in the course of transacting academic business. Of what are they a trace? Not of what the professor said in his lecture: to believe this would be placing time on its head: how can Monday's trace inform us of Tuesday's event? No, the lecture notes are the trace of what the professor intends to say in his lecture. They are also the traces of his knowledge and of his ignorance, of his opinion and prejudices; they may be the trace of the state of accepted history in his day, as reflected by his mind. The students' lecture notes are a trace—how faint!—of what the professor actually said. The question: of what, or for what, are the professor's notes a "source," could not have been so fruitful in results, unless a deliberate effort had been made to forget the metaphor it embodies, and that would have meant thinking, however inarticulately, in terms of traces. It is better to be frank and to clear up our vocabulary. Sources are a source of confusion.

The investigator's mind will proceed in the same way if it is applied to a charter, a Papal bull, a secret resolution of the States of Holland, or a letter from the Grand Pensionary Heinsius to William III. This is a trace. Of what events? Perhaps, merely, of the fact that someone committed a forgery. I have repeatedly used words like fact, state, condition, for that which leaves a trace. Let us not forget that the phenomena indicated by these words are also events. All things are occurrences or events, for all is motion.

This book is intended to be an introduction to history, an attempt to find out what it is and what is its place among the departments of human knowledge. It is not a handbook or a guide. Completeness is therefore not to be expected in the enumeration and description of the traces of the past that can be useful to historians. But the main lesson of this chapter stands out more clearly as a result of its incompleteness. It is that no comprehensive legislation can be laid down in the matter of handling traces. Right from the beginning the use of traces must be made in the full understanding that, however they may be labelled as a result of the classification favoured by those who preserve them or present them to the learned world, they are in fact specific, and will talk to us only if we look upon them as parts of the actual chain of events with which we intend to make ourselves acquainted.

Chapter II

DETECTING THE TRACES

§ I

HEURISTIC

THERE is a technique which helps us in looking for historical traces. It is called heuristic, from the Greek word *heuriskein*, which means to find. This name breathes scholarly optimism, since it looks forward to the successful result of the search. It must not cause us to overlook the actual search which can be tedious, and is not seldom fruitless. Heuristic is, as I said, a technique, an art rather than a science. It has no general rules, and knows few short cuts. It is, almost entirely, a deftness in the handling of specialized guide-books, a strong memory for bibliographical detail, severe self-discipline in the making, classifying and preserving of notes. No text-book of heuristic exists; methodologists devote chapters to it, but in these little more is to be read than that the art can be acquired by practice only: *fabricando fit faber*.[1] Bauer points out that a body of knowledge about heuristic has gradually developed, in which every detail helps, every aspect dovetails into another aspect.[2]

Material traces of the past will be found in museums, whose catalogues can be useful instruments of heuristic. But many are in private collections. The investigator must, somehow, get to know of them. Documents are kept in archives and in libraries: these, too, have catalogues. But catalogues are often incomplete out of date, or unmethodical. No heuristic will be successful without a solid and broad foundation of accepted history. What was done with Acts of Parliament in England? Unless we know, we may have difficulty in finding them in their original form.

[1] See Bernheim on heuristic, *op. cit.*, pp. 252–79. See also the following pamphlets of the "Helps for Students" series of the S.P.C.K.: Gilson, J. P., *A Student's Guide to the Manuscripts of the British Museum*, 1920; Johnson, Ch., *The Public Record Office*, 1921; Hearnshaw, F. J. C., *Municipal Records*, 1918–23; Roberts, R. A., *The Reports of the Historical MSS. Commission*, 1920.

[2] *Op. cit.*, pp. 193–7.

What was done in various countries with letters and reports from ambassadors and envoys abroad? As Halphen observes, heuristic is not a haphazard process; the dispersal of documents is in itself part of history.[1] A neglect of the accepted history of his own special subject would involve the historian in an unnecessary prolongation of the heuristic labour. We may learn, for instance, while preparing a biography, that certain documents were produced by someone upon a certain occasion. But they have since disappeared. Clearly, a knowledge derived from accepted history of the career and the movements of the subject of the biography will provide clues about the places and perhaps even the collections of documents where the manuscripts we require are being preserved. Written traces of the life of William III exist in the archives of the House of Orange-Nassau and at the Hague State Archive and in many local archives of the Dutch Low Countries. But they also exist at the Public Record Office in London, and in a number of British archives. It is clear that to work at a biography of William III one must begin not with research work, but by reading previous biographies of the Stadtholder-King and of people connected with him. Documents concerning the cloth industry of the Belgian town of Courtrai are found not only in Belgian archives, but also in the Archives du Département du Nord at Lille in France. At various periods during the Middle Ages Lille belonged to the county of Flanders, and under Philip the Bold, Duke of Burgundy, it was the capital and seat of the council. This is why much medieval archive material concerning Belgian Flanders is to be found at Lille. Political and constitutional history here provide the first heuristic guide for the telling of a fragment of economic history.[2]

None of the operations that have to be performed by the historian while he carries out his task can be isolated from the others, heuristic least of all. No sooner has the research worker found a trace than he must judge it. When the coastal fisherman

[1] *Introduction à l'Histoire*, pp. 39–40. In other words this dispersal is part of the past, and therefore, part of a sequence of events. And we know now that it will be the terminal of the sequence. The old nomenclature is not faulty. It is, merely, too metaphoric, in fact, too poetic, to provide a guide to rapid action.

[2] Espinas, G. et Pirenne, H., *Recueil des Documents relatifs à l'Histoire de l'Industrie drapière en Flandre*, I, pp. 647 *sqq*.

hauls in his trawl he unfastens the net and spreads his catch on the deck. He then handles every fish, judging it rapidly, throws overboard those that are too small or otherwise unsuitable, and keeps only those that can be sold. The research worker looks at every trace or parcel of traces as he finds it, and asks, not only whether it is a good trace, but also, and even before the first question, whether it is an historical trace at all. He subjects the trace to criticism.

§ 2

AUTHENTICITY AND EXTERNAL CRITICISM

Is this trace what I believe it to be? Is it what I am told it is, what it "claims" to be? In whatever form he couches it, this is the kind of question the historian must ask when he meets a material or written trace, or a set of traces, of the past. To answer the question in a systematic way, to settle a matter of authenticity, is to apply external criticism. At a later stage the historian will also have to ask: can I trust the message which this trace appears to be carrying, is it really the terminal of the sequence of events which, at first sight, it appears to be, or is there behind it a less obvious sequence? To answer this question the historian applies internal criticism.

The comparison between the two modes of criticism is instructive: let us carry it a little further. In this case the use of metaphors is helpful, provided, of course, we bear in mind the fact that a metaphor points the way but has no special virtue for placing us into immediate contact with the "essence" of things. Objects are no more endowed with speech than the little carp that was caught by Lafontaine's angler:

"Le pauvre carpillon lui dit en sa manière. . . ."

But it is useful to let them have their say. Here, then, is a florin. It says to me: "I am a coin from the reign of William and Mary, struck in the year 1689." This is an assertion to be tested by the process of external criticism. It also says that William and Mary were, "by the grace of God King and Queen of Great Britain, France, and Ireland." Does the coin tell the truth? I have been assured by a friend who once a year places flowers at the foot of the statue of Saint Charles I that in 1689, by the grace of God, James II and none other was King of Great Britain and Ireland. I also remember that in the same year a person called Louis XIV claimed to be King of France. Does my coin tell the truth? This question must be answered by internal criticism.

Internal criticism can be applied only where we are dealing with writing, whether in documents or in inscriptions on monuments, coins, medals or seals. Documents can be said, with less effort of the imagination, to speak a language. Here is a letter which announces itself as coming from my friend X, and which says that he is going away on business. External criticism confirms the first assertion: handwriting, signature, postmark, paper and ink tell their story of authenticity. But it is possible that my friend merely wants to avoid meeting me, and has no intention of going on a journey. The authentic letter may carry a false message; internal criticism may show that it is the trace, not of an intention to travel, but of a less obvious sequence of events, which can be ascertained only by comparison with the contents of other letters and of reports of the movements of X.

In carrying out external criticism we must remember that the only alternative to authenticity is fake or forgery. A sport of nature which faithfully reproduces a man-made object may be ruled out. The question to be asked is: who would carry out the forgery, and why? Could it be done, in the practical world of common sense? Objects might be forged for the purpose of selling them to amateur archaeologists. Documents have been faked, similarly, to be sold for gain. They have been faked, also, with a desire to deceive, as in the case of alleged medieval donations. A scholar has sometimes faked a document to provide a missing link in a sequence of events he had imaginatively reconstructed. Nowadays this is an extremely rare occurrence, because in the training of historians increasing emphasis is laid upon the fact that the historian's work can often not be checked, so that he is put on his honour in a way that could not apply to the natural scientist working in a world where experiments can fairly easily be duplicated.

External criticism can therefore be described negatively as

making sure that the alleged trace is not a fake or a forgery. The first rule is that there is safety in numbers. There are letters written by the first Duke of Marlborough at Blenheim, but also at The Hague (until recently!), in London, and in many other places. The hypothesis that, as a result of a gigantic conspiracy, a large number of forgeries was placed in all these archives and collections is much more improbable than that of the authenticity of all the letters. One may, therefore, with less strain upon credulity, postulate the authenticity of the bulk of the letters. Each individual letter will be like the others; it will show the same handwriting, clumsy style, poor spelling and other characteristic features. Moreover, as the hand of every man changes with the years, a chart could be established of the development of Marlborough's hand, and it could be seen that a new criterion becomes available for the approximate dating of the letters, which will agree with the date given on the letter. The historian who has familiarized himself with the letters of Marlborough will require no such chart: he can see at a glance to which period of the general's life any letter belongs. It is the concurrence of a number of indications of this sort that provides for each letter a guarantee of authenticity. Our coin of the reign of William and Mary can be compared from the point of view of shape, weight, workmanship, etc., with many other coins that cannot collectively be suspected of being fakes.

The touchstone of accepted history, the knowledge of the difficulty of faking, the confirmation provided by other objects of admitted authenticity, such are the instruments used in external criticism. They will never lead us to absolute or formal certainty, but to an empirical satisfactoriness. On such principles of mutual support given to each other by historical traces, research workers have in the course of time elaborated techniques of recognition which, in some instances, are nowadays so precise that they are sometimes reckoned among the sciences.[1]

[1] On external criticism, *cf.* Bauer, *op. cit.*, pp. 192–225; Bernheim, *op. cit.*, pp. 464 *sqq.* On forgeries, *ibid.*, pp. 230 *sqq.*, and Crump, *The Logic of History* (S.P.C.K. Helps for Students, 1919), pp. 37 *sqq.*; Marshall, R. L., *The Historical Criticism of Documents* (S.P.C.K. Helps, 1920), pp. 12–43; see also Lacey, G. J., on "Questioned Documents," in *The American Archivist*, October 1946, for an interesting ultra-modern development. Forgeries by the use of typewriters can be

§ 3

AIDS TO RESEARCH

I have referred to certain techniques used by the research worker in the course of his investigations. They play a part at every stage, from the heuristic to the narrative. The historian must also use the results achieved by workers in other fields of human knowledge. All these techniques and sciences are aids to the historian's work, but they are on different levels: some are servants, some allies. *The ancillary disciplines* (from *ancilla*, hand-maiden) are not sciences in their own right. In some cases history shares them with philology or other branches of knowledge.[1] Special treatises deal with each of these ancillaries. There are handbooks of chronology, palaeography, diplomatic, etc., which provide us, as Langlois and Seignobos observe, with "methodical repertories of facts." They are primarily digests of practical experience, and what we said about heuristic also applies to these disciplines: the best way to become acquainted with them is to practise them. Gradually the historian will apply them in the course of his research work without giving much thought to theory. A trained worker recognizes the date of a handwriting without analysing the shape of each letter. *Auxiliary sciences* are departments of knowledge in their own right. History makes use of them, just as they use history, or should use it, for their own purpose. They are allies of history. In a way, as Bernheim explains, every single science has every other as an auxiliary: this is the natural result of the unity of all human knowledge.[2] I may point out in passing that I use the words "discipline" and "science" without prejudice. Discipline, used in the medieval sense, signi-fies a systematized section of knowledge; a science is a discipline on whose behalf certain claims can reasonably be made. A pre-ciser formulation of the implications of the word may be post-poned till it is needed for the sake of our investigation. Let us now

detected by photographing typewritten letters under a ruled square, which shows the difference in width of hooks and length of crossings, as well as differences in design.

[1] Some methodologists call them auxiliary sciences (e.g. Langlois and Seig-nobos, *op. cit.*, p. 34). This leads to confusion.   [2] *Op. cit.*, p. 279.

pass in review the principal ancillary disciplines and auxiliary sciences of history.

Among the ancillary disciplines *chronology*, which takes charge of the very framework of narrative, the time element, deserves place of honour. It arranges the significant events which took place in the past in their time order and fixes the intervals that elapsed between them.[1] Chronology was probably invented in early ages for two equally utilitarian purposes: for fixing the dates of religious functions and ceremonies, and for timing agricultural operations. As in external criticism, results are achieved in chronology by the accumulation of data which provide each other with mutual support. For instance, the charters granted by the early Norman Kings of England usually bear the regnal year, but now and then the year of the incarnation is also mentioned, and the chronologist will not fail to make full use of the possibility this offers for linking up two different systems for reckoning time. The literal acceptance of Biblical chronology has for many generations impeded the development of chronology as practised in Western Europe. Complications like that arising out of the adoption of the Gregorian calendar in Great Britain and Ireland in March 1751, while it had been used in Continental countries from a much earlier date, or the medieval habit of dating documents by giving a Saint's-day, are dealt with by writers on chronology.[2] To illustrate some of the pitfalls that threaten the student of dates, Professor C. R. Cheney says in his *Handbook*: "Thus 28 December 1190 would be reckoned by the English chancery clerk of that day as falling in the second year of King Richard I, but for a clerk of the exchequer the accounts covering this date belonged to the Pipe Roll of 3 Richard I, and a Benedictine chronicler would include the events of that day in the year of grace 1191. Cervantes and Shakespeare did not die on the

---

[1] See the very useful article "Chronology" in *Encyclopaedia Britannica*, 11th ed. Also Bauer, *op. cit.*, pp. 189–92. Bossuet says: "De même que, pour aider sa mémoire dans la connaissance des lieux, on retient certaines villes principales, autour desquelles on place les autres, chacune selon sa distance; ainsi, dans l'ordre des siècles, il faut avoir certains temps marqués par quelque grand événement auquel on rapporte tout le reste" (*Discours sur l'Histoire universelle*, Avant-propos).

[2] The Royal Historical Society has issued a *Handbook of British Chronology*, by F. M. Powicke in 1939 and a *Handbook of Dates for Students of English History*, by C. R. Cheney in 1945.

same day, although each died on 23 April 1616, according to the computation of his country. An English document dated 28 January 1620 would be written on the same day as a document dated in Scotland 28 January 1621 or a document dated in France 7 February 1621."

Palaeography is the systematic study of old handwritings. The way in which men shape the letters of the alphabet has varied from period to period and from region to region. Palaeography describes the evolution of each letter in time and in space. The palaeographer can not only read old manuscripts, but can also date them and tell us where they came from. In the past as today education had the effect of standardizing the shape of letters used in each centre of culture. Even nowadays Belgians and Dutchmen use distinctive handwritings which are, again, very different from the average English hand. Palaeography also deals with the abbreviations used by scribes, especially in the Middle Ages. Nowadays certain abbreviations like "i.e." or "e.g." are in common use. Before the invention of printing the need for them was greater. There are dictionaries which list the abbreviations used in manuscripts.

Palaeography is as much an ancillary discipline of philology as of history. More than any other help to history it demands concentrated attention to detail. It gives scope to mental alertness, and to the development of empirical capacities, i.e. of an ability to face difficulties as they present themselves, without previous reference to general principles. A man who has done his share of archive work and of the deciphering of difficult documents is less likely to be carried away by superficial resemblances, to take external appearances for granted. His critical faculties have become sharpened.

Claims to systematize our knowledge of the relation which undoubtedly exists between character and handwriting are made by people who call themselves "graphologists." Too many factors apart from character—the material used, the place occupied by writing in a person's scheme of life,[1] etc.—influence the

---

[1] A man for whom writing is an unwonted exercise will express far less of his personality in the formalized characters he uses than one for whom writing is an habitual operation.

H

handwriting, for the claims of graphology to be justified. Never-theless it is a fact that the habitual practice of palaeography makes investigators more sensitive to every aspect of writing. It is obvious enough that the handwriting of a letter shows whether it was written in haste or at leisure, and that it can betray the sex of the writer, and whether he was young or old. Why should it not also inform us of the existence of certain intimate preoccupa-tions like hastiness of judgment, avarice, or self-indulgence? Such indications cannot be treated as scientific data, but they may be faint traces of past realities. I am convinced that the handwriting of the Dutch grand pensionary Heinsius, notwithstanding the haste which usually blurred his outlines, has given me an insight into his character. I would not treat such an indication as evidence, but it caused me to look for more tangible confirmation, and I think that I found it.[1]

Diplomatic is the systematic study of the form of official docu-ments. The word diploma, which originally meant a piece of writing folded in two, has gradually been adopted to indicate any kind of official writing, and has given rise to the name diplomacy as well as to diplomatic. It was observed as early as the seven-teenth century that official bureaux such as the Papal chancery used in the composition of letters and documents issued by them not only a rigid order for arranging the subject matter, but stereotyped formulas for every part of the document. Clearly, the clerks working in these offices possessed formularies with models to be copied on different occasions. This is still the habit observed for many routine matters in the Civil Service of today. As the nature of business changed with the years, the formulas had to be revised from time to time. Diplomatists study the form of official documents and establish lists of formulas used, and note the approximate times at which modifications were intro-duced. If a document presents itself as originating from a certain office, but does not follow the style prevalent in that office at the date which it bears, it is *ipso facto* suspect and will have to be criticized with the aid of every available ancillary disipline. On the other hand, our confidence in a document is greatly increased

[1] Anal complex. See Jones, E., *Papers on Psycho-analysis*, pp. 680–704; also Renier, *The Dutch Nation*, pp. 217–18.

if the findings of palaeography and of diplomatic coincide. Here, as happens so often in historical research, we have a circular argument: authentic documents are written in a certain form; this document is written in that form; therefore, it is authentic. The practice of research softens the crudeness of this argumentation. As in other cases, the individual document is supported by the bulk of documents which could not possibly have been produced by a universal faker. Still, the formal imperfection of the argument is a valuable reminder of the fact that the historian seeks practical conviction and not metaphysical certainty.[1]

Sigillography (or sphragistic) is the name of the study of seals and can be looked upon as a department of diplomatic. As we noticed in the case of the word *vestigium*, the word seal indicates an object and its visible trace: it signifies both the matrix which is impressed upon the wax (nowadays the shellac) as well as the object in relief which results from this contact. Sigillography describes the seals used for authenticating official documents. It takes cognizance not only of the form and aspect of the seal, but of the manner in which it is attached to the document, and of the material of which it is made. Wax was commonly used; but in warm countries like Southern Italy practical considerations made the use of lead preferable. Ancient seals are often objects of considerable beauty, and the images on them are traces of social habits, clothing and decoration. Many of the images found on seals can be described by the methods of *heraldry*, another ancillary discipline which describes coats of arms in its own romantic language and lays down the rules observed in their composition.

Epigraphy, which interests the philologist as well as the historian, is the palaeography and diplomatic of inscriptions placed upon monuments. To discover the events of which they are traces the research worker must have a thorough knowledge of the language in which they are written and of the system of abbreviations used in composing them.

The study of coins is called *numismatic*. The coin is obviously a

---

[1] See the excellent articles on "Palaeography," "Diplomatic," "Seals," "Autographs," "Heraldry," "Inscriptions," "Manuscripts," in *Encyclopaedia Britannica*, 11th ed. See Bernheim, *op. cit.*, palaeography, pp. 289 *sqq.*, diplomatic, pp. 299 *sqq.*, sphragistic, p. 306, heraldry, p. 307, numismatic, *ibid.*

trace of events, but can also be considered in its own right, and it is possible, for instance, to tell the story of the effect of the invention of coins upon prices.[1]

Archaeology has been defined as "the orderly arrangement of monuments."[2] This is true enough, provided the word monument is used for all material traces of the past other than those in writing. Archaeology is an ancillary discipline of history, but for ages which had no organized state-machine and used no writing it is a subject in its own right, and an alternative name for pre-history.

Since every branch of knowledge may at a given moment be used by the historian, we cannot give a full survey of the auxiliary sciences. It will be sufficient to mention those that are most inportant to history. *Geography* is indispensable because an event that is not situated in space is as difficult to incorporate in a story as one that is not situated in time. An historian should always have a map at his elbow.[3] *Sociology* needs history more than history sociology. We have noted before that the connection between *economics* and economic history is more intimate than that between sociology and social history. It is important that the relation between history and sociology should be clearly understood, since the left wing deviationists threaten to abolish history by identifying it with sociology. Sociology asks general questions such as: in what circumstances do populations rise or fall? To answer these questions concrete data have to be obtained from observations made by anthropologists, from events reported by historians, and, most of all, from statistics collected among existing communities. Sociologists will also want to know the advantages and disadvantages of a rise or a fall in the population, the efficacy of methods used for the deliberate influencing of such rises or falls. However great their devotion to "pure knowledge,"

---

[1] *Cf.* Jongkees, *De Uitvinding van de Munt*, 1946.

[2] Crump, *Logic of History*, p. 21.

[3] Bauer (*op. cit.*, p. 164) says that geography and history used to be intimately connected, and that it is only since the days of Alexander von Humboldt (1769–1859) that geography has become a science in its own right. This is an example of the exaggerated importance attached by a specialist to his own subject. Geography was an independent science at a much earlier date. See B. Varenius, *Geographia Generalis* (Elzevir, Amsterdam, 1664, p. 1): "Geographia dicitur scientia mathematica mixta, quae telluris partiumque illius affectiones a quantitate dependentes, nempe figuram . . . docet."

sociologists will be affected by eudaemonistic theories and by the desire to cope with practical issues. Nevertheless, they will, as is expected of them, report on their results in a generalized form. The historian's approach to matters of this nature is entirely different. His interest will go to the single and the concrete, because, like a newspaper reporter, he is out for a story. He will ask: did the population in a given area rise or fall during a specified period? When he has traced enough events, he will tell a story which is his reply to this concrete question. The story tells what happened and how. If it also tells why it happened, this will be supererogation. But if the historian begins by reading the views of sociologists, he may find it easier to search for relevant events. He will save time in the course of his preliminary investigation.

To *philology*, the study of languages in their present condition and in their past development, history owes an immense debt. The historical method was invented by early philologists. Like all intellectual workers, historians must know many languages. Philology gives them an insight into languages and helps them to detect the traces of the past which they contain. The history of place names is one of the many fields where historians and philologists labour in co-operation.[1] Outside England the intimate connection between the two disciplines is understood; at historical and at philological congresses a section is reserved to the practitioners of the sister-discipline.

One word about the sciences, by which English word the natural sciences, the *Naturwissenschaften* of Dilthey's nomenclature, are indicated. They can be extremely useful in the course of historical research and in the construction of the historical narrative. Medieval studies have benefited from data provided by botany and agronomy to pronounce upon the possibility of certain vegetables having been cultivated in certain areas; the microscope and certain processes of photography help to reveal forgeries, and medical studies of the morbid symptoms displayed by Roman Emperors or French kings have given us a better understanding of these monarchs. The assertion of Michelet that the reign of Louis XIV must be divided into two periods, "avant

[1] Bauer, *op. cit.*, pp. 170–5. Bernheim, *op. cit.*, pp. 284 *sqq.*

la fistule" and "après la fistule" can be disproved through the study of the diary kept by the physicians of the *Grand Monarque*. This manuscript, which was published in the nineteenth century, reveals that the health of Louis had been extremely bad for many years before a *fistula analis* was diagnosed, and that this new illness was not an exceptional phenomenon in the career of this coarse contemner of hygiene and sensible living. The chemical and biological examination of mummies has rendered similar services to Egyptian history. It is possible that the recent development of the science of statistics will one day revolutionize history. Much scepticism exists on this score among historians, which is probably due to a misunderstanding of the nature of the modern science of statistics, and ignorance of the fact that statistics is not a synonym for figures. The influence of right wing deviationism is at work in the distrust shown in the historical world towards those who take cognizance of the results of modern psychology and of the natural sciences in general. The best remedy for this situation is that scientists shall endeavour to understand the true nature of history. Scientists have the ear of those who hold the strings of the public purse. They may, one day, save history from the Marxists and historians from themselves.

Chapter III

FROM TRACE TO EVENT

§ I

THE TRACE AS EVIDENCE

DISCOVERED by the process of heuristic, provided with credentials by external criticism, the trace is now available to the investigator as the last of a sequence of events which may be suitable for inclusion in the historical narrative. The trace is, therefore, evidence of a sequence of events. Indeed, according to the *Oxford English Dictionary*, the word evidence was used in the past to indicate a mark or trace, as in the phrase "the evidences of ancient glacier action." According to the same authority, "information that is given in a legal investigation, to establish the fact or point in question" is called evidence. The lawyer, like the historian, uses evidence. Can the historian learn from the way in which the lawyer deals with his evidence? In an address delivered in 1939 to the Historical Association Lord Sankey expressed the view that there is much resemblance between the work of the historian and that of the lawyer. Both must call evidence and establish facts; their first task is research. Both end by telling a tale. While the historian's evidence, however, is generally documentary, that of the lawyer is given by a living person. If the lawyer is bound by the rules of evidence, which restrict him in his attempt to reach a conclusion, cross examination, on the other hand, protects him to some extent from error. Like that of the scientist, the historian's solution lacks finality.[1] Such is the gist of that part of the judge's talk which is relevant to our present enquiry.

Now this comparison between historians and lawyers would be much more instructive if we were as clear about the meaning of the word lawyer as we are about the word historian. If lawyer is taken as referring to a barrister, Lord Sankey is right in saying that evidence is, for him as for the historian, the material that

[1] Viscount Sankey, "The Historian and the Lawyer, their Aims and their Methods," in *History*, September 1936.

leads to the telling of a tale. But, as the speaker himself observes, the lawyer "may also be a judge or a professor who teaches law." The lawyer and his story are but part of the legal process, and lawyers do more with their evidence than historians, whose task is fulfilled when their story is told. The comparison will fail to be instructive as long as we do not take cognizance of those other ways of using evidence which are open to lawyers, but not, happily, to historians. Let us use that portmanteau abstraction, the Law, as one uses a mathematical symbol, knowing that it means nothing in itself, but stands for many things. Among the things it stands for are courts of law, the police, and prison governors. The embodiments of the law have as their collective task something that is not the mere telling of a story. Evidence is for a court of law material that will lead to decisions affecting the interest, sometimes the honour, possibly even the life, of a citizen. The verdict of the court is made effective, its sentence is carried out, within a brief period. History, on the other hand, is told at a leisurely pace, and its pronouncements are subject to perpetual revision. It is never too late to appeal from its verdict. Surely the final use to which history and the law put the evidence of which they dispose must greatly affect their attitude towards it. Is it not true that, knowing the issues that are at stake, the law, by its fastidious adherence to the rules of evidence, deliberately exercises self-control, and sacrifices, again and again, its chance of reaching a conclusion? In his inaugural lecture as professor of Netherlands Indies' criminal law and criminal procedure in the University of Utrecht, Mr. J. E. Jonkers complained that criminal law protects the claims of the individual to the detriment of the community.[1] Can one not truly say that the law is, justifiably, more exacting and more critical in its handling of evidence than the historian who lives in a world of relativity?

This is not the view taken by the late R. G. Collingwood. The self-same reason which leads me to expect severer standards from a court of law than from an historian makes him more indulgent towards those who are responsible for conducting the process of law. In one of the papers that were collected after his death under the title *The Idea of History* he wrote: "If any juror says: 'I feel

[1] *De Waarheid in het Strafproces*, 1939.

certain that a year hence, when we have all reflected on the evidence at leisure, we shall be in a better position to see what it means,' the reply will be: 'There is something in what you say; but what you propose is impossible. Your business is not just to give a verdict; it is to give a verdict now; and here you stay until you do it.' This is why a jury has to content itself with something less than scientific (historical) proof, namely with that degree of assurance or belief which would satisfy it in any of the practical affairs of daily life" (p. 268). And again, on p. 270: "The reader will recollect that in criminal detection probability is required, of a degree sufficient for the conduct of daily life, whereas in history we demand certainty." One might observe that detective work must necessarily allow itself more fluidity of thought than is permissible at a trial; the supreme penalty it can inflict is arrest and an indictment. The court has greater powers. And one might also observe that in demanding certainty for the historian Mr. Collingwood speaks as one who advocates the annexation of history to absolute idealist philosophy.

It cannot be denied that many lawyers are as emphatic as Collingwood in their view that history requires a greater degree of certainty than does the law. The real difficulty is that so few people can pronounce with authority upon the problems and the needs of both history and the law. It is not easy for the layman to surrender his mind to the specialized symbolism of legal thought, and on the other hand it really would appear that none but the practising historian has a chance of knowing what history sets out to do. Rather than consult their writings I have tried to seek guidance in the conversation of lawyers. The constant practice of the courts and the contact with minds less subtle than their own has developed in many lawyers gifts of exposition with which one would not credit them upon the evidence of their writings. I owe much, in particular, to a talk with my compatriot Mr. P. W. A. Immink, professor of the history of law in the University of Groningen.[1] He is not to be held responsible, of course, for the conclusions I have reached. They amount to a

[1] See his instructive inaugural lecture, *Recht en Historie* (1946) which does not, however, deal with the problem which occupies our attention.

realization that sane lawyers dwell as much in relativity as sensible historians. Lawyers, like scientists, know that to ask for absolute knowledge will lead them nowhere. They will be satisfied if their system works and produces results. However much the layman or the methodologist of history may be impressed by the fact that criminal law handles evidence with a view to immediate, and sometimes drastic, action, he soon perceives that the lawyer accepts evidence which the historian would look upon as repugnant, such as the testimony of illiterates. As for civil procedure, it cannot reasonably be expected to weigh evidence at all. For its concern is not with the precise "how," but with the relative validity of two opposing sets of arguments supported by evidence. With due regard to Plato, some of the arguments he lends to Socrates are childish. But they are immeasurably superior to those of the Sophists. So it is with civil procedure: the argument of lesser weakness wins the day.

We may conclude that a comparison between the legal and the historical handling of evidence is less instructive than might have been expected. If it teaches us one lesson, it is that caution is needed before we commit ourselves to a final statement about the relation between evidence and knowledge, between the trace and the sequence of events which it is supposed to reveal.

§ 2

THE DIFFICULT JUMP

To infer, from a perceived trace, the existence of a sequence of events that brought it about, and to which, by inverting the process of time, the research worker may now be led if he takes the trace as a starting point is, as our comparison between legal and historical evidence has suggested, an enterprise fraught with uncertainty and risk. It is not enough that the historian should, every hour of his working day, make the jump with a light heart and a clear conscience. The methodologist must try to persuade his friends the scientists that the jump will land the historian on solid ground, and that history is neither fable nor guess-work.

The trace that is most famous in Western European culture,

even though it does not belong to history, is the *vestigium* discovered on a fateful day by Robinson Crusoe. The great story-
teller Daniel Defoe conjured up the event with inimitable simplicity: "It happened one Day about Noon going towards my
Boat, I was exceedingly surpriz'd with the Print of a Man's naked
Foot on the Shore, which was very plain to be seen in the Sand;
I stood like one Thunder-struck, or as if I had seen an Appari-
tion; . . ." Did Crusoe, without hesitation, make the jump from
trace to event, did he accept the evidence? He first went back "to
observe if it might not be my Fancy"; but no, the trace was
there, directly perceived—Crusoe could not deny it. How was it
to be interpreted? To what event did it point? For some time he
played with the idea that it had been left by Satan, less fearsome
than an unknown human being. After a few days, however, he
reluctantly told himself "that it must be some more dangerous
Creature." Crusoe did not long persevere in this state of lucidity.
He tried to persuade himself that the trace had been left by his
own foot. By applying experimental verification, however, he
was constrained to discard this comforting hypothesis. Only then
did he finally resign himself to the obvious reconstruction: trace
—foot—man.

Fear, the mistress passion, may have clouded the brain of
Robinson Crusoe. Yet the procession of hypotheses passing before
his eyes like the row of phantoms that frightens a sleep-walking
child was merely a slowing down of the process of reconstruction
as it flashes through the mind of the research worker. Which
sequence of events will he adopt for placing at the back of his
trace? There will be various possibilities, one of which he will
choose by eliminating the others. This will happen so rapidly
that he is hardly aware of the operation. Such is the historian's
practice. But when the theory of history is examined, one of the
questions that occurred to Robinson Crusoe cannot be disposed
of so easily. Has the investigator any logical justification for supposing that his trace was indeed the result of an event? To begin
with, it is not universally admitted that every event leaves a trace.
The writer of the Book of Proverbs holds that some events do not.
"There be three things which are too wonderful for me, yea,
four which I know not: The way of an eagle in the air; the way

of a serpent upon the rock; the way of a ship in the midst of the sea; and the way of a man with a maid" (Prov. xxx, 18–19). Are we agreed, at least, that every trace is backed by an event?

Millions of men and women belonging to the Christian Churches or to the orthodox Jewish faith accept the story of creation told in the book of Genesis as an accurate account of past events. These fundamentalists are educated people, some of them are intellectuals and cultured. Liberal protestants may look upon the story as symbolic: an élite among Catholics may find it possible to reconcile a belief in evolution, guided by the Creator, with Catholic orthodoxy.[1] The majority of Christians clings to the literal interpretation of Genesis. This, however, is impossible unless one adopts the doctrine that traces can exist without being preceded by the sequence of events to which they seem to point. The great French writer René de Chateaubriand (1768–1848) made this clear in his *Génie du Christianisme*, published in 1802. How, he asks, can we explain the traces of antiquity that are visible in our world? "God must have created, and did no doubt create the world, with all the traces of age and derivation which it displays before our eyes." Thereupon Chateaubriand's melodious diction conjures up for us an idyll of the creation which is as convincing as it is charming and fresh. If the world was not old as well as new when it emerged from the Creator's hands, he says, morality would drop out of the scheme of things, for morality is inseparable from what is ancient. Naked, brand-new rocks would have looked preposterous. The sea-shore must already have consisted of sand mixed with crushed sea-shells. Are we to believe that all plants were just sprouting out of the ground, that all animals were newly-born? This would be too distressing to the poet! No! Adam must have been thirty when he was created, and Eve at least sixteen![2]

---

[1] Klug, I., *Het Katholieke Geloof* (1939), pp. 126 *sqq.*

[2] Livre IV, chapitre V. See also note K: "En effet, il est vraisemblable que l'Auteur de la nature planta d'abord de vieilles forêts et de jeunes taillis; que les animaux naquirent, les uns remplis de jours, les autres parés des grâces de l'enfance. Les chênes, en perçant le sol fécondé, portèrent sans doute à la fois les vieux nids des corbeaux et la nouvelle postérité des colombes. Ver, chrysalide et papillon, l'insecte rampa sur l'herbe, suspendit son oeuf d'or aux forêts, ou trembla dans le vague des airs. L'abeille, qui pourtant n'avoit vécu qu'un matin,

It is highly improbable that Philip Henry Gosse (1810–88) ever read *Le Génie du Christianisme*. Its oppressive sensuousness would have repelled him. We know him best through the uncomfortable but haunting portrait drawn by his son Sir Edmund Gosse.[1] A member of the Plymouth Brotherhood, he believed in the literal truth of the Bible and in the latest discoveries of geology. He managed to reconcile his two faiths—and, like Chateaubriand, he did it at the expense of the historical validity of traces. His doctrine is ably explained in *Omphalos, an Attempt to untie the geological Knot*.[2] The argument is lifted from the sphere of poetic intuition where it dwelt with Chateaubriand, and is given a basis of self-assured scientific logic.

Geology, Gosse readily admits, establishes that the earth's crust bears traces of a much longer time-process than is allowed for by the Biblical story of creation. Nevertheless, in geology "there is nothing but *circumstantial* evidence, there is no *direct* testimony to the facts sought to be established" (p. 103). "Where wast thou when I laid the foundations of the earth? declare, if thou hast understanding," Gosse says with Job (xxxviii, 4) to the geologists. And he makes bold to refute them with a very simple argument. He assumes one single postulate: the reality of creation. He then contends—as did Chateaubriand—that the creative act is unthinkable without the creation of traces which correspond to no actual past event. "Could not God have created plants and animals without these retrospective marks? I distinctly reply, No! not so as to preserve their specific identity with those with which we are familiar. A Tree-fern without scars on the trunk! A Palm without leaf-bases! A Bean without a hilum! A Tortoise without laminae on its plates! A Carp without concentric lines on its scales! A Bird without feathers! A Mammal without hairs, or claws, or teeth, or bones, or blood! A Foetus without a placenta!" (p. 349). The blood coursing through the arteries and veins of the first man, "implies the previous process

comptoit déjà son ambroisie par générations de fleurs. Il faut croire que la brebis n'étoit pas sans son agneau, la fauvette sans ses petits; que les buissons cachoient des rossignols étonnés de chanter leurs premiers airs, en échauffant les fragiles espérances de leurs premières voluptés."

[1] *Father and Son* (1907). See in particular p. 134.

[2] Published by John van Voorst, Paternoster Row, London, 1857.

of the reception of food" (p. 276). The skeleton pleads in favour of past events, more clearly still the navel (pp. 289–90).

Hence the name of the book, *Omphalos*, the Greek word for navel. I believe that learned men in past ages had already given thought to the need for providing Adam with a navel, lest he be an imperfect human being. Adam's navel, however, was not the trace of his foetal connection with a carnal mother, but of his connection with some unborn Lilith who lived in the Creator's mind only. Why, asked Gosse, should the first man, and earth on its first day, not have born traces of a past that never existed? "Admit for a moment, as a hypothesis, that the Creator had before his mind a projection of the whole life-history of the globe, commencing with any point which the geologist may imagine to have been a fit commencing point, and ending with some unimaginable acme in the infinitely distant future. He determines to call this idea into actual existence, not at the supposed commencing point, but at some stage or other of its course. It is clear, then, that at the selected stage it appears, exactly as it would have appeared at that moment of its history, if all the preceding eras of its history had been real" (p. 351).

In his fine novel, *The World of William Clissold*, H. G. Wells has devoted a couple of pages to *Omphalos*. He considers that the author overcame his difficulty "lucidly, simply, and completely." But he points out that Gosse overshot the mark, since "for all I can demonstrate here, I may have been created even as I write here, created with the illusion of past memories in my mind. Or the reader may have come into being in the very act of reading this sentence."[1] Memory also is a trace, and here, carried to its logical extreme, is the doctrine that no trace whatever need correspond to an actual sequence of events situated in the past. If Philip Gosse is right, a fundamentalist Christian can be a scientist, but it is impossible for him to be an historian. Even if it remains innocent of evolutionism, Christianity must, with Chateaubriand, admit the trace that corresponds to no event. The nihilistic view of the relation between trace and event goes hand in hand with the certitude that is born of faith.

Christianity, the lawyer's relativism, the historian's inability

---

[1] Book I: § 11.

to produce experimental confirmation for his conclusions, they all conspire to impose upon the student of method the need for a thorough investigation of the jump from trace to event. Here is an epistemological problem: we must make up our minds about the nature of historical knowledge.

Chapter IV

CERTITUDE, DOUBT
AND COMMON SENSE

HISTORIANS may be satisfied that their methods lead them to generally acceptable results, but the previous chapter should remind them that, from the outside world and in particular from the scientists, questions are to be expected about the justification of the passage from traces to events. The historian may dislike speculation, but whenever he builds up his story he adopts, at least by implication, an epistemological theory, and he approaches his subject in a certain way. Can we classify the various approaches to history, and is it possible to choose among them one which is more consonant than the others with the main function of history? This is the task which, as a result of the uncertainty brought about by the problems raised in the previous chapter, we must now try to carry out.

§ I

PRIMITIVE CERTITUDE

The language of the less educated shows that they possess a high degree of mental security. "Of course," "didn't you know?" —not to mention the strange use of the word "definitely" at moments when the Rabbi of Nazareth would merely have us say "yes." Their own taste, a matter of perpetual hesitation among the cultured, is an open book to them. Even their doubt is dogmatic. They disbelieve with all the fervour of belief, on grounds that are purely psychological. As Hume observes: "The greater part of mankind are naturally apt to be affirmative and dogmatical in their opinions; and while they see objects only on one side, and have no idea of any counterposing argument, they throw themselves precipitately into the principles to which they are inclined."[1] Scruples about the justification of the jump from

[1] *Enquiry concerning Human Understanding*, Section XII.

128

trace to event are not to be sought among the simple-minded. "They say that" is, in their language, the equivalent of "it is established, it is certain, that." Legends and early theogonies owe their existence to the disinclination of the primitive mind to entertain doubt. To quote Hume once more: "No weakness of human nature is more universal and conspicuous than what we commonly call credulity, or a too easy faith in the testimony of others."[1]

The primitive inclination to certainty and to dogmatism as well as the readiness of the untutored to take every assertion for granted inevitably affects the attitude of some people towards historical studies; professionals of history are not entirely free from it. As Langlois and Seignobos remark, "men have a spontaneous tendency to believe assertions and to reproduce them, without as much as feeling the need to establish a clear distinction between them and their own observations."[2] These authors consider that spontaneous credulity is so strong that it even affects trained historians and causes them to overlook some of the contradictions they meet at every turning of the road.[3] Collingwood also warns us against dogmatism, though he is less free of it than of credulity. He condemns "the common sense theory which bases history upon memory and authority."[4] Such a theory would indeed enthrone accepted history without allowing for the possibility of its being improved by addition, or corrected, or refocused. But surely ever since the Renaissance gave us the rudiments of historical criticism, credulity has ceased to be "common sense." To argue against it is to tilt against windmills. Dogmatism is responsible for graver and more recent misdeeds.

Let us, in fairness, recognize that dogmatism has assisted the development of the human mind. Dewey points out that by saving us from vacillation it has encouraged action.[5] But it does

---

[1] *A Treatise of Human Nature*, I, 3, ix.   [2] *Op. cit.*, pp. 48–9.
[3] *Ibid.*, pp. 130 *sqq.*   [4] *The Idea of History*, p. 238.
[5] He also explains the precise place to which the dogmatic attitude is entitled in the life of the intellect: "As the scientific spirit develops, we see that it is we who lend fixity to the ideas, and that this loan is for a purpose to which the meaning of ideas is accommodated. Fixity ceases to be a matter of intrinsic structure of ideas, and becomes an affair of security in using them. Hence the important thing is the way in which we fix the idea—the manner of the inquiry

this only if we handle it consciously, and realize that it is a tool, to be put down as soon as it has performed its valuable office. The moment we surrender to our dogmatic inclinations we lay ourselves open to primitive temptations which invite us to mental laziness, and we find ourselves looking out for magical short-cuts. Applied to history, the dogmatic mentality will reveal itself by the naïve demand that it shall reproduce the whole of the past as it really did occur. Poor Ranke is often accused of having given countenance to this preposterous expectation. Anyone who will take the trouble to examine the context of his *wie es eigentlich gewesen* will realize that he did nothing of the sort.[1] The dogmatic approach to history which Ranke wished to avoid in his own work also tries to lure the historian, as Ranke warns us, into formulating with an air of certain knowledge the laws according to which past events are supposed to be connected with each other. For those who suffer from this mentality claim that history is a science.

Whether history is indeed a science, whether its methods are, at least, akin to those of the natural sciences, is a problem that must be reserved for later investigation. At the present moment we are concerned with a notion of science which is primitive and superannuated. The dogmatists who claim that history is a science mean by this that it achieves secure knowledge which can be formulated through laws. A reviewer in *The Times Literary Supplement* declared, in the course of the justified demolition of a book on seventeeth century history, that the method of fitting historical material in with what an author considers is dramatically plausible "can perhaps be justified by those who do not regard history as a science, but as a form of mythology."[2] Myth-

which results in definition. We take the idea as if it were fixed, in order to secure the necessary stability of action. The crisis past, the idea drops its borrowed investiture, and reappears as surmise." *Essays in Experimental Logic* (1916), pp. 191–2.

[1] In the preface to his *Geschichte der romanischen und germanischen Voelker, 1495–1535* (p.v.), he says that history has been allotted the task of directing the past towards instructing our own world for the sake of years to come. But he will have nothing to do with this left-wing deviationism. His purpose is merely to say how things actually did happen, or, to translate this into our nomenclature, to give an accurate story.

[2] January 4, 1947: "Cromwell kills the King."

ology or "science"? It remains to be seen whether this is a true dilemma that exhausts all possibilities.

Bernheim devotes many pages to refute the notion that history is a natural science.[1] Bauer tells us, most sensibly, that any attempt to reduce the whole past to causation and determination is bound to fail, and that it would be advisable to assign a considerable role to chance.[2] He quotes as an example of the dogmatic approach a book published in 1883 by Adolf Rhomberg, *Die Erhebung der Geschichte zum Range einer Wissenschaft*,[3] which, as the title indicates, attempts to make a science of history. On page 21 Rhomberg lays down an "historico-critical" axiom which appears most convincing at first sight. "When two or more contemporary witnesses, whether ocular or aural, report, independently from one another, one and the same event, with a number of particulars which are the same in each version, although they have no necessary connection with the main event and do not invariably occur when an event of this nature takes place, but are merely accidental—then these two reports must be true, in so far as they agree, provided the particulars concerned were so clearly observable that there could be no mistake about them." This rule has a truly scientific ring. Bauer, who is ready to adopt it, calls it the pivot of all higher "source-criticism." But he permits himself one observation. Before applying the rule we must, of course, make sure that the coincidence between the two reports does not rest upon contagious contemporary opinions, illusions, preconceptions or partisanship. He also wants to be assured, he tells us, that the mutual independence of the two witnesses is not merely apparent, but real. Now this means that, from the safety of a generally valid principle, we are transferred once more to the risks of empirical investigation. Bauer's proviso plays havoc with the axiomatic quality of Rhomberg's rule, and rightly so. For it is no more than a rule of thumb, a practical hint to craftsmen.

[1] *Op. cit.*, pp. 101–45.

[2] *Op. cit.*, p. 26. He quotes Hans Driesch (*Wirklichkeitslehre*, 1917), who considers that there is no real development in the past, but, as he calls it, a *Kumulation*, in which one stage merely produces the prerequisites for the next. Bauer also gives a survey of the doctrines of those who argue that historical events are determined by laws in the same way as scientific events (*ibid.*, p. 20).

[3] *Ibid.*, pp. 334 *sqq.*

When you notice a coincidence of testimony such as has been described, ask yourself whether you cannot say that . . ., but do not forget that you must also find out whether . . . This leaves nothing of the certitude which Rhomberg wanted to call science.

The word science is used by the dogmatists as a magic formula which gives repose and security. We have no room for this primitive craving in the realm of history. We have read *Le Génie du Christianisme* and *Omphalos*. We must admit, with the great Michel de Montaigne in his *Apologie de Raymond Sebond* that "l'impression de la certitude est un certain tesmoignage de folie et d'incertitude extrême."[1] As an antidote to dogmatism Hume, in his *Enquiry concerning human Understanding*, from which we have already quoted, recommends "a mitigated scepticism or academical philosophy, which may be both durable and useful." Langlois and Seignobos, in the modern idiom, advise the historian to approach every affirmation with *a priori* distrust. The historian, they say, must begin by doubting.[2]

§ 2

FERTILE DOUBT

Reflective minds must have turned away at an early stage from primitive confidence and certitude at the sight of the unedifying clash between discordant dogmatisms.[3] Thus was born the systematic scepticism of Pyrrho of Elis, of Protagoras, which could not possibly interest the methodologist of history. By its uncompromising denial of the possibility of attaining truth it invites the formal refutation wich points out that the sceptic is compelled to exclude the duty to doubt from the notions that have to be doubted. There is another kind of scepticism—we might call it practical scepticism—which is simply a psychological attitude, an *approach* to knowledge. Those who profess it are inclined to uphold the theoretic possibility of doubting every-thing, but their doubt has no ferocity. They are not afraid of minor formal contradictions. As Anatole France once said: "the

---

[1] *Essais*, II: xii.　　　　　　　　　　　　　　　[2] *Op. cit.*, p. 132.
[3] In the new universities in England one witnesses sometimes dogmatically conducted existences that are a sermon in scepticism.

true sceptic is ready to believe anything—le vrai sceptique est celui qui est prêt à tout croire." F. C. S. Schiller considers that, "so far as theory goes, there is no harm in universal doubt. If anything, it is beneficial. For doubt is the chief stimulus to enquiry, to research, and so to discovery." This logician tells us that the use of doubt must be subject to two conditions. We must never doubt all things, "but only such things as we purpose to investigate," and "our doubts . . . should not diminish our confidence in the truths we accept or take for granted." For, he adds, "doubt sets in only when an alleged truth has ceased to satisfy us."[1] At an earlier date, Alfred Sidgwick said that the right scepticism "consists of a recognition of the defects of knowledge only in the hope of helping knowledge forward. Among its leading principles," he continued, "are these: that doubt is always lawful but not always expedient; that human fallibility is only worth remembering for the sake of discovering and correcting actual errors; and that beliefs may be unquestioned without being unquestionable. So far from using the notion that man is fallible as an excuse for despair, or for tendering the advice that nothing should ever be believed, we use it as a justification of the effort to improve our knowledge little by little for ever."[2] Such is the practical scepticism which is infinitely more fruitful than dogmatism. It never acts as a dissolvent upon the legitimate claims of the intellect, and it deserves a hearing from the historian who, undismayed by genuine theoretical difficulties, seeks upon which foundations he may build his story.

Numerous attempts have been made to apply systematic (or universal) scepticism to the processes of history. The objectivity as well as the utility of history has been denied at one time or another by Agrippa van Nettesheim, Pierre Bayle, de Fontenelle, Volney, d'Alembert, Schopenhauer, Du Bois-Reymond, and Max Nordau.[3] Descartes did not believe that it was possible to acquire a knowledge of past events. Bernheim tells of the Jesuit Jean Harduin who, towards the end of the seventeenth century,

---

[1] *Our Human Truths* (1939), pp. 77–8.
[2] *The Use of Words in Reasoning*, p. 233.
[3] Bernheim, *op. cit.*, pp. 197 *sqq.*; Bauer, *op. cit.*, p. 20; Van Schilfgaarde, *op. cit.*, pp. 130–1, 150.

looked upon Thucydides, Livy, Terence, Ovid, as well as upon the whole history of the Franks, as forgeries, and who distrusted any historical evidence apart from that of coins. There also was, at the beginning of the nineteenth century, a German called P. J. F. Muller who, in a published work, stated that the story of the German people had been completely falsified as a result of an international conspiracy, and that the whole body of medieval documents had been invented by people who were jealous of the German nation, and had succeeded in making the world forget that the Germans were once the most civilized as well as politically the most powerful unit in Europe.

Apart from these radical sceptics, undistinguishable in spirit from the dogmatists whose spiritual descendants are now British Israelites, or "Baconians" ranting about the clown Shakespeare, history has had and still has its practical or relative sceptics. There was Droysen, for instance, who held that history must be forever satisfied with possibilities and probabilities. Enough has been said about scepticism in general to show that practical scepticism can be a friend of historical research. This does not mean, of course, that scepticism is necessarily the last word in wisdom. It has another aspect which should not be ignored: it is the ambivalent companion of dogmatism, and makes its appearance, sooner or later, wherever we meet with dogmatism. I shall explain the notion of ambivalence at a later stage.[1] It means that, as heads and tails belong to the same coin, so do psychological opposites like love and hate point to the same disturbance: love and hate are both extreme preoccupation with an object. Dogmatic and absolute doctrines carry within themselves the seeds of scepticism. Doubt is cast upon the principle of causation, not by humdrum empiricists, but by ethereal idealists. Historical scepticism is met with in the most unexpected quarters.

Happier than the Calvinists, whose sole "source" of knowledge is the Bible, the Catholics possess the double certitude that resides in God's written word and in the unbroken apostolic tradition of their Church. Rome can, therefore, afford to fish with a net whose meshes are wide enough to let unwanted facts go through. In theory Rome pays tribute to the rules of historical

[1] Below, III: iii: § 2.

method. Father Charles Boyer has some admirable pages on certitude in history in his handbook of philosophy. In practice, however, Catholic history disregards awkward facts and produces stories which are original, and not infrequently artistic rather than accurate. Hilaire Belloc's *Robespierre* is an example. The Calvinist Mr. Cadoux, to whom I have already referred, could disregard all the work done about the history of the Low Countries since Motley, because his knowledge resulted from intuition and faith rather than from the study of traces. And if we think of the legerdemain which goes by the name of history in the Soviet Union we shall have to agree that doctrinal dogmatism is not inseparable from a Pyrrhonic disregard of facts. The skill with which Trotsky, the saviour of Leningrad, has been conjured out of Russian history books ought to settle the question whether history is a science or an art, at any rate as far as Soviet history is concerned.[1]

I wish to illustrate the real meaning and the importance of practical historical scepticism with a brief study of the doctrine as it appears in the works of its leading modern exponent Anatole France (1844–1924). At present he is under a cloud in his own country. While he lived and could purr or scratch at will his reputation was safe enough. After his death his stock fell abruptly. There appeared a spate of studies and biographies, most of them somewhat ironical,[2] and the French were easily persuaded that their great man was not above their own stature. In the 1920's the French were tired of classicism, and the formal beauty of the master's writings no longer moved people who could listen patiently to actors of the Comédie Française reciting the immortal lines of Racine as though they were prose. But the French have failed to understand that when a culture transcends its original frontiers it ceases to be the monopoly of its makers. French culture now belongs to the world, and the world refuses to take part in

---

[1] Another false dilemma, of course, about which more will be heard.

[2] Among others: Le Goff, Marcel, *Anatole France à la Béchellerie*, 1924, with an interesting chapter on France's historical knowledge, pp. 57–77; Ségur, Nicolas, *Conversations avec Anatole France ou les Mélancolies de l'Intelligence*, 1925 (superfluous); Brousson, Jean-Jacques, *Anatole France en Pantouffles*, 1926, and *Itinéraire de Paris à Buenos Ayres*, 1927, both of them intelligent, witty, spiteful and pathological.

the conspiracy of silence which surrounds the memory of Anatole France. It is not only in Holland that intellectuals still read his work and understand its value.

Anatole France, who enjoyed a sound classical education, understood the process of philological research and was, therefore, no stranger among the mysteries of historical method. He was a poet and a critic, a lover of art, which implies a curiosity about its origins and its development. He loved, also, the traditions and the glories of his country. History fascinated him throughout his long existence. At the same time he was a disappointed lover of certitude, for he began his career as a nationalist, a militarist, almost a religious believer. He escaped from these convictions by the deliberate cultivation of systematic doubt. It was not a pose. His enquiring mind was shaking off the trammels of dogmatism.

The sceptical approach had to be applied to history as it was to other subjects that preoccupied Anatole France. He formulated his doctrines for the first time in his early novel *Le Crime de Sylvestre Bonnard*, in 1881.[1] Curiously enough, he chose a student of the Ecole des Chartes to proclaim them (pp. 308–10). Ten years later, in the course of one of those delectable rambling critiques which he contributed to the great daily *Le Temps*, Anatole France reproduced the pages on history which, he said, he had "jetées légèrement et par badinage" into his little novel. This time, however, he made it clear that he accepted responsibility for them. "Je vois qu'elles valent quelquechose." He published this essay in the second volume of *La Vie Littéraire* which appeared between 1888 and 1892 (II, pp. 116–17).

"Is there such a thing as impartial history?" asked France. "And what is history? The written reproduction of past events. But what is an event? Is it any kind of occurrence? Certainly not! It is a noteworthy occurrence. Now how is the historian to judge whether an occurrence is noteworthy or not? Arbitrarily, accord-

[1] A work of considerable charm, with the quality of timelessness that is such a surprising aspect of the versatile personality of its author. At the beginning of his career France shows himself before our eyes as an old man, just as, at its close, he will show us, in *Le Petit Pierre* and *La Vie en Fleur*, France as a child. Sylvestre Bonnard is what France would have been, if circumstances had allowed: an erudite and a collector.

ing to taste and whim, in his own way, in short, as an artist. For occurrences do not, by their own nature, divide themselves into those that are historical and those that are not. An occurrence is in itself infinitely complex. Is the historian to reproduce occurrences in the fulness of their complexity? This would be impossible. He must strip them of most of the particularities of which they consist, and as a result they will be truncated, mutilated, and different from what they were. As for the relation between occurrences among themselves, let us not talk about them. If a so-called historical occurrence is caused, as is possible, indeed probable, by one or more occurrences that are not historical, and therefore unknown, how then is the historian to notice the way in which these occurrences are actually related and linked together? And while saying this I am taking for granted that the historian has unexceptionable testimony before his eyes, whereas in reality he is being deceived and he trusts one witness or another merely for reasons of interest or sentiment. History is not a science, it is an art. One can be successful at it only through the use of imagination."

About a year afterwards, in *La Rôtisserie de la Reine Pédauque*, one of his favourites among his own works, France allowed his mouthpiece, the gentle and erudite abbé Jérôme Coignard, to propound the habitual thesis of historical agnosticism with some new embroideries.[1] The following year he published his sceptical breviary, *Le Jardin d'Epicure*, in which he reprinted his paradoxical challenge to history. In this tidy garden of doubt the weeds of action and belief peep through in more than one place. Even the passage on history had to undergo one or two subtle emendations before it could be placed like a cherished sun-dial among the shrubs. The historian was no longer allowed to establish a distinction between historical and non-historical events according to his whim: his decision was dictated by his temperament. No longer did he prefer one witness to another according to interest or sentiment. He was allowed to be disinterested: sentiment alone was to guide him. Such concessions are not without significance. The arch-sceptic was taking the world into account, and had no desire to offend it.

[1] 1893, pp. 220-9.

In 1903 France published *Sur la Pierre Blanche* which contains his socialist Utopia, a sensible and plausible piece of writing. More than ever he revealed in this book his preoccupation with the problems of historical method and of the philosophy of history. The sceptical statement was once more given its place; it had, by now, become part of the mask which Anatole France presented to the world, of the role he played for his own delectation more even than for that of others. One of the workers in Utopia was allowed to declare that as a science statistics had taken the place of history. This, by the way, would imply that history had been a science, in the days before the revolution which introduced Utopia, in other words, in the days of Anatole France. But the Utopians were not morbidly consistent. Another statistician proceeded to give, a moment later, a lucid account, in the allegedly superannuated historical form, of the political and social development of mankind during the previous three centuries. In another part of the book Anatole France, attentive to the demands of scepticism, excluded prognostication from the tasks with which an historian can be entrusted. "It is certain, anyhow, that our too imperfect knowledge of past events does not provide us with the elements that would be needed for an exact determination of events still to come" (p. 191). Surely, in this case, doubt has dictated the only posssible answer to the question: can history foretell the future? France adds that, precisely because some of the past is known, some of the future may be foretold. We can observe circumstances in which certain social phenomena occurred, and lay down, in consequence, the circumstances in which they will occur again. Thus one deals, not in certainties, but in probabilities.[1]

At the age of 74 Anatole France drew up his final account with the muse of history. That was in 1918, in *Le Petit Pierre*, the first part of his last autobiographical novel. Dealing with his own

[1] Here is another example of the inevitable breakdown of absolute scepticism, almost a profession of faith in the rationality of the world, taken from the same book: "Je n'entends pas dire . . . qu'il y ait une justice au monde. Mais on voit d'étranges retours des choses; et la force, seul juge encore des actions humaines, fait parfois des bonds inattendus. Ses brusques écarts rompent un équilibre qu'on croyait stable. Et ses jeux, qui ne sont jamais sans quelque règle cachée, amènent des coups intéressants" (pp. 211–12).

childhood and with the uncertainties of its chronology, he wrote: "Chronology and geography, they say, are the two eyes of history. If this be true, there is every reason to believe that, in spite of the Benedictines of Saint Maur who invented the art of verifying dates, history is, at best, one-eyed. Might I add that this is the least of her shortcomings? Clio, the muse Clio, is a grave personage with a somewhat forbidding aspect, whose words instruct us, or so it is said, interest, move, entertain us. One could listen to her all day. But, by frequenting her most assiduously, I have observed that she allows herself to be caught, too frequently, in the act of being forgetful, vain, partial, ignorant and mendacious. These defects have not prevented me from loving her very much. I still love her" (pp. 46–7).

That the arch-doubter should have tried his hand at a substantial piece of historical reconstruction may seem surprising. But when we reflect that Anatole France's reiterated doubt was an expression of his preoccupation with history, when we hear the reluctant but repeated declarations of love he addressed to Clio— but most of all when we come to understand that doubt is not a doctrine, but an attitude, an approach which need not preclude action, then we take up *La Vie de Jeanne d'Arc* with a pleasant sense of anticipation. This work came between the socialist *Sur la Pierre blanche* of 1903 and the somewhat anarchistic *Ile des Pingouins* of the end of 1908. We should avoid, however, establishing too close a connection between it and France's public life. Too much has been attributed, in his career, to the courageous part he played in the Dreyfus affair. His conversion to positive beliefs, and in part to socialism, dates from the early 1890's, well before the *Affaire*.[1] The great master's evolution from scepticism to action is natural. Scepticism is the royal road to wisdom, but wisdom is not for those who sit down by the roadside. France did not sit down. He loved history too much. And once an earnest and perspicacious mind begins to handle the material traces left

[1] *Cf.* Braibant, Ch., *Le Secret d'Anatole France*, 1935. This is by far the best book about Anatole France. At the time when he was writing *Jeanne d'Arc*, the influence of Madame de Caillavet, sometimes beneficial, often baneful, as is manifest in the dreary novel *Le Lys Rouge*, of 1894, was on the wane. See Pouquet, Jeanne M., *Le Salon de Madame Arman de Caillavet* (1926).

by the past, his deepest human impulses will move him towards a sane reconstruction of the events that hide behind the traces, and the use of these events in the telling of a story.

The sceptic tackled his job in the right way. He made himself thoroughly acquainted with the accepted history of his subject, a task in which he was helped by his unusually retentive memory. He made use of preparatory studies by a young historian, Pierre Champion, while his secretary Jean-Jacques Brousson, a trained philologist, distilled for him "the somewhat acrid honey of erudition," as he described the preparatory work of history in an earlier book.[1] Many a professor has made similar use of the work of research students, and Mr. Churchill, in our day, sent his young historians to the archives of Europe to do the spade-work for his *Life of Marlborough*. Langlois and Seignobos, as we have seen, look upon this kind of division of labour as legitimate and even advisable, but I think it should remain an exception. France consulted some of the foremost historians of his day, Paul Meyer, Lavisse, Petit-Dutaillis, Langlois, and others, and made good use of their advice. As the collection of excerpts and précis increased, he meditated upon the impending task. His scepticism warned him of certain pitfalls. Historical figures are subject to continual transformation, because the general public finds ancient personages interesting only if it can endow them with its own sentiments and passions.[2] Here France perceived a first danger of distortion. Distortion threatened from another quarter also, from the scholars. "To have about Joan of Arc the insight of a Quicherat or an Henri Martin three centuries had to pass with absolute monarchy, the Reformation, the Revolution, the wars of the Republic and of the Empire, and the sentimental neo-Catholicism of the men of '48. It is through so many brilliant prisms, underneath all these layers of varnish, that romantic historians and generous palaeographers have discovered the figure of Joan of Arc, and it is asking too much from that poor Dauphin Charles . . . to expect that he should have seen Joan as she was made and completed by the centuries."[3]

So he worked, ever on the alert, but unmindful of his favourite

[1] *Le Crime de Sylvestre Bonnard*, p. 20.
[2] *La Vie de Jeanne d'Arc*, Vol. I, p. lxiv.   [3] *Ibid.*, I, p. liii.

theory about the distinction between events that obtain admission into history and those that do not, and about the arbitrary character of this distinction.[1] He worked like an ordinary historian, preoccupied before all else by the desire to tell a story that was as accurate as possible. He saw that the testimony of contemporaries of the Maid of Orleans is awkward and contradictory, that official documents of the period were subjective and unreliable. More than once he reached a cross roads where there was no pointer, and where, like the most orthodox historian, he had to listen to the promptings of his own mind in deciding which way to go. Is the subjective character of this choice somewhat more in evidence in *Jeanne d'Arc* than it would be in the publications of orthodox historians? Not more, I should imagine, than in the work of Carlyle or of Michelet. The story does remain personal, his conclusions do not invariably command the agreement of expert readers. Its value is real, nevertheless. Gabriel Monod, Salomon Reinach, Lefèvre-Pontalis, gave it serious reviews, and suggested improvements which were incorporated in subsequent editions. Halphen and Saignac rank the book among the serious contributions to our knowledge of the story of Joan of Arc, even though they warn the student to exercise caution in using it.

Anatole France's handling of the figure of Napoleon, to whom he frequently refers in his writings, is another illustration of his historical knowledge and insight.[2] Kant has observed somewhere that scepticism is not a permanent dwelling for human reason. Anatole France confirms this view. In action he ceased to be a sceptic. What is true in his case is true of history in general, History is action, because it is the telling of a story. The sceptical approach does not inhibit activity. It is, on the other hand, the cure of certitude, of the pseudo-scientific dogmatism that kills the desire for action. But doubt does not solve the great problem with which we are still faced. It tells us nothing to justify the

[1] Cf. *Les Opinions de Jerome Coignard*, p. 223.

[2] Anatole France felt at the same time repelled and fascinated by the figure of Napoleon. He always came back to it, both in his works and in his conversation. He said strikingly true things about Napoleon, and showed how much he had read and meditated about the conqueror. The development of France's views on Napoleon deserves to be studied one day in the light of contemporary French politics and of the evolution of the personality of Anatole France.

jump from trace to event, even though it does not paralyse us when we attempt it.

§ 3

COMMON SENSE

The dogmatic or pseudo-scientific approach to research is utterly sterile. The sceptical approach achieves results by ignoring its own premises. The methodologist whose main task is that of justifying before the non-historical world the actual manner in which the historian carries out his duties will have to ask himself sooner or later where lies the middle way between these two approaches. That it exists he knows from the rows of volumes on the history shelves of every library, and from the fact that chairs of history are endowed, and occupied. There *is* a way. Where does it lie?

Is not the way of the historian simply the way of common sense? Huizinga is not far from taking this view, since to prove that history is not subjective he points out that it is based, as a rule, upon agreement among people with trained minds.[1] Many working historians take for granted that the epistemology of history is that of common sense. It would be comforting, if we could in all conscience end our enquiry at this stage, finally brush aside the doctrine of *Omphalos* as the crazy perversion of a few individual minds, and proclaim that the passage from trace to event is not a *salto mortale* but a safe step sanctioned by common sense. There are a few difficulties, however, even for those who cannot agree with Bernheim that to proclaim the equivalence of historical method and common sense carries us nowhere, since it merely states the obvious fact that everything in the world is common sense.[2]

What do we mean by common sense? Is it indeed something that is common or at least general? The Dutch do not speak of common sense, but of healthy understanding—*gezond verstand*. Both the English and the French have a synonymous expression, good sense, *bon sens*, which indicates a belief in the quality of untutored judgment rather than in the virtue of a statistical

---

[1] *De Wetenschap der Geschiedenis*, pp. 128–9.   [2] *Op. cit.*, p. 180.

average of public opinion. This way of looking upon untutored judgment is even more dangerous than the Gallup poll conception. It makes good sense or common sense the prerogative of the wholesome man with a vigorous brain (similar to our own) and regards it as a direct communion with the world of simple, uncontrovertible values. Good sense is the court which sanctions men's intuitions, their "hunches," as they like to call them. The trust they place in their own good sense is a mere variant of the primitive uncritical certitude which holds out so little promise to the methodologist in search of the right approach to the problems of historical research. On the other hand, to attach a special virtue to the largest common denominator of the mentality of a group or a period presupposes a general level of enlightenment which no actual study of the mental processes of the masses will confirm. Anatole France is right when he observes that "le sens commun est rarement le sens du juste et du vrai."[1]

Yet, when all is said and done, the fact remains that men have in common certain notions which, at first sight, would seem to be self-evident: thing, the same or different, kinds, minds, bodies, one time, one space, subjects and attributes, causal influences, the fancied, the real,[2] and the aggregate of these notions is in actual fact what goes by the name of common sense. But, as William James, from whom I take this list, observes, these notions are not self-evident to children. "They may have been successfully discovered by pre-historic geniuses," he says, "they are but sublime tricks of human thought, our ways of escaping bewilderment in the midst of sensation's irremediable flow." In short, common sense is a complex system of postulates which it must have taken mankind centuries to develop. It is "a collection of extraordinarily successful hypotheses," and not in the least "the mother tongue of thought." Such a doctrine is not derogatory to common sense. It is certainly not a plea for its abolition. "For all utilitarian practical purposes these conceptions amply suffice," says William

---

[1] Jeanne d'Arc, I, p. 327.

[2] James, W., article on "Common Sense" in Pragmatism (1907), pp. 165–194. "There is probably not a common-sense tradition, of all those which we now live by, that was not in the first instance a genuine discovery" (The Meaning of Truth, pp. 61 sqq.).

James. Common sense, says Schiller, comes from an ancient stock and has a long history behind it. "The common sense view of the world is the outcome of a long development and the embodiment of much racial experience: the view which man and his ancestors have successfully evolved for dealing with the world in which they have lived and have managed to survive. It has therefore the highest pragmatic sanction and should not be lightly set aside."[1]

In the light of this interpretation, however, we must renounce the attempt to obtain from common sense an easy solution of our methodological problem. If it is not a set of intuitions, but a collection of assumptions that have become a habit, if it is eminently practical—then it will cease to operate the moment it is called upon to guide thought instead of action. No sooner does common sense begin to reason, than it merges with philosophy. This is the view put forward by Alfred Sidgwick when he says that "philosophy is only common sense with leisure to push enquiry further than usual, while common sense is only philosophy somewhat hurried and hardened by practical needs."[2] We shall therefore define philosophy as the leisurely investigation and the systematization of any problem presented by life, which agrees with the provisional definition we ventured at an earlier stage. But once we accept, with Sidgwick, that common sense and philosophy are at bottom the same thing, we shall refuse to restrict philosophy to speculative enquiries into the possibility of activity, causation, knowledge, personal identity, motion, or change. Such problems belong to the branch of philosophy called metaphysics. One can be a philosopher, or, at any rate, a philosophically minded person, even if one restricts one's enquiry to practical issues.[3] In brief, as soon as we appeal to common sense we appeal to philosophy.

Where is the methodologist of history—let us not forget that

---

[1] Schiller, *Our Human Truths*, p. 322.

[2] *Distinction and the Criticism of Beliefs* (1890), p. 35. "We are here concerned with the war between two methods sharply opposed in idea though not in their actual manifestations; the method which loves a short cut, and the method which aims at taking the utmost care" (*ibid.*, p. 40). "Philosophy is inherently criticism. . . . Criticism is discriminating judgment, careful appraisal," Dewey, *Experience and Nature*, p. 398.

[3] *Cf.* James, W., *Some Problems of Philosophy* (1931), chapter V.

he should be a working historian and not a professional philosopher[1]—to find the philosophy that will help him out of his
difficulty? He sees a bewildering number of conflicting schools,
most of which delight in metaphysical subtleties that leave him
indifferent, as indifferent as the philosophers remain to his practical preoccupation with traces and with the manner in which
they lead to a knowledge of past events. The more he seeks to
thread his path through the labyrinth of philosophical speculation, the more he will feel inclined to agree with the verdict o
Hume: "I have long entertained a suspicion, with regard to the
decisions of philosophers upon all subjects, and found myself a
greater inclination to dispute, than assent to their conclusions."[2]
Luckily, it is unnecessary for the uninitiated mind with an inclination towards leisurely and systematic investigation to take
cognizance of the philosophy of the schools.

There is, in point of fact, no difference between the classical
systems that divide professional philosophers. They were all born
of a pathetic desire to escape from the uncertainties of life, of a
passionate longing to endow our contradictory world with
meaning, of a quest for certainty. To quote Dewey, in an abridged
form but in his own words: "If classical philosophy says so much
about unity and so little about diversity, it may well be because
the ambiguousness and ambivalence of reality are actually so
pervasive. Upon their surface, the reports of the world which
form our different philosophies are various to the point of stark
contrariness. These radical oppositions suggest that all their
different philosophies have a common premise; variant philosophies may be looked at as different ways of supplying recipes
for denying to the universe the character of contingency which it
possesses so integrally. Quarrels among conflicting types of
philosophy are thus family quarrels."[3]

The historian turned methodologist finds his task beautifully

---

[1] Above, Foreword.

[2] *Essays*, I: xviii. He will also tend to agree with Montaigne's "Et certes la
philosophie n'est qu'une poésie sophistiquée" (*Essais*, II: xii), and with Anatole
France who says: "La métaphysique a cela d'admirable qu'elle ôte au monde tout
ce qu'il a et qu'elle lui donne ce qu'il n'avait pas" (*Le Jardin d'Epicure*, p. 93).

[3] *Experience and Nature*, pp. 46–7. See also his *Quest for Certainty*, chapters I, II
and III. "The quest for certitude has determined our basic metaphysics" (p. 25).

simplified by Dewey's analysis. He need not give up his desire, indeed his right, to philosophize, but he will philosophize regardless of the schools and of their doctrines. This does not mean that he will despise or ignore the results they have achieved. He will have no difficulty in admitting that the old philosophies have for twenty-five centuries exercised the wits of men and made them nimble, while they also perfected the linguistic matrix of their thoughts. He will know, moreover, that the variations of philosophical doctrine belong to the history of ideas, and that the story of human experiences which ignores them is incomplete.[1] He may even like to know that by thinking at leisure and systematically he is contributing to the collective thought of his own age.[2] But remembering that the historian is a man with a task to accomplish, the methodologist will look for a system that guides action and does not ask men to devote their energy to speculation.

§ 4

THE WAY OF THE SCIENTIST

Seeking for a philosophy that accepts the imperfections and limitations of the world in which we actually dwell instead of trying to escape from them, the methodologist of history notices the success of his fellow intellectuals, the scientists, and the way in which they work, in the full enjoyment of the respect of society and of their own self-esteem. No one, least of all they themselves, questions their methods, since they achieve tangible results. What are these methods, on what philosophy are they based, and can the historian also be guided by them? My sub-

---

[1] "Les philosophies sont intéressantes seulement comme des monuments psychiques propres à éclairer le savant sur les divers états qu'a traversés l'esprit humain" (Anatole France, Le Jardin d'Epicure, p. 133). See in Schiller's Formal Logic, pp. 189–91) the origin of the syllogism as a method for forcing the opponent to confess himself beaten in a public debate. For the effect of the existence of slavery in the Greek world upon the development of Greek thought see Dewey's Experience and Nature, pp. 93 sqq.

[2] "Betrachtet man Philosophie als das zu einem System zusammengefasste Denken einer Zeit, einer Menschengruppe, dann arbeitet jeder oder doch jeder halbwegs selbständig denkende Mensch an dem jeweiligen Aufbau der Philosophie mit," Bauer, op. cit., p. 41.

146

mission is that the scientific method implies a philosophy which can guide the historian in every one of the operations in which he engages, and which takes in its stride the passage from trace to event.

Earlier in this chapter I referred to the fallacy that looks upon science as the possession of final knowledge. This antiquated aberration belongs to the pre-experimental ages when, ignorant of the technique of observation, learned men drew their certitude from authorities. The French abbé Barthélemy (1716–95) tells us, in the introduction to his *Voyage du jeune Anacharsis en Grèce*, that in his youth he had known an ancient priest with a vast library and a great erudition. The old man one day talked about the Parthians whose arrows, he said, flew so fast that their metal heads melted by friction with the air. Young Barthélemy ventured to express a doubt, whereupon his friend rose and took an ancient Greek work from his bookshelf. He found and read aloud the passage in which this story was told, shut the book and put it away, with the words "that settles it." Those cautious methodologists Langlois and Seignobos have not travelled much beyond the mentality of the old priest, for they imagine that, difficult though it may be to achieve, there can be found, in the end, a science that gives incontrovertible knowledge.[1] Credulity and certitude go hand in hand. They are symptoms of the disease called metaphysics. It is an ancient disease. Dewey warns us against it when he says: "There is something both ridiculous and disconcerting in the way in which men have let themselves be imposed upon, so as to infer that scientific ways of thinking of objects give the inner reality of things, and that they put a mark of spuriousness upon all other ways of thinking of them, and of perceiving and enjoying them."[2]

If we listen to contemporary scientists explaining their work and their problems, we detect in their words as little self-assured-

[1] "La science est une économie de temps et d'efforts obtenue par un procédé qui rend les faits rapidement connaissables et intelligibles; elle consiste à receuillir lentement une quantité de faits de détail et à les condenser en formules portatives et *incontestables*" (my italics, *op. cit.*, p. 228).

[2] *The Quest for Certainty*, p. 131. Huizinga tells us that according to Wendelband and to Rickert we must not expect absolute certainty from the scientific method (*De Wetenschap der Geschiedenis*, p. 33).

ness as inclination to metaphysics. The surgeon realizes that in many cases biochemistry is more powerful as well as kinder than the scalpel. Medicine is aware of the doubtful value of many laboratory experiments concerning vitamins.[1] Some biochemists show a concern with electronics which may one day sweep away the distinction between their own subject and physics. "It may surprise those who are not anatomists to hear that one of the great attractions of the subject is that whatever part of the body you study you soon find that very little is known about it, at least from current points of view," says one anatomist.[2] In modern science all is modesty, hesitation, undogmatic suggestion, revision. Let us ask one of these undogmatic scientists, Professor H. G. K. Westenbrink, of Utrecht, to tell us in his own words how he looks upon the task of the scientist. "What do we mean by 'knowing'? Primary knowledge concerns exclusively our own inner self (*ons eigen innerlijk*), our own 'I'. All that lies outside it we can only learn to know by making observations. This 'learning to know' means nothing else and nothing more than that the human mind has the capacity of constructing a system of ideas which, without inner contradiction, connects the observed facts with each other in such a way as to draw up an image that conforms with nature. This image is in a state of constant development. Those who drew it up must not for one moment lose contact with observed facts. Through the discovery of new facts the image will constantly expand and display even more delicate gradations. If it is ascertained at any time that a new observation does not fit in with the accepted structure of ideas, this structure will have to be modified in a lesser or greater measure. Such an event may shake the foundations of the system; it may in the end require the construction of an entirely new building upon different foundations, of a new system of ideas which makes it possible to incorporate the new discovery logically into the whole. The accuracy of the theory, i.e. the measure of con-

[1] Nuboer, J. F., *De Heelkunde aan den Tweesprong* (Utrecht, 1946), p. 10; Langen, C. D. de, *Bezinning by de snelle Ontwikkeling der Geneeskunde* (Utrecht, 1938), *passim*.

[2] Young, J. Z., *Patterns of Substance and Activity in the Nervous System* (inaugural lecture, London, 1946), p. 14. The whole of this paper illustrates the point I am trying to make.

formity between the structure of ideas and reality, is established by the success of predictions, or, to put it differently, by the confirmation through new observations of conclusions drawn from the theory."[1] A resemblance will, no doubt, be observed between Westenbrink's "accepted structure of ideas" and our notion of "accepted history." May we expect the resemblance between the work of the historian and that of the scientist to apply to other aspects of their work also? We hold a clue, and we shall not be overlong in finding out where it leads.

Some philosophers have taken notice of the practical and unassuming ways of scientific investigation. Dewey points out the contrast between the methods of science and the search of classical philosophy for certainties that are supposed to reside outside our experienced world. "Science," he writes, "has advanced in its methods in just the degree in which it has ceased to assume that prior realities and prior meanings retain fixedly and finally, when entering into reflective situations, the characters they had prior to this entrance."[2] Schiller holds that "the application of Scientific Method is universal. . . Scientific Method is the only genuine method of knowing, and will tackle anything knowable."[3] These philosophers, and all those who adopt the philosophical approach that has become known under the name of pragmatism, proclaim that their epistemological system is the method of science as it is described to us by modern methodologists.[4] This method is also that of history, and this is why pragmatism has been for generations the philosophy of historians, though they are as unaware of it as M. Jourdain was of the fact that he talked in prose. Historians are pragmatists whenever they take the step from trace to event, whenever they detect and arrange their events, whenever they answer the questions society asks through them about its past experiences,

---

[1] *De Wetenschap om haar zelfs Wil* (Utrecht, 1946), p. 4.
[2] *Experimental Logic*, p. 244. See also *The Quest for Certainty*, pp. 236–7.
[3] *Logic for Use*, pp. 386–7.
[4] "It is not too much to say that on one side Pragmatism means the discovery of the method of Science. But the method of science, rightly understood, is the method of all knowing and all living, and the scientists themselves, misled by the false formal logic of intellectualist philosophy, had not understood it. They only practised it, instinctively. . . ." Schiller, *Must Philosophers Disagree?* p. 71.

and whenever they tell the story which society requires from them. Any thinking human being who, through a course of scepticism, has been cured of absolutist longings and of the pseudo-scientific indolence of dogmatism, will find in pragmatism a comforting attitude of mind which is prepared to treat his sceptical leanings with understanding, provided he does not allow them to inhibit his activity. Pragmatism holds that even legitimate doubt cannot save us from the necessity to act, because life is activity from beginning to end. It looks upon action as the justification of every intellectual system, and as the sole available method for testing the validity of our knowledge.

The name pragmatism chosen for the philosophy of provisional verification by action has led to confusion. William James, the first consistent interpreter of the pragmatist frame of mind, said that pragmatism is "a new name for some old ways of thinking." He confessed that his choice was not fortunate, but by the time he had come to realize this the name had caught, and all efforts to change it were in vain.[1] Schiller tried to launch the name "humanism," because it is "the attitude which makes man's standpoint central," and Dewey calls his system instrumentalism, because it looks upon ideas as tools or instruments to solve problems. Sidgwick, the veteran logician who administered a mortal wound to the reputation of the syllogism and denied the claims of formal logic to conduct men towards the possession of unchallengeable truth, was the most significant of a number of forerunners. William James, who began his career as a physician and an experimental psychologist, was listening to the promptings of filial piety and attempting to prove to himself that the mysticism of his remarkable father was not a philosophical absurdity. The profound charity and kindness of heart of William James, which stands out in every page of his correspondence and struck all who met him,[2] is the key-note of his system. For it is a system that attempts to show men how unimportant are their disagree-

---

[1] "I dislike 'pragmatism,' but it seems to have the *international* right of way at present." *Letters of William James*, Vol. II, p. 271. "A most unlucky word," *ibid.*, p. 295, also p. 298.

[2] Logan Pearsall Smith says in his *Unforgotten Years*: "I need not try to describe the charm of the most charming man I ever met" (p. 104).

ments, how significant is their common desire for happiness and righteousness; it is a system full of toleration and liberalism, which recognizes every man's right to believe. There is in William James's early work much groping after imperfectly apprehended wisdom, much use of the very human (and very scientific) method of trial and error. F. C. S. Schiller, a great fighter to whom William James once wrote: "I think that your *gaudium certaminis* injures your influence,"[1] proved to be a loyal and doughty supporter. In Schiller's battle against "absolutist" philosophy with its "copy-book" theory of truth as the reproduction of reality, the historian will recognize many features of the ceaseless action that has to be fought against the pseudo-scientific dogmatism with its dreams of an integral reproduction of the past. Schiller also showed that absolutist idealism and extreme scepticism are ambivalent diseases of the mind. John Dewey is a pragmatist who has carried the method of criticism by action into new fields such as ethics and social science.

This is how William James formulated his doctrine of knowledge: "The absolutists . . . say that we can not only attain to knowing the truth, but we can *know when* we have attained to knowing it; while the empiricists think that although we may attain it, we cannot infallibly know when. . . . Objective evidence and certitude are doubtless very fine ideals to play with, but where on this moonlit and dream-visited planet are they found? . . . There is but one indefectibly certain truth, and that is the truth that pyrrhonistic scepticism itself leaves standing—the truth that the present phenomenon of consciousness exists. . . . No concrete test of what is really true has ever been agreed upon. . . . But . . . when as empiricists we give up the doctrine of objective certitude, we do not thereby give up the quest or hope of truth itself."[2]

Philip Henry Gosse and René de Chateaubriand now look far less threatening. Comforted by the possession of a philosophical system that can lead us to such knowledge as human beings may

---

[1] *Letters*, II, p. 271. For the controversial character of early pragmatist logic see Dewey, *Experimental Logic*, p. 20. It is interesting to note that William James looked upon H. G. Wells as a pragmatist. (*Letters*, II, p. 257).
[2] *The Will to Believe*, pp. 11-17.

hope to possess—William James said: "One of pragmatism's merits is that it is so purely epistemological"[1]—realizing that knowledge is forever held subject to the test of practice, we shall cease to despise Robinson Crusoe's hesitations and contradictions in the presence of his *vestigium*. The passage from trace to event will be taken at the prompting of a judicious mixture of doubt and of the human impulse to act. Working in the honourable company of the scientists, serving society by action as they do, the historian will tell the story that is going to become increasingly accurate without ever presuming to offer a faithful tracing of the past. Without the help of the pragmatist approach the honest historian who reflects upon his craft is at a loss. How clear this becomes when one reads Bauer's chapter *Die Grenzen und die Sicherheit des Geschichtlichen Erkennens*.[2] Bauer admits the existence of uncertainties but is unable to offer a satisfactory way out. To an historian trained in the Anglo-Saxon world empiricism comes naturally, and A. F. Pollard, a man of considerable awareness, revealed his healthy pragmatism when he wrote: "The truth that deals with concrete things is always relative; absolute truth is an abstract ideal not attained in practical human affairs, and therefore not attainable in their history."[3]

Before attempting in the following chapter to examine in

---

[1] *The Meaning of Truth*, p. 215. Schiller observed that "if infallible judgment and absolute final knowledge were given to man, the whole business of judging, reasoning, etc., would come to an end" (*Logic for Use*, p. 225). See for a brief statement of the whole logical theory of Schiller: *Our Human Truths*, p. 283. A neat definition of pragmatism (without the name), in A. Sidgwick's *The Use of Words*, pp. 99–100. Finally, see Dewey's *Experimental Logic*, pp. 210–11: "With the development of empirical research, uncertainty or contingency is no longer regarded as infecting in a wholesome way an entire region, discrediting it save as it can be brought under the protecting aegis of universal truths as major premises." [2] *Op. cit.*, especially pp. 98–100.

[3] Quoted Williams, *Historians*, p. 44. In the notes for the preface to Vol. IV of *La Réforme*, which appeared after his death, Imbart de la Tour wrote: "L'histoire a une grande vertu d'appaisement. Je ne me flatte point d'apporter des solutions définitives. L'histoire, comme toute science, recorrige sans cesse, et tout érudit devrait avoir devant les yeux la belle devise de Fustel de Coulanges: *quaero, je cherche*" (Vol. IV, p. xi). "It is only the worn-out cynic, the devitalized sensualist, and the fanatical dogmatist who interpret the continuous change of science as proving that, since each successive statement is wrong, the whole record is error and folly; and that the present truth is only the error not yet found out" (Dewey, *Experimental Logic*, pp. 101–2).

detail the manner in which pragmatism guides and justifies the historical method, I must clarify one or two subsidiary issues. It is occasionally suggested that the non-professional who chooses pragmatism as his philosophy is a lazy thinker who will not take the trouble to acquaint himself with the body of classical philosophy. Do we expect a man who knows the length of one side of a triangular field and the degrees of the two adjacent angles to walk along the two other sides with a surveyor's chain? Historians and methodologists of history have the fullest right to adopt a philosophy which satisfies them entirely and which they have applied in practice even before they became aware of its existence. We must remember, of course, that pragmatism is not the only system of modern philosophy which adopts and sanctions, for philosophical and other enquiries, the approach to knowledge that prevails in modern science. A. J. Ayer's logical positivism has much in common with pragmatism, and its epistemology never conflicts with that of the pragmatists.

Of far greater importance than the fancied obligation for a serious intellectual to refrain forever from philosophical thought unless he reads all the classical philosophers is the ethical problem raised by the acceptance of a relativist philosophy. To the pragmatist the act of knowing appears entirely free from metaphysical elements. On the other hand, as Schiller has repeatedly observed, it cannot be divested of certain purely psychological elements. But psychology, which is the study of human behaviour, increasingly reveals an inability to ignore judgments of value. The logic and epistemology of pragmatism are profoundly ethical. It is opportune that intellectual investigation and scientific research should go ahead. In the absence of formally compelling canons of certainty the investigator must look upon it as a moral obligation to make his margin of error as narrow as possible. Therefore he must practise the utmost honesty at every stage of his enquiry. Dewey supports this view in a convincing passage. "The engineer, the physician, the moralist," he writes, "deal with a subject-matter which is practical; one, that is, which concerns things to be done and the way of doing them. But as far as personal disposition and purpose is concerned, their inquiries are intellectual and cognitive. These men set out to find certain things; in order to find them out, there has to be a purgation of personal desire and preference, and a willingness to subordinate them to the lead of the subject-matter inquired into. The mind must be purified as far as is humanly possible of bias and of that favouritism for one kind of conclusion rather than another which distorts observation and introduces an extraneous factor into reflection."[1]

Intellectual honesty is even more important for the historian than for the scientist, for unlike the scientist, the historian cannot submit his conclusions to the test of experiment. He knows that his work may go unchecked for generations, and that he is therefore put on his honour. Here, by the way, is a real difference between history and science. In most sciences experiment is an essential part of the process, in all of them there is prediction and its verification by ulterior observation. But, as we shall see, the historian can never predict. So it would appear that history cannot be called a science, even after we have corrected our notion of science. But the debate whether history is a science is about as important as the question whether the Albert Memorial will survive a Third World War.

We may conclude that the methods of science are not those of history, but that both science and history approach their method in the same spirit, and that this common approach receives its philosophical formulation in the writings of the pragmatists.

[1] *The Quest for Certainty*, pp. 67–8.

Chapter V

OUR KNOWLEDGE OF EVENTS

§ 1

THE PRAGMATIST SOLUTION

WITH the scientist and the pragmatist philosopher we shall henceforth adopt the view that we can acquire knowledge sufficiently secure to justify the carrying out of our task; that this knowledge will never be absolute, never definitive, always subject to partial or even radical revision, and finally, that the control of our knowledge is to be sought in the success of its practical application, in the satisfactory carrying out of our task. What this means in actual practice is that the historian is entitled to introduce into his story events which he infers from the traces that have come to his knowledge if this enables him to carry out his social task to the satisfaction of his conscience. The historian's criterion will be practical and ethical; it will never be metaphysical. There is nothing esoteric in our admitting into the story past events which we did not witness and which are no longer directly to be observed. A. J. Ayer remarks that "if one is justified in saying that events which are remote in space are observable in principle, the same may be said of events which are situated in the past."[1]

We shall now look once more at the historian while he is at work, but this time we are going to observe him in the light of the methodological principles we have just established. We must on no account forget that, as the scientist is in possession of accepted science, the historian is in possession of accepted history,

[1] *Language, Truth and Logic*, preface to 2nd edition, p. 19. Ayer also says: "it must surely be admitted that, however strong the evidence in favour of historical statements may be, their truth can never become more than highly probable" (*ibid.*, p. 37). There is no contradiction here, since Ayer himself adopts a pragmatist solution of the problem of historical knowledge. He refers to a pragmatist justification of historical knowledge in Lewis, C. I., *Mind and the World-Order* (1929), pp. 150–3. The views of Lewis are comforting, but he does not see history through the eyes of the working historian, with the result that he does not tackle the problems of historical procedure at close quarters.

and that he is now going to retell part of it in such a way that
the hitherto unknown events which he has discovered fit into it.
He has been guided in his search for events by the questions
society has asked through his agency. As we know, he obtains a
knowledge of events by the traces they left. We have defined a
trace as the still perceptible termination or culmination of a
sequence of events or of several sequences of events.[1] This provisional definition must now be expanded and, if possible, given
greater precision.

A trace is an event or occurrence of a special nature. There is,
as we noted before, no essential difference between event and
occurrence. If we bear in mind that every occurrence is itself a
sequence of occurrences of a lesser order, and part of a sequence
of occurrences of a higher order, we can say that a trace is an
event which continues to be perceptible in the present—and the
present, we know, is an elastic conception that cannot be fixed
within precise limits. The reason that makes the event perceptible
for the time being is that, provisionally, it forms the terminus of
a sequence. It is an event that has become concrete. We can use
another metaphor, and say that it has become congealed. Here is
an icicle. Water has been running into the gutter, and the matter
suspended in this water finally obstructed the outlet. More water
arrived, and the gutter overflowed. At this moment frost set in,
and drops became congealed in the act of running over the side
of the gutter and of falling down. The icicle is the termination of
this sequence. Not for ever: it may be broken off, or it may melt
away. Meanwhile it is there, the trace of the sequence I have
just indicated, evidence that justifies us in accepting as true a
narrative of this sequence of past occurrences or events. In this
particular instance, confirmation of the narrative will come with
the thaw, when the sequence will be resumed and water will
overflow once more from the gutter. Before this happens, our
reconstruction will already have led to action. We shall attempt
to remove the obstruction from the outlet of the gutter. Nevertheless, our knowledge, based upon the observation of the trace,
is not absolute. It is conceivable that this particular icicle was the
trace of the occurrence of a burst in a pipe. Attempted verifica-

[1] Above, II: ii: § 3.

tion by action may establish the untruth of our first story, and compel us to adopt the second.

Here is another example. We see a building, perhaps one of the Pyramids. It is an event that has become concrete. It disintegrates all the while, but so slowly that it creates an impression of permanance. It is a trace, not of one, but of a number of sequences of events. The need was felt for this particular kind of building, there followed a desire to satisfy this need, and a decision to fulfil the desire. This is one sequence. There was a plan; there may gave been several plans. One of them was given preference over the others. Steps were taken to carry one particular plan into effect. Here is a second sequence. The construction of the building was carried out by human agents. These agents were collected by the exercise of economic pressure, more probably by violence and the making of slaves, or by other means. This third sequence, mentioned here in generalized terms that make it look like one event, must have left other traces apart from the building itself. We should look for them in hieroglyphic inscriptions or in written documents. Material was used which arrived on the spot as the result of occurrences such as its collection by purchase, capture, or otherwise. Of some of these events the geologist may be able, by examining the material, to detect trustworthy traces. The construction followed a system that was not only technical, but also social and economic, perhaps religious and ritual. When the monument was finished it was the trace of all these sequences of events. Then it was modified by use, by adaptation to purposes for which it was not originally intended, and probably, in the end, by neglect. Its present state is a bundle of traces left by these subsequent events.

The mind which contemplates these traces sets to work at once. It ceases to look upon a trace as being merely the end term of a sequence of occurrences. It gets hold of the trace and makes it the starting point for an inference.[1] For the trace can be

[1] "Strictly speaking, data (as the immediate considerations from which controlled inference proceeds) are not objects but means, instrumentalities of knowledge: things by which we know rather than things known. It is by the colour stain that we know a cellular structure; it is by marks on a page that we know what some man believes; it is by . . . the scratches on the rock that we know that ice was once there, . . ." (Dewey, *Experimental Logic*, p. 43).

accepted, by anyone who knows how efficaciously experimental science makes use of its data, as an event connected by a "natural law" with another event earlier than itself. It is true that this natural law is merely a well-established hypothesis, but it suffices for the purpose of moving inferentially from the trace to another event or set of events. The events in this set are not, or need not be, continuous. The point is that they can be looked upon as typical of events between which there is a regular connection. Thus the historian feels justified in constructing the story of these events at the same time as he continues to look for other confirmatory traces, i.e. for other events that can also form a legitimate starting point for an inference leading to the same event or events already inferred from the first trace or set of traces.[1]

The question may be asked what is the nature of our knowledge of traces. It will, however, not be asked by historians. The man in whose mind a doubt about reality can arise was not born to be an historian. He was destined for philosophy, or for a nervous breakdown. Pragmatism is content to leave the question of the reality of the world as we perceive it to the metaphysician.[2] It begins to be interested in our process only when it finds us preoccupied with the passage from trace to event, or, as we must now formulate it, with the ascent from the latest and still visible event to the sequence that led to it and is no longer visible to us.

How do we come to know our events? How can we feel reasonably secure in this knowledge of which we know that it must remain provisional? The pragmatists tell us that knowledge

[1] Bussemaker realized that research works in the opposite sense of historical narrative, since, as he puts it, it begins with a result and seeks its causes. In this way it establishes facts which have in turn been brought about by causes (*Over de Waardeering der Feiten*, p. 23).

[2] "Knowledge of sensible realities comes to life inside the tissue of experience. It is *made*" (James, *The Meaning of Truth*, p. 106). "It is reality's part to possess its own existence; it is thought's part to get into 'touch' with it by innumerable paths of verification" (*ibid.*, p. 214). "Realities are not *true*, they *are*; and beliefs are true *of* them" (*ibid.*, p. 196; also Dewey, *Experience and Nature*, pp. 323–4, and *Quest for Certainty*, p. 190). Those who might think this too easy a way out may consult Ayer's *Foundations of Empirical Knowledge* (1947) with its conclusion: "So long as the general structure of my sense-data conforms to the expectations that I derive from the memory of my past experience, I remain convinced that I am not living in a dream" (p. 274).

and its verification must come to us through action. "Knowing is only one way of interacting with reality and adding to its effect," says William James.[1] Dewey considers it a mistake to believe that "knowledge is a grasp or beholding of reality without anything being done to modify its antecedent state." To him, knowing is to participate: "Knowing is itself a mode of practical action."[2] The practical action which provides knowledge and the verification of knowledge, is experimentation, in the case of the scientific worker, and in that of the historian it is the telling of the story.[3] It is only as he tells his story that the historian finally weighs his evidence, pronounces on the quality and reliability of his traces, and exercises his critical function to the fullest extent.

Does this mean that, to tell an accurate story, the historian must tell an accurate story? In the realm of absolute certainty it does. By the rules of the superannuated logic of the schools, we have, here, a perfect *petitio principii*. But why should we wish to enter the realm of certitude where the rules of thought are provided by Aristotelian or absolutist logic? That realm holds no place for historical knowledge! Where historical knowledge is deemed possible, that is in the sphere where scientific procedure is admitted, the story of past events will be granted access when it satisfies the ethical requisites to which I have already referred. The judge of the story is the historian's own conception of honesty, and that of other historians. They must feel satisfied that accepted history, as modified by the introduction of newly detected events, becomes acceptable to them. The story must pass muster before the intellectual integrity of the men of the craft, and this is the equivalent of the experiment in science. The historian weighs the evidence presented by the traces he has detected. He will be helped by the experience he has acquired in weighing the evidence presented by other traces, as well as by the powers of reconstruction of his imagination. For him imagi-

---

[1] *The Meaning of Truth*, p. 96.

[2] *The Quest for Certainty*, pp. 188 and 104. See also Sidgwick, *Distinction*, p. 193.

[3] The idea that the historian's reconstruction is justified when it leads to the telling of the satisfying and sufficiently accurate story is reached by implication in Crump's excellent brochure *The Logic of History* (1919), p. 52.

nation will certainly not be the final arbiter, as it seems sometimes to be for Croce or Collingwood. It will do no more than provide him with suggestions. The sequence that presents itself to his imagination may be obvious, not to say inevitable. It may not be too convincing. Indeed, more than one arrangement into sequences may suggest itself. Among the possibilities the historian will choose the most probable, that which combines all available data in the least artificial way, that which is supported by the best established and soundest analogies taken from accepted history. It may well be that several different combinations lead to equally plausible stories. In that case the historian is free to make his own choice, provided he makes it clear that there has been a free choice, and that the resulting hypothesis is even more provisional than the rest of the story.[1]

We are also entitled to demand from the historian that, if carried on, his story shall lead back to existing traces without being incompatible with any of them. Let us remember the existence of immaterial traces, such as institutions that are still functioning. They rarely provide the historian with a fruitful starting point for the reconstruction of a sequence of events, but they are eminently suitable for use as a control to the story.[2] In short, the historian's reconstruction of the past is justified, not by any particular virtue of his traces, but by being acceptable to trained minds. And it will be acceptable if no one can seriously challenge its right to be included in the body of accepted history, even though, as a result, a section of this accepted history becomes superannuated.

Collingwood reports a statement by Bradley that "the historian's criterion is something he brings with him to the study of the evidence, and this something is simply himself; . . . his cri-

---

[1] Bernheim, *op. cit.*, p. 619. F. C. S. Schiller also points out that if the historian has a choice between alternative stories which satisfy his requirements he may adopt whichever version seems to him best (*Logic for Use*, p. 425).

[2] Clearly, a history of the British Parliament which would lead, if continued to the present day, to a Parliament constituted and functioning differently from the present Parliament would be inaccurate or incomplete. " . . . all history must be such that acknowledged present facts can be derived from it" (Schiller, *op. cit.*, p. 425). "History is an hypothesis to account for the existence of facts as they are" (Crump, C. G., *op. cit.*, p. 11).

terion is therefore never ready-made; the experience from which it is derived is his experience of historical thinking, and it grows with every growth of his historical knowledge."[1] But Collingwood uses this wise saying in a manner of which we cannot approve. "Historical thinking" leads him to the illusion of certitude, while it brings us to the awareness of provisional knowledge. Perhaps our "historical knowledge" is what, in another connection, William James has called "concatenated knowledge."[2] All things in our perceived world are, somehow, somewhere, connected with all other things. No event stands isolated. There is no knowledge of an event without the knowledge of many other events. No sooner do we perceive an event than we obey an impulse to place it in a concatenation. One such chain is already familiar to us, the time sequence. But there are many others. Events can be connected into logical series, and of these the best known and most used is causation. We frequently link up several events by saying, and believing, that they were brought about by one of them, or by another event, or that each of them was the result of another one in the same series.

Serialization is the method by which the historian constructs his story. As long as he looks upon his events as sovereign or autonomous, and leaves them in isolation, he can tell no story. The serialization without which there is no story is directed by principles that cannot be called purely logical. F. C. S. Schiller observes that "it is a mistake to represent any enquiry which terminates in a judgment as a cold, calm, dispassionate verdict of pure intellect." He also says: "No situation would be enquired into, if it did not seem questionable, . . . unless it could somehow make a personal appeal to the mind that raises it. . . . Hopes and fears steer the course of exploration. . . . Hence the mind is not unbiased or unprejudiced, and its thought experiments are tried in a definite order, an order of attractiveness, while the more repellent or improbable ones are postponed *sine die*."[3] All this is equally true of the enquiry which terminates in a story.

This time we appear to have reached a clear-cut conclusion. While absolutist logic and the belief in the possibility of attaining

---

[1] *The Idea of History*, pp. 139–40.
[2] *Some Problems of Philosophy*, pp. 129–30.   [3] *Logic for Use*, pp. 200–1.

certitude must forever preclude the passage from trace to past event, the pragmatist doctrine that justifies historical method and is implied in it hardly sees this passage as a problem. The trace is the legitimate starting point for an inference that leads us to the knowledge of previous events with which it is connected. We obtain our knowledge of these events thanks to the ability of following up traces which we have acquired in the practice of common life and in our previous historical work. This knowledge is forever subject to correction. We serialize the events of which we have acquired a knowledge according to a number of principles to which we adhere by sentiment and preference at least as much as by our reason. Thus serialized, our events enter naturally into a narrative. The value of this narrative is constantly tested by the degree to which it fits in with other narratives based upon other traces, but more still by the integrity which, as intellectual workers, we bring to our task.

§ 2

INTERNAL CRITICISM

When the historian examines traces of past events, he criticizes them, which means that he judges them. He judges them first of all from the point of view of their authenticity, and asks whether they are what they purport to be. This operation, which we have discussed in an earlier chapter,[1] is called external criticism. The trace is looked at from the outside; its value as a material object is judged. If the trace is written, if it is what we call a document, it is then looked at from the inside with the purpose of finding out whether the message it carries is genuine. This is internal criticism. Internal criticism is not a separate operation. It takes place each time we come across a bundle of traces that forms a document, and is in actual fact a part of the process by which we pass from trace to event.

External criticism tries to make out whether a document is the trace of a forgery. Internal criticism tries to determine whether the document contains lies or errors. In external criticism there

[1] Above, II: ii: § 2.

is an argument from multiplicity, a realization that each document is vouched for by all similar documents preserved with it and elsewhere. As the number of documents of the same nature grows, so does the probability that each of them is authentic. Internal criticism, on the other hand, is individual in its method. The genuineness of each document, like its freedom from error, has to be assessed on its own merit. The process by which this takes place is that described in the previous section: trial and error, the use of accepted history, the application of acquired experience and skill, the belief in physical science.[1] It is always guided by moral standards and a code of honesty which compels the instant relinquishing of an hypothesis that becomes untenable in view of the emergence of new evidence.

We may conclude this section by looking at a document which means something different from what it appears to say. No real problem of criticism is raised by it because the accepted history of the subject is too well established to leave any room for doubt. But the instance will show that the uncritical reader of a document might easily be led astray although those responsible for it had no intention to deceive. The patent which created the famous University of Leyden tells a story that is very different from the accepted history of this event. We know that since 1572 the provinces of Holland and Zeeland were in open rebellion against their sovereign King Philip II of Spain. In 1574 the Spanish general Francisco de Valdez invested Leyden with troops consisting mainly of Spanish and Walloon mercenaries. The blockade lasted from May to early October. Leyden suffered from famine and plague, but a determined minority prevented the disaffected elements in the population from forcing a sur-

---

[1] "The two sources of our empirical knowledge are memory and induction. It is not possible to *prove* the reliability of either without circularity, and each depends on the other. We use induction to test memory (e.g. by consulting written records: it is an inductive hypothesis that the words written in my diary do not change of their own accord). And conversely, all inductive hypotheses involve trusting memory at some stage. For our ground for holding any hypothesis to be established is ultimately always that such and such events have occurred in the past. Thus historical beliefs involve beliefs in physical science (beliefs about the property of parchment, ink, print, stone, etc.) and belief in the properties of physical science involve beliefs about what happened in the past." (Note contributed by Professor A. J. Ayer.)

render, and the Spaniards were finally compelled to withdraw after the Dutch troops belonging to the States of Holland had flooded large tracts of territory around the town. At the time Leyden emerged from this ordeal the nascent state ruled by Calvinists and irreconcilable enemies of Spain was in great need of a university at which future Calvinist divines could be trained. Prince William of Orange agreed with the States of Holland that a university must be founded, and among the towns which competed for the honour and the advantage of housing this institution Leyden was deemed the most deserving owing to its recent sufferings undergone for the common cause. The patent establishing the University of Leyden, dated January 6, 1575, is kept in the archives of the town of Leyden. It has been published more than once,[1] and no question arises concerning its authenticity.

When, however, we read the original Dutch text a bevy of problems presents itself. The patent for the establishment of this rebel university states in so many words that it is granted by King Philip! It reports that the recent lengthy warlike operations have deprived the Counties of Holland and Zeeland of all good instruction and edification of the young with the result that the inhabitants are obliged to send their children to study in other provinces where a different religion is practised from that of Holland and of Zeeland. It refers to troubles caused by the Duke of Alva and his supporters, and points out that as the citizens of the King's town of Leyden have recently undergone with great fidelity considerable sufferings in the course of these troubles, they deserve to be gratified and assisted by every possible means. Having taken the advice of his beloved cousin William, Prince of Orange, his stadtholder and captain general in Holland, Zeeland, etc., the King therefore orders that a university shall be founded at Leyden. All this sounds like a hoax. Clearly, the document is not what it purports to be, the trace of certain reflections and decisions of the King of Spain. The answer is that the document does not emanate from the King of Spain, but from the secre-

---

[1] Most recently in Molhuysen, P.C., *Bronnen tot de Geschiedenis der Leidsche Universiteit*, Vol. I, 1913, appendix, pp. 7–9. *Cf.* Fruin, R. "Over de Leidsche Universiteit," in *Verspreide Geschriften*, Vol. VIII, pp. 389–403.

tariat of Prince William, who refuses as yet to admit that the new Dutch Repubiic has cut itself off from its obedience to its legitimate sovereign. The fiction that all acts of government are taken in the name of the King is therefore upheld. Leyden is supposed to have resisted the Duke of Alva, but not the King, to whom it is still faithful, and William is still supposed to be the King's legitimate representative. The difficulty presented by the unexpected form of this document is therefore solved by recourse to accepted history.

We have, now, determined our criterion of knowledge. In the next part of this book we shall see how the historian fulfils his mission towards society by telling his story, while providing at the same time the final test by which its accuracy can be assessed.

Part Three

TELLING THE STORY

Chapter I
RELEVANCE AND SERIALIZATION

§ I

NARRATIVE, THEORY, AND CRITICISM

WHEN the historian begins to write his report he enters upon the culminating stage of his activity. He is, at last, carrying out his social task, the recording, for future reference, of some of the collective experiences of a human society. We must remember, however, that the telling of the story has begun long before the historian put pen to paper. From the earliest stages of research the story led an inchoate existence in his mind. Each time he read accepted history, each time he observed a trace, he inferred a fragment of story, and tried to gauge the extent to which it would fit in with other stories, with inferences from different traces. On the other hand, his critical function does not come to an end when he begins to write.

As the story takes its final shape, it becomes more than a mere narrative. We know already that it cannot be told without the admixture of explanatory and speculative elements. It is in these static parts of the story that the writer will refer to the criticism that checked his inferences, if he chooses to refer to it at all. He may mention some of the arguments that guided him in constructing his story. These will be the passages that reflect his preconceived notions and his predilections, the temperament he brings to his work, and all the subjective contents of his mind which he dignifies with the name of theories. Thus there will have to be two aspects to the critical operations that accompany the telling of the story: *a priori* theories will be used to check inferences, and inferred events must check the theories. It is only by the faithful and fearless application of the second kind of check that the historian proves his intellectual integrity. His ethical standards may at any time command him to suspend or even to discard a beloved theory, if it proves incompatible with events that have been satisfactorily established. As must so frequently happen in the course of intellectual labour, the writing of an historical report implies a circular mental process. Theories, as I just observed, check events, and events check theories. This shows, once more, that absolute knowledge is not within the historian's reach, that absolute accuracy cannot be achieved by him. There can only be a gradual elimination of error, and this never leads to certitude.

It is clear, therefore, that two threads must run through the final stage of the historian's work: the construction of the narrative out of events, and the criticism of events through the narrative. Method, however, implies simplification and distinction; this is why the final part of this survey will concentrate upon the telling of the story, and more often than not take the critical operation for granted. At the same time the reader must realize, and not forget for one moment, that this Third Part will, in the nature of things, be much more subjective than the previous parts of this work. We have now reached the aspect of the historian's task in which a personal and individual treatment is not only legitimate, but unavoidable and indeed highly desirable. There is, in the telling of the story, no other choice than that between freedom and regimentation. The historian is in possession of a large number of events. Among them he must select those he will use, and the resulting selection must be arranged. In these operations the historian *must* be guided by his personality, his views, his theories. One qualification only can be made to this statement: the historian's conscience has a prior claim to his loyalty; his theories occupy second place. But conscience also is private and individual.

When I say that the historian must select his events and use certain methods for serializing them into a story, I formulate what I consider to be a fundamental rule of historical method. As soon, however, as I discuss the manner in which events can be serialized, I become subjective. Every historian will have a different system for giving contents to the principle of causation. He will use his imagination, and it differs from that of other historians. He will see human behaviour through his own eyes, which are not those of his colleagues. He will construct his own philosophy of history. I can, in actual fact, explain no more than the working of my own imagination, present my own view only of human character, give instances of my own philosophy of history. These individual opinions cannot be printed in italics or green ink. The reader is invited to remember that henceforth his disagreement with my views is a confirmation of my methodological doctrine.

§ 2

SELECTION

We have decided upon a methodological simplification. We shall imagine the historian in possession of a considerable number of events, and, eliminating from our minds the problem of criticism, we shall observe how he works them into a story. To enter more fully into the situation we may imagine that we are taking part in one of those parlour games that are occasionally inflicted upon defenceless visitors by hosts who are aware of their own conversational limitations. We are presented with the following paper:

"Within the lapse of half an hour and within the radius of two miles the following facts or events have been observed:

1. It is a November morning;
2. The weather is dull, there is neither wind nor rain;
3. At 11.02 a.m. a loud bang is heard;
4. About 11.10 a missel-thrush, seen on the branch of a tree, is observed singing at the top of its voice;
5. A little footbridge across a narrow canal is broken and the canal has to be crossed by a punt;
6. At 11.30 the fire brigade of T. is fighting a fire which has broken out at a garage as the result of the explosion of a petrol tank.

"Indicate in brief outline the different stories or reports that can be constructed by connecting two or more of these detached items."

One answer should suggest itself at once to every mind and save the visitor from the awkward necessity of handing in that blank paper which is a vote of censure upon the sense of fun of his hosts. He can serialize his events chronologically by introducing an imaginary narrator who has witnessed every single item on the list. Unless the narrator is a born essayist, his report will be a bald narrative rather than a story. "I went for a walk," he will say, "one morning in November. The weather was dull. It was not raining, but there was no wind at all. Just after 11—I happened to look at my watch at that moment—I heard a loud bang. I wondered what it was. Less than ten minutes later I saw a missel-thrush. It was sitting at the top of a tree, and singing merrily. When I reached the canal I found that one could not use the wooden footbridge: a number of boards were missing towards the middle, the entrances to the bridge had been roped off, and there was a notice saying: 'No passage. Use punt below.' There was a small punt attached to a chain that stretched across the canal. I used it. It was quite simple. You merely pulled yourself along the chain, and there was a rope fixed to each end of the punt and tied to a stake on each bank, so that anyone could pull the punt back if he needed it. I then walked on, and as I turned the corner of the road I saw firemen playing a hose on the garage. They told me there had been an explosion. That explained the bang, of course."

This last remark came to the narrator before he knew what he was saying. To his bald narrative, he was adding an explanation. By using his imagination, he filled in gaps between detached items. A second answer to the question had occurred to him. Every participant in the game was bound to establish this connection between items 3 and 6. They had thought of a second story, that of an explosion and a fire, which might be of interest to a newspaper reporter or to a police investigator wanting to establish the precise time at which the explosion took place. For the purpose of this second story, the items 1, 2, and 4 will be discarded as being irrelevant. A question will arise, however, about item 5. Is it connected with the explosion: was the little footbridge damaged as a result of it? If the version adopted by the imaginary chronicler of the first story is adhered to, the answer is in the negative. The alternative provided for crossing the canal could hardly have been improvised within twenty minutes of the explosion.

A third connection between some of the items will occur to an ornithologist, who will note the items 1, 2, and 4, and will disregard the items 3, 5, and 6. He will observe that it is unusual for a missel-thrush to sing at the top of its voice on a dull autumn day. Apart from the mating season, it also sings when it feels stimulated by a strong wind: hence its popular name of "storm-cock." The ornithologist will now look at item 3, the loud bang. Is it not a fact, he will ask, that an unusually loud bang sometimes stimulates birds into singing, or at least twittering, at unwonted times, and is this not particularly true of the missel-thrush? The bang becomes significant to the ornithologist, but he disregards item 6, which explains its origin, as irrelevant for the purpose of telling his own particular story.

Finally one may imagine a physicist looking at our list of events. He will at once establish a connection between items 3 and 6, and a number of questions will arise in his mind. He will certainly want to find out many more events before he can use these two in a report about the perception of sounds. He would even think of fixing the precise moment of the explosion in item 6, by measuring the distance between the garage and the place where item 3 was noted, if the observer had noted the time in a scientific way.

In each case, therefore, the narrator or reporter selects certain events, and, unless he is a mere chronicler, he rejects certain other events. He will not act in an arbitrary or haphazard manner, as Anatole France suggests, nor will he consult the eternal scheme of things, as Van Schilfgaarde seems to expect of him.[1] He will make his selection in accordance with a double criterion: the relevance of events, and their suitability for serialization.

Let us first examine the criterion of relevance. It applies to other than purely historical investigations. Schiller devotes a whole chapter to the matter.[2] He argues that the practical man requires the notion of relevance, that the lawyer calls relevant anything that is helpful to his purpose. But the use of relevance has several important implications. It is and remains subjective, because what is selected is a part, an extract, and the whole of the matter is not given. Selection is risky, and its product can be

[1] Above, II: iv: § 1, and § 2.
[2] *Logic for Use*, pp. 75–94. See also Sidgwick, *The Process of Argument*, pp. 56–7.

queried or disputed. Relevance implies usefulness instead of giving us a grasp of the "essence" of things. It "makes no pretence of turning the usefulness of things for our purposes into an attribute of the things themselves." Schiller also observes that "in general, what is relevant to an enquiry is variable, and varies as the inquiry proceeds." We should never lose sight of the fact that "selections other than those we prefer are thinkable, and others may prefer them." Dilthey was aware that selecting and editing are operations necessary not only in historical work but in all human studies. We select what we consider to be important, and in the last analysis, he points out, our standard of importance is our own standard of values.[1]

The fact that the historian cannot avoid selecting among his events those which appear to him important from the point of view of his judgment of values means that he is placed, once more, in the necessity of making a choice between two extremes, that he must aim at the golden mean outside which there is no wisdom. He selects, and this means that he is subjective, that his results are partial and may have to be corrected. The historian who imagines that he can reach final results or that he has risen above partiality lives in a fool's paradise. It is better, therefore, far better, that he should confess, to himself and to his readers, the nature of his approach, display his bias, lest he assume an air of finality and objectivity which will put his readers off their guard.[2] But subjectivity, though unavoidable, is no passport to licence. It does not justify distortion. When two historians like Taine and Arthur Lévy draw of Napoleon two portraits that could hardly differ more if they applied to two different men,[3] one of them at least has allowed expediency rather than importance to be his criterion of relevance. We are back again to our only paramount criterion, which is not logical but ethical. The narrator of the story that is required by society must practise intellectual integrity. He must not cheat.

Those events are important in the eyes of the historian, and therefore relevant to his purpose, which will enable him to tell

---

[1] Hodges, *Wilhelm Dilthey*, p. 81.
[2] We shall return to the subject of bias in III: vii: § 1.
[3] Geyl, *Napoleon* (1949), p. 169.

an accurate story in reply to questions asked by society. An episodic story is irrelevant, unless it throws some light upon the main problem raised by the enquiry. The elements that would make up such an episode will therefore usually be discarded. The views expressed by Torcy on ecclesiastical policy in his diary are irrelevant for the purpose of narrating the conduct of foreign relations by the Government of Louis XIV, the activities of a Swiss during the War of the Spanish Succession may be ignored by an historian of Dutch diplomacy at that period. But Napoleon's attitude towards the Papacy may be highly relevant to our knowledge of his policy towards Austria. No general ruling can be given, and relevance must forever remain a matter to be settled by each individual historian in each individual case.

We must now examine the second criterion of selection, the suitability of events for serialization. Serialization is the method by which the historical narrative is constructed. While the events form the substance of the narrative, serialization is its life and soul.

§ 3

PRINCIPLES OF SERIALIZATION

We have learned from William James that all knowledge is "concatenated,"[1] and we have noted that there can be no knowledge of any event without the knowledge of many other events. The historian is unable to narrate an event without connecting it with certain other events. He fits each of his events into a series.

Where will the historian find the principles upon which he builds these series, what will be the patterns according to which he will serialize his events? They will not be the result of a profound study of the human past, and here, though it is by no means original, is one of the fundamental doctrines put forward in this book. To draw conclusions from the study of past events, to build generalizations upon them, to formulate the "laws" of history, may be the task of the philosopher of history or of the sociologist. The historian's task is the telling of a story. He comes to his facts with preconceived notions, which he has gathered by

[1] Above, II: v: § I.

observing the present-day world, and which he may have strengthened or modified in the course of previous historical work. It cannot be stated with sufficient emphasis that the historian's principles of serialization are introduced into history by him, not deduced from it, that, in short, they are *a priori*. Needless to say, the ethics of intellectual life demand that the historian shall be ready at any time to reformulate or to give up any principle which fails to account for ascertained events.

Methodologists are aware of the importance of serialization in the historian's work. Louis Halphen refers to the concatenation (*l'enchaînement*) of the facts discovered by research.[1] To effect this serialization, he says, the historian is entitled in many instances to argue by applying to past events data from his own experience. There should, however, be no attempt to arrange past events in accordance with a single and all-embracing formula such as Taine's race, environment and moment, or geographical determinism, or Marxist philosophy. Life, concludes Halphen, cannot be reduced to formulas of such excessive simplicity.

In his textbook Bernheim mentions more than once the part played in the historian's work by generalizations and by the use of so-called "laws." It is not the historian's purpose, according to this authoritative methodologist, to discover or to infer them from his study of the past. They are for him instruments or tools.[2] They provide a most valuable point of view from which events, common origins, analogous motives, can be appreciated. This is equally true for individuals and for collectivities.[3] Bauer agrees with Bernheim that the historian comes to his subject with preconceived notions. "Historical investigation," he writes, "directs itself primarily towards the individual, not towards the general. How revolutions come into existence is not an historical problem, but the special conditions in which the English, the

[1] *Introduction à l'Histoire*, pp. 48–56. They must, he says, form "des séries bien agencées de causes et d'effets."

[2] *Op. cit.*, p. 628: "Der Forscher darf . . . allgemeine Kategorien nur heuristisch verwerten, um vorläufig die einheitliche Erfassung der Zusammenhänge zu ermöglichen, immer bereit, sie durch das Tatsachenmaterial zu korrigieren und verändern oder sie zugunsten anders sich ergebenden Zusammenhänge fallen zu lassen."

[3] *Ibid.*, pp. 142 and 168: Generalizations are to be used "als Hilfsmittel."

French, Revolutions came into being—these interest the historian. Of course, for the treatment of these events he must possess a general conception of the essence of revolution, but the historical discipline does demand that attention should be given to the individual."[1]

It will be appreciated without the need for argument that if the historian brings to his events methods of serialization based upon his reading of the world in which he lives, upon his experience, and therefore upon his beliefs, these methods will belong to one of two categories: they will either be acceptable to all historians, or depend entirely upon the historian's personal outlook. It would be difficult to imagine a history written by one who does not accept the common-sense views of time and causation, or who does not ask his imagination to provide hypotheses for bridging the gaps between ascertained events. But when it comes to the historian's theories about human behaviour, about the regular appearance of certain sequences in the past, we must expect differences to arise. For even the most rigorous cultivation of intellectual integrity cannot make all men think alike. Historians will serialize their events according to different principles, and the interpretations which are bound to find expression in the non-narrative passages of their story must diverge. This means, also, that these interpretations can and will be rewritten forever, unless indeed the minds of men, owing to the triumph of communism or some other fascist system, are to be manufactured all on one pattern.[2]

Let us not forget that, apart from being the architect of the story, serialization fulfils an important critical function. The

---

[1] *Op. cit.*, pp. 18–19. Bauer also says that it is better for the historian to possess some flexible notions about tendencies than to be wedded to abstractions formulated in the shape of laws. "Ohne solche rein empirisch gewonnene Einsicht in eine, wenn auch nur beschränkte und bedingte Regelhaftigkeit historischen Werdens, kommt die Geschichte nicht aus. Sie leitet den Forscher und führt ihn dazu, sobald er daran geht, historische Typen zu bilden und grössere Zusammenhänge zu gewinnen, Lücken auszufüllen, Zeugnisse der Vergangenheit richtig zu werten" (*ibid.*, p. 30).

[2] This does not preclude the possibility of there being final histories, but final from the point of view of form and presentation: histories that are artistically perfect, even though they have to be excluded from the body of accepted history, like the writings of Motley.

selection of events is guided not only by their relevance, i.e. their importance from the point of view of the historian's purpose, but also by their suitability for serialization. A genuinely isolated occurrence is of no interest to the historian, because he cannot make it fit into his story. Knowledge, as we have agreed, is knowledge only if it is "concatenated," and an isolated fact can, therefore, never receive the ultimate sanction of fitting into a story. There is a pitfall in this, and the historian must be careful to avoid it. An event must not be eliminated merely because it does not agree with a preconceived principle of serialization, in other words, because it clashes with a theory. The isolated occurrence may well present itself with strong credentials which forbid us to ignore it. In such a case the clash must be taken as a warning that more research is needed. We shall then have to look for the traces of events that can be connected with our isolated case. If we fail to find such traces, we shall feel compelled to mention our failure, and to make it clear, at any rate in a footnote, that our generalization is provisional, and that we are faced with an unsolved problem.

Chapter II

SOME METHODS OF SERIALIZATION

Some of the methods available for linking up the events which the historian has inferred from the traces discovered by him could not easily be neglected or rejected without making the telling of the story wholly impossible. Time and causation appear to be essential to the purpose, while imagination, though a tool that can be dangerous, must be used at some stage by anyone who ventures to formulate an hypothesis. We shall examine these three methods in the present chapter.

§ I

CHRONOLOGY

E. M. Forster defines a story as "a narrative of events arranged in their time-sequence." He explains that "daily life is full of the time sense," and that it is practically composed of two lives, "the life in time and the life by values." The novel, he says, includes life by values, but "the time-sequence cannot be destroyed without carrying in its ruin all that would have taken its place; the novel that would express values only," he concludes, "becomes unintelligible and therefore valueless."[1] We have seen at an earlier stage that chronology, which arranges significant events in their time-order, and fixes the intervals that elapsed between them, provides the very framework of history.[2] More is needed, nevertheless, to make a story than merely to follow a time-sequence. Even in indicating the time factor the story-teller does not content himself with a perpetual "then, and then, and then." He establishes connections, and says "meanwhile, before this, subsequently, afterwards."

The historian does not care whether time is an essence or a category. For his purpose it is a measure of the speed or slowness

---

[1] *Aspects of the Novel*, pp. 40, 43, 45, 61. [2] Above, II: ii: § 3.

with which things happen.[1] He accepts on empirical grounds that there is a simultaneity or succession in all occurrences. He clings to the common-sense notion of time as a succession of moments. To him the metronome, the pendulum, are symbols of the time element which carries the totality of events in which he is interested. He knows that, whatever other principles he may adopt for the serialization of events, it is essential that he should know when, before or after or together with certain other events, an event did occur.

§2

CAUSATION

Every story-teller takes for granted that certain events are linked together by a special relationship which is indicated by the name of causation. He frequently uses words like "because," "owing to," "as a result of," and these words seem hardly less indispensable to the story than the words "then," "subsequently," "meanwhile." Causation is a familiar tool in the hands of the historian, and methodologists are unanimous in looking upon it as an essential feature of the historical discipline. Halphen points out that most official documents, such as deeds concerning sales, donations or exchanges, sentences of courts of justice, administrative decrees, enactments, etc., indicate in their preamble the causes of the decision which they embody.[2] "Instinctively, and truly without there being much chance of a mistake," says this author, "the historian is led to establish between certain facts, i.e. events of which the text has given him no more than the order in which they occurred, causal links which he infers by examining the circumstances in which they took place." Thus, for instance, the obvious link between the geographical position and the economic life of a population. Here is a principle for serialization which is universally admitted and which produces results in the shape of histories bearing every mark of accuracy.

We might be content with this, were it not that the normal interpretation of causation contains dangerous elements which

[1] "C'est que les dates sont tout en cette matière" (Bossuet, *Discours sur l'Histoire Universelle*, II, 28).　　　　　　　　　　　　　　　　[2] *Op. cit.*, pp. 48 *sqq*.

threaten the basic quality of the historical narrative. There exists a feeling that a cause "occupies a position superior in reality to its effect."[1] This may well lead to the acceptance of an erroneous scale of values, with an undue emphasis placed in the story upon events which are dignified with the name of causes. The greatest danger, however, of an uncritical acceptance of the principle of causation is the tendency it encourages of looking upon the detection of causes as the real purpose of history, instead of treating it as an instrument useful for the performance of the historian's task, which is the telling of a particular kind of story.

There is but one step from this misunderstanding to the superstitious belief that, by carrying on his causal series beyond the present, the historian is able to forecast the future. We shall find it useful, in view of these difficulties, to take a careful look at the current or common-sense notion of causality, and we must try to find out whether a better understanding of the principle may not help us to apply it more efficiently.

A number of guesses has been made as to the origin of the principle of causation in the minds of men. William James is of the opinion that we acquire the notion of cause and effect by observing how we ourselves want to achieve results, and how we make efforts and overcome obstacles in order to do so. The desire of the end, of the results, assumes the status of an efficient cause that produces the end.[2] In Dewey's opinion labour and the use of tools provide a sufficient explanation of the belief in causality: the tool invariably enabled men to carry out a certain task. It was felt, therefore, that a relation existed between the tool and the accomplished task.[3] Whatever its origin, causation is regarded by pragmatist thinkers as one of those ancient beliefs, acquired by men after centuries of tentative formulation, which we dignify by the name of common sense.

As held in the world of common sense, the notion of causation implies an anti-nominalist metaphysical system: it endows an abstract word with a life and with virtues of its own. Aristotle formulated this common-sense notion of causation, and the Scholastics adopted his definitions and divisions, in particular that

---

[1] Dewey, *Experience and Nature*, p. 262.
[2] *Some Problems of Philosophy*, pp. 208 *sqq.*   [3] *Experience and Nature*, p. 84.

of an "efficient cause," upon which they look as "that which produces something else by a real activity proceeding from itself."[1] Once the abstraction "cause" had been promoted to the rank of reality it was natural that men should look for a quantitative equivalence between cause and effect. "Causa aequat effectum," said the Scholastics. Here was a view which implied that nothing can happen without a cause, and therefore also, that there could be no novelty in the world. Occurrence was nothing but a series of equations between the "virtue" received by an event from its efficient cause and that transmitted to its effect. This led, rather naturally, to the opinion that the historian's task consisted principally or entirely in formulating these equations. Here is our old friend pseudo-scientific or dogmatic history, the concomitant of ignorance and of fascistic communism.

It is, therefore, with a genuine sense of relief that the methodologist, who believes that history must approach its problems in the spirit which inspires the natural sciences, welcomes recent trends of thought that have rocked the foundations of the common-sense conception of causation. Idealist philosophies have long since distrusted causation, because it can find no adequate expression in terms of rational concepts. For once, the pragmatist methodologist feels a sneaking sympathy for the absolutist philosophies. He is grateful to the physicists who have observed that certain components of the atom seem to behave in an undetermined way, and who are convinced that in the present condition of physical science no situation can be foreseen in which they could be observed to behave otherwise. They consider that, as a result, the belief in unlimited causation must be given up. Professor L. Rosenfeld of the University of Utrecht observed in his inaugural lecture that "the principle of causality is nothing but the formulation of a methodological requirement, of a logical scheme according to which phenomena can be arranged as succinctly as possible according to their reciprocal relations; in this way," he said, "this principle acquires meaning only through the concrete contents which it is given, and these contents vary with the progress of our knowledge of nature."[2]

[1] James, W., op. cit., pp. 190 sqq.
[2] Rosenfeld, L., Ontwikkeling van de Causaliteitsidee (1942), p. 12.

When sweeping novelties arise in the field of human knowledge they have psychological repercussions which go far beyond the immediate logical conclusions that can legitimately be drawn from them. The cause which radiates its virtue into its effect, whether immediately or through a continuous chain of intermediaries—and the effect which absorbs and utilizes the concrete, tangible, ponderable virtue of its causes, are being relegated to the museum for superannuated instruments of human thought. Nowadays causation is the name given to the regular appearance of the same succession of events. We call cause an event *a* after which we are reasonably entitled to expect the appearance of another event *b*. This regularity of occurrence which may reasonably be expected, is not, however, a "law" or a "canon": it is a postulate. A postulate is a notion freely accepted by our will, which implies that we are also free not to accept it. It is conceived independently of experience, and while it may be confirmed by experience, the lack of such confirmation does not necessarily make it useless.[1] Schiller tells us that "men may gradually have succeeded in disentangling certain sequences of events which may with reasonable confidence be regarded as guides to other events, and . . . this is all that causal analysis does or aims at doing."[2]

Expelled from the paradise of ontology, causation must moderate the claims it dare make upon the historian's exclusive attention. It can no longer be argued that the historian must make it his primary task to acquire a knowledge of the causes of events or of things. Instead of wondering all the time why events did happen, he can give his attention to the question "what did actually happen?" and this will greatly improve the quality of the story he has to tell. He will still look for the anterior event that "guides" him to the subsequent event. He will still have recourse to the postulate of causation as to one of the methods available for the serialization of his events. But he will do it in a spirit of

[1] Schiller, *Formal Logic*, p. 126.
[2] *Ibid.*, p. 274. See, as being highly relevant to the historian's preoccupation, the whole chapter on causation, pp. 272–309 in this book. Alfred Sidgwick has a useful passage in *The Process of Argument*. We distinguish for practical purposes between antecedent and consequent, but the distinction is artificial, says Sidgwick. "They are more or less ill-defined parts of a whole which it suits us to pull asunder."

freedom. Causation, properly understood, will also be a guide to the discovery of traces of hitherto unknown events. If I infer from its traces the existence of an event *b*, shall I not be able to find, somewhere, traces of its habitual antecedent *a*, or if I know *a*, shall I not find traces of its habitual consequent *b*? This shows that, even when writing the story, the historian not only continues, as we have seen before, his critical task, but that his heuristic labour is not necessarily terminated.

In his *Introduction à la Philosophie de l'Histoire*, Raymond Aron contributes an intelligent and useful discussion of historical causation in which he examines the problem of retrospective probability. To explain what has been, he says, the historian must ask himself what might have been. If I say that the Victory of Marathon saved Greek culture, I mean that a Persian victory would have prevented the miraculous efflorescence of Greek life which followed that battle. Greek life would have been different from what it actually was. Therefore, the victory of Marathon was one of the causes of Greek culture. What we have been doing has not been simply to add together the antecedents of a culmination of Greek cultural life. We took one of its antecedents, "thought it away," and tried to imagine what would have happened in this hypothetical situation. If really the consequent event had then assumed a different aspect, the antecedent is at any rate one among the causes of this particular effect. But this does not lead us beyond a formula of probability. A Persian victory will be called the adequate cause of a theocratic regime. An immediate antecedent, Aron also says, is not called the cause, but the occasion of an event, if, in the opinion of the historian, the event in question had to take place anyhow in view of the general historical situation (pp. 164–5). The postulate of causation is still very helpful in this conception, but it remains a mere instrument, and one which never leads those who use it beyond the sphere of relativity. Geographical factors, for instance, which are so useful for our understanding of past events, will explain possibilities, as Aron remarks, but they can never put us in possession of necessities (p. 192).

Raymond Aron also appears to sense the value of the principle of causation as a story builder. "In what cases, at which moments," he asks, "do we suspend the story to substitute for a judgment of reality a judgment of necessity or, at any rate, of virtual necessity? Almost inevitably," he answers, "when the story seems to interrupt itself of its own accord, when an individual does not act in character, when a political decision does not fit in with the circumstances, when a course of evolution is determined, initiated, or arrested by an accident. Let the deed be confronted with the personality, the personal decision with the environment, the historical movement with the accident; reality possesses the structure implied by causal analysis, and the analysis suffices, not for an exact measurement, but for an appreciation of the efficacy of an antecedent or the contingency of a fragmentary datum. Now the historian usually does not claim to reach other results. No one will ever know what might have taken place if the Archduke had not been assassinated in 1914" (p. 185).[1]

§ 3

IMAGINATION

Mommsen said that phantasy is the mother of history; Michelet called history a resurrection.[2] Every methodologist admits that imagination must play a part at some stage of the historian's work. When it comes to the practical application of this principle, we meet with fundamentally divergent views. For Croce and Collingwood the imagination is the source of historical knowledge, while Halphen soberly envisages the possibility of "seeking in our own experience the necessary correctives to the insufficiency of our documentation."[3] I wish to advocate the use of imagination as one of the systems for serializing into a story the events which we have inferred from our knowledge of their traces.

We speak of creative imagination, but this is a misleading expression. No doubt, the imagination can produce works of fiction which, in their entirety, do not correspond to reality. But not a single one among the elements of which fiction consists

---

[1] Aron makes a useful distinction: "La recherche historique s'attache aux *antécédents* d'un fait singulier, la recherche sociologique aux *causes* d'un fait susceptible de se reproduire" (*op. cit.*, p. 229, my italics).

[2] Bauer, *op. cit.*, p. 80; Halphen, *op. cit.*, p. 15.   [3] *Op. cit.*, p. 61.

has been created. They were present in the author's mind. "Imagine the indignation of Belinda's father!"—By all means, provided I possess, stored in my memory in such a manner that they can be made available, experiences about indignant people, about a father, about a number of other relevant occurrences. *Nemo dat quod non habet* goes for my memory, and therefore also for my imagination. We call imagination the process by which we deliberately bring into our immediate awareness impressions stored in our memory. It varies from one individual to another. Some see their past impressions vividly, perhaps even in rich colours. Others, and they are probably the majority, see them dimly. This explains why the monochrome cinematograph does not strike us as ludicrous: it corresponds with the products of the visual imagination of most of us. In the case of some people what was heard is recalled more intensely than what was seen. There are tactile imaginations, muscular imaginations, and others. The whole process of imagining still baffles the psychologist. This, however, can be asserted: so long as we are not subject to hallucinations, our imagination does not create.[1]

The statement that the imagination provides a method for serializing events detected through research means that we may attempt to find those hooks and eyes that connect separate events by comparing them with experiences stored in our memory. Thus, as we shall see when dealing with human nature, we may compare actions we know to have taken place in the past with actions we have witnessed ourselves; we may, by analogy, form hypotheses about unknown aspects of past actions. But we may, also, by much reading of accepted history, by re-enacting past events in our minds, by dwelling in meditation upon the mentality of men of a bygone age, upon the material and social atmosphere of a period, have accumulated in our memory images of the past which are accurate, but more vivid than those with which we have not familiarized ourselves to the same extent. When we wish to connect some events which we have inferred from their traces we can then call upon our rich store of historical memories, and bring them into the field of our immediate awareness. This will suggest to us a way of making our newly

[1] Probably not even then.

discovered events fit into the picture. We shall conclude that at some moment in the past a man must have spoken in such a manner, and certainly not in such another manner. We shall feel certain that such an action, such an attitude, is out of tone in a certain country or in a certain class at a given time, just as we spot and reject coarser anachronisms such as a gas-lamp in 1740. We shall deem it probable that, instead, the action, the attitude in question, will have been of this nature or that. Imagination, in short, will provide us with a number of hypotheses constructed by analogy, and of a lower order of cogency than other more rationally constructed inferences like those that led us to a knowledge of the events we are now trying to connect.

Whereas inference from traces is a logical operation which leads us to a knowledge of events previously unknown, the use of the imagination is a psychological process, that provides no new knowledge, but brings into action knowledge previously acquired. The imagination operates in a way that is less patent and obvious than the process of inference. The difference between the two is like that between the way in which a man and a dog find their way to a house. The man identifies the house by its address, its architectural features. He need never have visited it before. The dog can find it only if he has been there already. He may be able, then, to identify it from indications he receives from its *Gestalt*, a vague complex of smells and other data. This difference, described by William James in his *Principles of Psychology*,[1] is the same as that between the manner in which a person in a normal frame of mind and a subject under hypnosis identify a passage they have been shown in a book. The normal person will have to think of the chapter or the page, the context; he may consult the table of contents. The hypnotized subject goes straight for the passage. In his single-minded condition he has unconsciously noted, and with amazing accuracy, an array of indications such as the distance of the page from the front and the back cover, the distance of the passage from the top and the bottom of the page, etc. His success is preternatural in appearance only. It is precisely in this way that the historical imagination operates. Bauer tells us that Ranke had an uncanny gift for reconstructing

[1] II, pp. 348 *sqq.*

187

the past—i.e. for constructing an accurate story of the past—even when using imperfect or partial sources like the *Relazioni Veneziane*. He did it "mit schlafwandlerischer Sicherheit"—with the certainty of a somnambulist.[1] Precisely! But he could not have done it without the encyclopaedic knowledge of a Ranke.

What happens when we are convinced that we have acquired a sense of the atmosphere of a fragment of the past? Our interest grows keener, our attention is stimulated, we have greater ease in conceiving hypotheses that will shed further light upon the period. Our power of inference, our heuristic flair, will respond to the stimulus of a lively imagination. We shall detect new and fruitful traces and interpret them with greater success. Our story will gain not only in interest, but also in accuracy. Causal connections will present themselves to our vision with greater plasticity; our chronological sense will grow more alert and save us from pitfalls like anachronism or the temptation to eliminate with excessive readiness seemingly irrelevant events.

Once the nature of imagination is understood there is no need to warn the historian against its dangers, to tell him that it must be disciplined. Since the imagination is nothing but the mobilization of the contents of our memory, we must familiarize ourselves with the notion that it cannot run riot and lead us astray with inventions. It is no longer what the French have called it, *la folle du logis*. It is the least risky of all the systems by which we can serialize our motley collection of events. It is the guarantor of the accuracy at which the story-teller must aim.

[1] *Op. cit.*, p. 81.

Chapter III

HUMAN BEHAVIOUR

§ I

DOES HUMAN NATURE CHANGE?

THE historian tells a tale of human collectivities going through active and passive experiences, and of individuals who lived in societies, influenced them, were influenced by them. All history is about men.[1] Whenever the historian arrranges his events into series that will enable him to construct his story, he must picture men in action and in the course of being acted upon, he must attribute motives to them, apply the postulate of causation to their behaviour. Clearly, the hypotheses he adopts must be based upon his knowledge of the way in which men felt, thought, behaved. But where is he to find this knowledge, except from the knowledge he has of himself and of the men who live around him in his own time? Can he apply this direct knowledge of the present to the past, unless the men of the past were like the men of today? Obviously not.

"How incomprehensible history would be if human nature had not remained the same," observes Powicke. Happily, it has remained the same, he thinks, because "when man somehow became a rational creature, one of the processes of evolution came to an end."[2] A dogmatic assertion unsupported by evidence. However useful they may be, our guesses should be presented less apodictically. Sceptical Anatole France is more elegant with his tentative suggestion that "il y a en nous un fonds d'humanité qui change moins qu'on ne croit. . . . We differ little," he continues, "from our grandfathers. For our tastes and our feelings to undergo a transformation it is necessary that the organs which produce

---

[1] "Das Individuum als seelische Einheit ist die wahre Crux der modernen Geschichtstheorie" (Bauer, *op. cit.*, p. 62). "History is a generalized account of the personal stories of men united in bodies for any public purposes whatever" (Acton, "Essay on Buckle's Thesis," in *Historical Essays and Studies*, p. 305).

[2] *History, Freedom and Religion*, p. 17.

them should themselves become transformed. This is the work of centuries. Hundreds and thousands of years are needed for a noticeable alteration to occur in a few of our characteristics."[1]

It is, however, not universally admitted that human nature has remained unaltered. Collingwood argues very plausibly that it has altered and that it could not help altering.[2] All things are in a flux, and why should human nature alone be an exception to this universal rule? Collingwood insists that human nature is not uniform but diversified, that as it varies in space, so it varies in time, and is therefore "not a datum, but a problem."[3] We solve the problem, not by seeking to understand human nature, but by discovering it through Collingwoodian imaginative apperception. The view that human nature has changed, that men have become modified out of all recognition as the result of an unceasing process of growth, does not appear unreasonable. Is it, or is it not, a fact that classical antiquity shows us men of strong character, powerful in their single-minded membership of a collectivity; that medieval men, whether saints or knights or artisans, were as stereotyped as the figures on Borobudur, and that modern man has become diversified and individualized to the point of anarchy? Were not the nervous systems of the men of the sixteenth century, who suffered torture joyfully for the sake of religion, different from those of twentieth century people who are pampered with hygiene and anaesthetics? One might reply that fascism, falangism and communism have provided numerous men and women with an opportunity to show themselves as steadfast under torture as the martyrs of the sixteenth century. And should we not say that the differences between ancient, medieval and modern men are more apparent than real, that our conception of ancient and medieval men is distorted as a result of the idiosyncracies of the contemporaries who wrote about them?

Writers of classical antiquity were articulate—how articulate we learn, for instance, from the fiendish cleverness of Seneca's

[1] *Le Jardin d'Epicure*, p. 147.   [2] *The Idea of History*, pp. 81–5.
[3] *Ibid.*, pp. 91–2. He seems to echo Montaigne's "Certes, c'est un sujet merveilleusement vain, divers, et ondoyant, que l'homme. Il est malaisé d'y fonder jugement" (I, i), and the same author's "veu la naturelle instabilité de nos meurs et opinions, il m'a semblé souvent que les bons autheurs mesmes ont tort de s'opiniastrer à former de nous une constante et solide contexture" (II, i).

prose—their portraits of those who played a part in public life are skilfully drawn, rich and round. We can read into the minds of the Romans: Cicero and Horace are living beings for us. Suetonius seems to have sensed the importance of factors that were not understood till the Viennese psychologists looked into them. We are left with the problem of the amazing group-consciousness of the ancients, but this does not compel us to believe that since them human nature has changed. There is merely a difference in the purposes towards which human nature directs its activities. As for the puzzle of medieval impersonality, can it not be brought home to the stammerings of writers who used an unfamiliar language and whose powers of expression were circumscribed by clumsiness and inexperience? What do we know of the personality of Charlemagne, whom we see as one of those effigies without relief that adorn the tombs of wool-merchants in the church of Chipping Campden? Only the little we are told about him by Einhart in his *Vita Karoli Magni*. But Waitz, who edited the *Vita* for the *Monumenta Germaniae Historica*, has shown how in his imperfect knowledge of the Latin language and in his justified distrust of his own literary ability this author[1] copied numerous extracts from Suetonius's *Vita Divi Augusti* and used them with as little change as possible for his portrait of the Frankish Emperor. Charlemagne was laid on a Procrustean bed. He was made to limp because Augustus limped! While the study of documents has taught us much about Charlemagne's work, his personality is known to us only through the distorted projection elaborated by a medieval plagiarist. Is it not reasonable to argue that if medieval men appear to us so different from modern men we must attribute this to our ignorance of them rather than to a change in human nature?

Human nature changing or immutable?—these are alternatives about which psychologists and philosophers may argue if they want to, but between which historians cannot make a choice based upon data provided by their own discipline. Faced with

---

[1] Oman once wrote about "Eginhard's well-written *Vita Karoli Magni*—a testimonial to the excellent Latin taught in Charlemagne's Palatine School"! Einhart, by the way, was educated at Fulda, not at the Palatium Regale, where he arrived as an adult.

such a situation no scientist would cross his arms till the controversy had been finally settled. He would adopt the more promising of the two hypotheses and hope that experiment would ratify his choice. Such ratification by action is also the course which the historian will have to take. Action, in his case, is the telling of the story. He can tell—for ages he has told—an acceptable story based on the assumption that human nature has not changed, not, at least, out of all recognition. He takes for granted that human nature in the past was what it is now, and acts in consequence.[1] Pirenne used to say: "La nature humaine, en tant qu'elle intéresse l'historien, ne change pas." This leaves the theoretical problem where it was, and settles the practical issue. Another inroad is made upon certitude, a further reason is given to the historian for remaining modest, for becoming tolerant of the results achieved even by those with whom he does not agree. But it means at any rate that he can go ahead and use his knowledge of human nature as a method for the serialization of events into a story.

The area of the similarity between past and present which has to be taken for granted can be restricted if we agree to dispense with the abstract notion of human nature. What, after all, do we mean by human nature? Is it the name of what is common to all men? But men share many of their characteristics with other animals. If we take the words to mean that which distinguishes men from the brutes we are left with a vaporous phantasm to which we cannot even attribute acquisitiveness, humour, superstition, or pride, none of which is a human monopoly. It will be more practical to look at human nature—whatever it may be— in the one aspect which actually matters to the historian, at human nature in action, in other words at human behaviour. What interests the historian is not what human beings were, but

---

[1] "Die Identität der Menschennatur ist das Grundaxiom jeder historischen Erkenntniss," says Bernheim (op. cit., p. 192). "Si les faits rapportés dans les documents n'avaient pas été analogues à ceux que nous observons, nous n'y pourrions rien comprendre," says Seignobos (La Methode historique appliquée aux Sciences Sociales, 1901, p. 120). Bauer, from whom I take this quotation, comments: "Nur unter der Annahme, dass die Vorgänge im Bewusstsein der Menschen unter gleichen oder ähnlichen äuzeren und inneren Bedingungen sich gleich oder ähnlich abspielen . . . ist es uns möglich, zu historischen Ergebnissen zu gelangen" (op. cit., pp. 77-8).

what they did and had done to them. We never know, anyhow, what our neighbour is, but only how he behaves. The only assumption that is required for the serialization of past human actions according to the principle of causation is that men behaved in the past much as they behave today. To make such an assumption will put no strain on anyone's intellectual integrity.

§ 2

PSYCHOLOGY

How do historians acquire the understanding of human behaviour which they will need for the sake of explaining the behaviour of men who lived in the past? We have agreed that human behaviour is human nature in action. There will be no difficulty in our agreeing that character is habitual behaviour. If a man commits a cruel action I cannot with certainty call him cruel. If he is in the habit of acting cruelly I can say that he has a cruel character. I shall assume, in that case, that having committed a series of cruel acts in the past, he is likely also to act cruelly in the future. Passing judgment upon character implies the making of a prediction. If time verifies this prediction our judgment about character is correct. To acquire an understanding of human character and of human behaviour means, therefore, to become skilful in predicting successfully the actions of one's fellow human beings. This skill can be acquired by observation, from literature, and from the doctrines of psychologists.

We observe our own behaviour, and that of other people. Every man indulges in introspection, but our introspection is often unsystematic and prejudiced. If we have a trained mind the chances of gross mistakes are less, but in the case of cultivated people this advantage is easily neutralized by passions or neuroses. Yet the somewhat uncertain results of our introspection play an important part in the shaping of our judgment of the character of others. We tend to use our reading of our own character as a norm. We continually pass judgment upon others by comparing their behaviour with our own. While some people, especially those who are particularly self-centred, are poor readers of character, others strike us by their apparently uncanny intuition. They possess no esoteric powers for piercing the heart or the brain of their fellow human beings. The process they apply is rational, but unusually rapid. They are endowed to a high degree with the particular form of imagination needed to get under the skin of other people. This means nothing more than that when considering the behaviour of others, when trying to explain it to themselves, to assign motives to it, to make predictions about it, they allow their imagination to mobilize memories of their own behaviour in similar circumstances, and of their own motives. They take it for granted that the vivid memories of their own past are similar to what is happening inside the man of whom they are thinking. They share his longings, his fears, his shame. They produce no novel images, but they know that the images of themselves are valid also in the case of their brother. This is how they "get under the other fellow's skin."[1] They realize that a large store of indulgence is the best equipment for the understanding of character, that sympathy is a safer guide than distrust.[2] But those who are less gifted in this direction can develop and improve their judgment by practice. They must follow a method of trial and error, predict, observe the future behaviour of the object of their experiment, compare it with their predictions, and, finally, try to detect the origin of their mistakes.

There is an obvious connection between a man's facial expression and his character. Experience has shown that careful observation of facial expressions enables certain people to read the thoughts of those they encounter, and will even guide them towards a sound reading of their character. Yet the data provided by face reading cannot be looked upon as being more than an initial indication which must be controlled by consequent obser-

[1] The control of such "hunches" is provided by the outcome of the predictions to which they give rise. It is possible, of course, to understand, by the same imaginative process, the behaviour and character of certain among the higher mammals, like dogs, whose minds differ from ours quantitatively, but not qualitatively.

[2] Does this, perhaps, explain why so much bad history is written? Might academic life conceivably not be good for a man's soul? Emulation and the petty sides of administration harden the heart, and there can, of course, be no understanding of men without love, while there can be no good history without understanding.

vation. "La physionomie n'est pas une règle qui nous soit donnée pour juger les hommes: elle nous peut servir de conjecture," said La Bruyère.[1]

Women are better judges of character than men, till their passions, which are easily roused, obscure their powers. Perhaps the best judges of character are men with a strain of feminity in their psychological make-up, provided the strain is not too pronounced. A certain freedom from metaphysical obsessions facilitates the understanding of character, although the Jesuits are proof that this rule is not universally valid. The study of history, both in the form of intensive reading of accepted history and of research and the handling of traces, particularly written traces, increases our powers of psychological insight. This means, of course, that our friend the circular argument once more steps unashamed into these pages. But however disreputable his pedigree, he is an untiring and most helpful path-finder. History holds up to our eye a procession of human beings in action. We can understand them to the extent to which we can understand our contemporaries. But the people of the past will in their turn fill our case-books and increase the volume of causal sequences at our disposal. Thanks to this material our knowledge of contemporary character increases.

We must widen the scope of our survey of character as much as we can. The most inspired reader of character remains tied to his own personality; the subjective element can never be completely evicted from his judgment. To correct this subjectivity we are in constant need of comparing our findings with those of others. Much of the seemingly pointless conversation of people of all classes and every level of education, the gossip which delights the village grocery and the Senior Common Room, consists of such a comparing of notes about the behaviour of human beings. While pure bookishness may blind us to the humanity around us, there is a form of literary culture which implies a power to lift our eyes from our books and to look over the rim of our spectacles. It is the culture that transforms the world into a stage where plays are performed for our benefit, and that makes us the familiars of great minds without bringing

[1] "Des Jugements," in Les Caractères ou les Moeurs de ce Siècle.

about the submersion of our own. This culture, like the study of history, adds to our own directly acquired knowledge of human character the knowledge accumulated by great thinkers throughout the ages.

Literature and the drama portray human beings in action, but are not ruled by the need for accuracy which determines the nature of historical narrative. They may be products of the imagination, but, as we have seen,[1] imagination does not create out of nothing. Literature and the drama give us their authors' considered opinion on human character. Essayists and critics present us, more systematically, with the same substance. Poets and portrait painters do it in their own way. We shall not learn equally from every work of art. Provided, however, our interest is kept alive, our attention stimulated by the human problems which preoccupy an artist, his work will have assisted the growth of our human understanding. A comparison between the static characters of Homer and the ever-mobile humanity of Shakespeare will compel us to make a choice between two very different approaches to the subject, and like Shakespeare, Rabelais compels us to decide whether we believe human character to be an immutable datum. Montaigne, La Bruyère, La Rochefoucauld, whether they portray individuals or types, will continually put questions to any reader whose mind is not lazily surrendering to whichever author he spends an hour with. When reading Swift or Sterne we are carried from the work to the author, whose own character is a problem of greater fascination than that of their heroes.

Some authors like Balzac, Zola, Proust (and Saint-Simon, whose work exercised such influence upon Proust), do not portray characters copied from life in every detail. No novelist was less realistic than Zola. The types created by these authors, complex and composite personages like M. de Charlus, are not normal

---

[1] Above, III: ii: § 3. In the introduction to his *Outline of Psychology*, McDougall says that the words used in popular psychology are vague and ill-defined. The literary art has refined the common speech and made it more appropriate for the expression of psychological doctrines. No antagonism is necessary between literary and scientific psychology. "The wise psychologist will regard literature as a vast storehouse of information about human experience, and will not neglect to draw from it what he can."

human currency. If we familiarize ourselves with these types, and classify the people we meet under the headings provided by the great writers of fiction, we may not be put in touch with the essence of human character, but we shall be able to form fertile hypotheses about the habitual behaviour of individuals.[1]

We can say, then, that the knowledge of human character which we acquire by observing ourselves and others can be enriched and vivified by familiarity with the works of graphic and literary artists, but we must admit that none of their works can lead us to safe knowledge. We may subtilize our perceptions, enhance our powers of observation, provide ourselves with a collection of types that will assist us in passing judgment upon individuals we meet, but we have still found no way of liberating ourselves from the prison which is our own character and temperament.

Can science break the ring of subjectivism? It observes, counts, measures, records, makes provisional generalizations and tests their validity with experiments. Does psychology, which uses these methods and, though young and uncertain, is a science, hold out hopes that it will provide us with generally valid rules for reducing human behaviour to regular sequences? Can the historian ask psychology to help him in carrying out his task?

The practical historian fights shy of scientific psychology. Accepted history has managed to do without it for centuries. Need the historian now take cognizance of doctrines that lift so many veils, that discard the reticence which has become second nature to him owing to the fact that he is mainly preoccupied with affairs of state? Does he not distrust social history because it lays too much emphasis upon the human factor? Like so many ordinary human beings the historian feels a resistance against the new psychological doctrines that make such inroads upon his carefully nurtured dignity. Though steeped in human occurrence, he tends to become increasingly impersonal. Moreover, he can point with good reason to the multiplicity of tendencies and schools that divide the modern psychologists. Why should he believe the one rather than the other? How is he, a layman, to

[1] See Agatha Christie's *The Murder at the Vicarage*, chapter xxvi, for intelligent comment on the use of types for the understanding of human behaviour.

choose between these incompatibles; why should he accept psychoanalysis rather than *Gestalt* psychology, Watson rather than McDougall? Psychology is unconvincing, it is unsavoury, it speaks with many voices, it is unnecessary. Surely, evidence handled according to the rules of historical method is all that matters. To advocate the application of the results of contemporary psychological investigation in a circle of English historians is to expose oneself to accusations of amateurishness and lack of "scholarship."

If, however, the view put forward in the preceding pages is accepted, and a knowledge of human character is considered necessary for the understanding of men who lived in the past, historians must, at the very least, consent to examine the claims of contemporary psychology. It offers us a systematic *exposé* of results achieved by experienced observers. Psychology is to everyday practical observation of human behaviour what philosophy is to common sense: a more leisurely and more systematic way of doing what, in ordinary existence, is carried out more hurriedly and incompletely.

Present-day psychologists tell us either that they study human consciousness or that they study human behaviour. Human consciousness is of no interest to the historian as such. He is not concerned with the essence of human character. He wants to be informed about human behaviour, and will take notice only of those schools of psychology which tell him something about it. Now it is a fact that psychologists are at variance among themselves concerning the mainsprings of human behaviour. But, just as many practical psychiatrists achieve excellent results by adopting an eclectic attitude towards competing doctrines, the historian will obtain useful hints from the works of even those psychologists with whom he cannot bring himself to agree.

On one point there is no disagreement among psychologists. They consider that, as a result of modern investigation, less and less human actions remain unexplained. To explain an action is to situate it in a causal sequence. This means that more order can be introduced into our picture of human behaviour. Mystery and guesswork are receding together with their references to chance, free choice, temperament, providential intervention, or the whim of the gods. Actions can be classed into categories with other actions as a result of a resemblance which amounts to a suitability for being placed into similar causal sequences.

Although different schools of psychology favour different causal sequences, the differences are often enough merely verbal. There may be agreement about the importance of a symptom even when it is explained by different causes. The Freudian pleasure-principle and the Adlerian power preoccupation explain the relationship between parents and children each in its own way, but both explanations recognize the fundamental importance of the relationship, and its effects in practical life. Psychologists can resort to experiment, and are, as a result, much less tied up in their theories than if their discipline were purely speculative. Nor can their use of a specialized jargon be regarded as an affectation. It has considerable advantages. Before a technical term can be applied to a human action or to a human condition, certain well defined questions have to be answered. Loose thinking is thereby prevented, and the dangers of subjectivity are reduced.

The serious student of human character will ask psychology to provide him with categories that will apply to the results of his own observation and of his reading. To study the writings of professional psychologists will, moreover, provide a useful mental gymnastic that will develop his awareness in matters of human behaviour. He may adopt none of the current doctrines, and yet become familiarized with subjects that are ignored by serious-minded people, and realize the existence of stirrings in the unconscious mind which do not betray themselves in conscious behaviour even though they influence it secretly. He will take less for granted, but he will, also, be less subject to surprise and to indignation, which are both enemies of accuracy. He will acquire a little more tolerance than if he lived in ignorance, and tolerance is one of the virtues that are most conducive to human understanding. Thus, by understanding a little, he will learn to understand still more.

When the historian whose understanding of character has grown by all these methods discovers in the past the occurrence of a trait, of an action, isolated or habitual, concerning an individual or a group, he will fit it into an hypothetical sequence of human actions. Into this sequence he may then find it possible also to introduce other ascertained events which, without an understanding of psychology, would appear to be totally unconnected with the sequence. He will also feel moved to go in search of traces of other events which would fit into the new hypothetical sequence.

Each historian works out his own theory of human behaviour, each historian makes his own rules for the reading of character. The rules remain personal to him. A dangerous situation would arise if all historians were agreed on these matters. All incentive to search for alternatives to the universally established doctrine would be killed by complacency, and the resulting stagnation in one branch of human knowledge would spread to other disciplines. This is what happens invariably to intellectual life under totalitarian régimes. Truth is discovered by chance, and before it is universally established it is out of date. It would be a mistake, therefore, to claim universal validity for any approach to the reading of human character. The most a methodologist can do is to show as an illustration which kind of generalization possesses significance in his own eye.

In the matter of determinism I believe in a double standard. While judging my own actions on the assumption that my will is free, I look upon the behaviour of others, dead or alive, as totally determined. This does not mean that I can always see how determination works. The motives of other people's actions are in many cases a mystery to me, but sometimes I am satisfied that one of the ideal causal sequences I have constructed provides a suitable home for a case I have observed. Aware of the fact that there are fashions in psychology, that the relative importance, for instance, of heredity and environment varies fron one decennium to another, I try never to cling rigorously to the categories I have selected. Being as disinclined to apply moral censure as I am ready with intellectual condemnation, I hold it no sin against the paramount law of imaginative charity to attribute lowly motives to the behaviour of my fellow mortals. I accept, therefore, as a rough-and-ready guide the saying that there is no smoke without fire, and am inclined to accept most of the slander I hear. Judging by my own character and by my observations, I believe in original sin as wholeheartedly as the most hell-minded Calvinist. I cannot, for instance, bring myself to imagine that the Christian ideal of chastity has ever been put into practice on a large scale. But human weakness is to me a fact to be noted, not a shortcoming that demands condemnation, still less punishment. Evil, surely, is the intention to hurt, and this intention I have never diagnosed unless ignorance or mental disease had prepared the way for it.

I have the impression that the sequence which occurs most regularly in human behaviour is one which I indicate by the name of symbolization. I use the word in no accepted scientific sense, but in its etymological meaning.[1] Symbolization is the act of throwing together upon a token a number of characteristics and connotations that do not belong to it, but to something else. It uses these ancient methods of comparison and of metaphorical thinking that belong to the oldest mental habits of mankind. It places before our conscious attention an object or an idea, which represents a very different object or idea held in our unconscious mind only. The symbol becomes the patent aim of our endeavours, whereas our real desires and appetites reach out towards an altogether different goal of which we are not consciously aware. What, by the way, is this unconscious mind which frightens those who prefer to think of human beings as subject to no laws except those of religion, convention, and, no doubt much to their regret, of physiology? The distinction between the conscious and the unconscious is fictitious and purely methodological. For all their complexity human beings are integral units. But there are at least two aspects of our being that must be distinguished by different names. Socrates was aware of the fact that he possessed a *daimon* which advised him independently of rational inference. The "self beneath the threshold" was known to French psychologists of the nineteenth century. We need it, at any rate as a fiction, when we think of the purpose that is

[1] This word covers what professional psychologists might call projection, introjection, identification, transference, symbolization, and, more particularly, displacement.

hidden beneath the avowed purpose of our actions. "We see," says Montaigne, "how the soul in its passions will deceive itself, putting up some false and phantastic subject, even if it does not believe in it, rather than not be active in some direction or another."[1]

There is a symbolization in which the unconscious plays but a subordinate part. We find it in the significance attached to the flag. It may seem absurd that men should die or grow angry or elated about a few strips of coloured silk or cotton sewn together. But, as they themselves know, the flag is the symbol of their country, their nation, their community, and, most of all, of a way of living that is so dear to them that they would die rather than give it up. In morbid cases symbolization is not infrequently of a sexual nature. Freud describes many instances of what I call symbolization in his lectures on psychoanalysis. Stekel offers a convincing theory about what he calls the "Don Juan complex," which explains the extremer sorts of philandering by a deep-rooted dislike of women. In very normal individuals a constant and elementary symbolization occurs, shaping their dreams and dominating many aspects of their waking life. The house thus becomes the symbol of womanhood or even of motherhood. This explains in part the popularity of the House of Orange among the Dutch people and their strong attachment to the matriarchal form of constitutional monarchy. The behaviour of Louis Bonaparte, King of Holland, to his brother Napoleon is not easy to explain on political or economic grounds. Those who understand the working of symbolization as well as that of ambivalence, which I shall presently describe, must see that the hostility of the King of Holland to the Emperor of the French was symbolic of a younger brother's desire to liberate himself from the preponderance acquired by an older brother in the days when, at the beginning of his career, he stood to him in place of a father. Father Buonaparte was a shadowy figure, frequently absent from the family circle, and more than one of the Bonaparte's sought in an elder brother a substitute, i.e. a symbol, for

[1] "Et nous voyons que l'ame en ses passions se pipe plutost elle mesme, se dressant un faux subject et fantastique, voire contre sa propre créance, que de n'agir contre quelquechose" (I, iv).

the unsatisfactory father.[1] The doctrinal differences between Arminians and Gomarists in the Dutch Republic at the beginning of the seventeenth century were so slight that they cannot possibly explain the political commotions to which they gave rise. These, and the hatred that characterized the struggle between the two parties, can be understood only when it is realized that the views on predestination held by their supporters symbolized the profound difference in their general attitude towards religion and towards life in general. The obvious is often the worst conceivable explanation of human behaviour.

Human behaviour has another regular characteristic, the knowledge of which greatly facilitates the serialization of events. It is ambivalence—this time I am using a recognized technical term of scientific psychology—the characteristic of certain attitudes and frames of mind which act unaccountably in opposite directions. Common sense looks upon certain tendencies as incompatible opposites, while they are, in reality, the ambivalent or complementary and alternating aspects of the same psychological phenomenon. Thus courage and fear, as we saw when we dealt with military history, avarice and extravagance, love and hate, are ambivalent doublets. The spendthrift usually has his pet meanness, perhaps an irresistible desire to save railway or bus fares, or a fear to strike matches. The miser often has a white elephant upon which he lavishes money: a house, or an unworthy friend. Connoisseurship and collecting may gradually change a spendthrift into a miser; a miser may through them become extravagant. But neither will ever, unless perhaps after a successful but difficult analysis, acquire a sane and balanced attitude towards possessions and towards money. Both are obsessed by money or property. Love and hate are ambivalent. They are not each other's opposite, for their opposite would be a sane attitude towards the object which obsesses them. "Car ce qu'on hait," wrote Montaigne, "on le prend à coeur."[2] Saint-Simon showed that he knew this truth when he wrote, in the portrait he drew of

[1] For the complicated relations between the members of the Bonaparte family and the light they throw upon political events at the time of its ascendency, see Masson, *Napoleon et sa Famille*, I, pp. 16 and 25, and Lévy, *Napoleon Intime*, *passim*.   [2] I, Essay on Democritus and Heraclitus.

the Regent Duke of Orleans: "Le nerf et le principe de la haine et de l'amitié, de la reconnaissance et de la vengeance, est le même."[1] The historian who understands ambivalence will not be surprised or led astray by what seem at first sight unaccountable vagaries of human behaviour. Sudden changes of allegiance, revolutionary changes of policy, Othello's murderous love, Panurge's cowardice and passion for dangerous adventure, encourage us to look for the common origin of apparently incompatible forms of conduct.[2]

It is possible that the behaviour of collectivities shows in some respects a qualitative difference from that of individuals. It may be, on the other hand, that the difference merely consists in a greater suggestibility of individuals when they find themselves to be part of a crowd, a mob, a nation. In that case a society is perhaps not more than the sum total of its parts. The historian ought to have an opinion of his own upon this matter, if he is to write political and, still more, social history. He should hold his opinion provisionally, subject to correction. But he should have reached it before he begins to tell his story, for it is not his task to extract from history generalizations about human behaviour. That is the task of social psychology, which studies persons in their interactions with one another. The problems with which it deals are not always easily distinguished from those that concern sociology or the philosophy of history, which will form the subject of the following chapter.

[1] Ed. Hachette, Vol. VII, p. 349.
[2] Ambivalence is described by Freud in his essays on *Totem and Taboo*. The Dutch poet Hélène Swart has in her volume *Poëzie* a poem called "Mijn Haat" (my hatred) which begins with the line

> Ik ben met mijn Haat door het leven gegaan
> (It is with my hatred I went through life)

and ends with the line

> Gij zijt met uw Liefde door 't leven gegaan
> (You walked throughout life with your love).

Chapter IV

THE HISTORIAN'S PHILOSOPHY
OF HISTORY

§ I

NO DILEMMA

AT this stage of our survey we have come to realize that the historian will not be hampered in his task of story-telling by a lack of methods for serializing the events that have come to his knowledge. Time provides him with a necessary and obvious starting point. Causation, imagination, and his understanding of human character link together events that would, without them, seem isolated, and therefore unfit for use in a story. These are not alternative methods. The postulate of causation is all-pervading: every series appears as a sequence in which events follow upon each other not by chance, but in conformity with some inescapable regularity, apprehended by the historian's imagination. The historian does not invent, but perceives the connections suggested by his general knowledge and his experience of life. There is at his disposal at least one other method for formulating his general views, and therefore another system for serializing events. This method also fits into the picture made by causation and perceived through the imagination. It is the historian's philosophy of history.

Describing spiritual life in the Dutch Republic during the first half of the eighteenth century, the historian Blok, whom no one would call a wild or enthusiastic generalizer, wrote: "Material decadence usually goes hand in hand with decadence of a spiritual nature; indeed, it often reveals itself as a result of spiritual decadence."[1] This is *a priori* reasoning. Blok looked at events in the light of a principle that was real to him even before he knew them. He used it for the serialization of events of which he had become aware. He approached his task with a preconceived

[1] *Geschiedenis van het Nederlandsche Volk*, III, 2nd ed., p. 394.

notion about the way in which things happen in the world. He professed a philosophy of history which no Marxist·could accept, to which more than one non-Marxist would also refuse to subscribe. It is natural and right that P. J. Blok should have possessed a philosophy of his own, whatever its content. "A man with no philosophy in him," wrote William James, "is the most inauspicious and unprofitable of all social mates."[1] We have seen at an earlier stage that there is a way of understanding, or of trying to understand, the course of historical events as a result of reflection and leisurely examination.[2] If this reflective and leisurely examination is systematized, it is called by the name of philosophy of history, a discipline which belongs to philosophers and not to historians. But because he is an intellectual, the historian will necessarily, in the course of carrying out his work of research and story-telling, reflect upon the subject matter with which he deals, and form, for himself, certain more or less systematic generalizations about it. Every historian has a philosophy of history.

The late Sir Charles Oman, an eminent English historian, would not have subscribed to this view. He hated the idea that there could be a philosophy of history. "Popular phrases about the 'Philosophy of History,' " he wrote, "leave me very cold."[3] Not so very cold, it would appear, for he added: "The philosophers are the enemies of history, trying to make, out of a series of strange and perplexing happenings which we have before us, something logical and tending to an end."[4] Against these alleged absurdities Oman placed his own uncompromising opinion: "History . . . is (I think) a series of happenings, not a logical process." And he repeated himself: "History is not a tale of logical processes or necessary evolutions, but a series of happenings."[5] Here, let it be noted in passing, Oman uses the word "history" to designate, not the tale, but its contents. Having disposed of the philosophy of history Oman treats us, a little further in his racily written book of reminiscences, to his own, positive, views of what we should understand history to be.

---

[1] *Some Problems of Philosophy*, p. 8.   [2] Above, I: iii: § 2.
[3] *The Writing of History* (1939), p. 9.
[4] *Ibid.*, p. 84.   [5] *Ibid.*, both on p. 8.

"Let us never talk of the world stream, or inevitability, but reflect that the human record is illogical, often cataclysmic, anything rather than a regular process from the worse to the better down all ages."[1] Is this not a succinct but complete statement of a systematic view upon the course of past events, of a particular and personal philosophy of history? It is indeed, and no one could call it absurd. It might be termed, to use Oman's own word, the cataclysmic conception of history. It proclaims the view that the course of human affairs in the past has followed a series of progressions, each of which was invariably interrupted by some cataclysmic occurrence. We meet it also in Anatole France's *Ile des Pingouins*, in the *Zadig* of Voltaire, in the work of Spengler, and perhaps in Professor Toynbee's Apocalypsis. It explains, by the way, why Oman became a military historian.[2]

§ 2

MUTABLE DOGMATISMS

In the parliament of historians, where the extreme right is represented by the shade of Oman with his denial of the possibility of a philosophy of history, the other extreme consists of those for whom the philosophy of history is the purpose and culmination of all historical activity. The most thoroughgoing among them, the Marxists, abolish history as an autonomous discipline and annex it to sociology. Being in possession of the state machine in a number of countries governed by totalitarian methods, they enforce this attitude upon their historians. They convert the brilliant and fertile hypotheses of Marx and Engels into a Revelation which bears no qualification, and forget the eminent reasonableness of the fathers of Marxism. "A system of natural and historical knowledge which is all-embracing and final for all time is in contradiction to the fundamental laws of dialectical thinking," wrote Engels.[3] The new Marxists would,

---

[1] *The Writing of History*, (1939), p. 98.

[2] "For war of all things proceeds least upon definite rules, but draws principally upon itself for contrivances to meet an emergency" (Thucydides, I, 122).

[3] *Herr Eugen Dühring's Revolution in Science* (Transl. Emile Burns, p. 31).

of course, not reject this statement contained in one of their sacred texts. Stalin has written: "Engels said that 'materialism must take on a new aspect with each new great discovery.' We all know that none other than Lenin fulfilled this task, as far as his own time was concerned, in his remarkable work *Materialism and Empirio-Criticism.*"[1] But the "we all know" finds its sanction in dismissals and concentration camps. The philosophy of history which absorbs history may be dialectically variable, but the variation is dictated by force, not by free investigation. While it prevails, it enjoys a monopoly. This situation is a denial of scholarship and science.

Looked upon in the right way, as a maker of series needed for story-telling, Marxism is perhaps the most useful of all philosophies of history. Nevertheless, its insistence upon materialism and economic factors as the cause of every conceivable social condition is fatiguing. Methodologically, it is cumbersome. Whether ideas spring from social and material circumstances, or whether these circumstances are the result of ideas—this is one of those school controversies which may sharpen the wits of those who engage in them, but shed no light upon reality. We have seen how Powicke declares himself a supporter of the priority of ideas and makes disarming admissions in favour of the opposite view.[2] The whole debate is trivial, and Marxism is, in this respect, as trivial as its opponents. Ideas and circumstances are the two ends of a stick. There is no question of holding the stick by the wrong end; whichever way we seize it, we are in possession of the two ends and of the element that joins them. Marxists ought to know this. Did not Engels write: "Everything which sets men in motion must go through their minds; but what form it will take in the mind will depend very much upon circumstances."[3] It matters very little whether in telling the story the historian wishes at all costs to serialize his events by referring to ideas born from circumstances, or to circumstances that work through the ideas to which they give rise. Life is one, but it has many aspects.

Life's many aspects are reflected in a multitude of philosophies,

[1] Quoted in the official London Edition of F. Engels's *Ludwig Feuerbach*, p. 36, note 1. [2] Above, I: ii: § 2. [3] *Feuerbach*, p. 60.

and a vast choice is offered to the historian. There is a rabbinic philosophy of history, mainly ethnographic, which differs little, except as regards the identification of the chosen nation, from that of the Dutch Calvinists of the seventeenth century or that of the Nazis of the twentieth. No doubt there exists a Confucian philosophy of history, and would not a West African or Zulu witch doctor find one ready at hand if he undertook to tell the story of his tribe or his nation? Most of these philosophies lead men astray by their exclusiveness and by an excess of certitude. Each of them contributes to the variety of the historical picture and adds to it an element without which it would be even more incomplete than it is at present. The Dutch professor Sneller, a great economic historian and a great Calvinist, who looks upon the philosophy of history as "a search for the meaning of history" —a definition with which no one could disagree—finds the criterion of this meaning in the Calvinist revelation. "Only a personal God who directs the course of events towards the goal determined by himself can give repose to the thought of the philosophers of history; only in the intentions of God does the meaning of history manifest itself."[1]

I have already referred to the Roman Catholic approach to history, when I pointed to its kinship with scepticism.[2] Rome feels so sure of itself that it can disregard facts. I should like to bring out one or two other characteristics of the Roman Catholic philosophy of history because they are equally surprising to those who think of Rome as the rock that never moves. They illustrate the weakness of dogmatism when it has to cope with reality. Rome is variable, and Rome is eminently human. Like Marxism, the Roman Catholic philosophy of history is subject to change, because all things are subject to change. But there is a difference. Marxism makes a dogma of its mutability, tries hard to be immutable nevertheless, and changes, as a matter of fact, all the while. Rome, on the other hand, is most vocal in its professed immutability: it condemns Loisy, a fine historian and a clear thinker, and Tyrell, because they taught that, being a living organism, the Church is bound to change. Meanwhile, Rome sways with every wind.

[1] *De Zin der Geschiedenis* (1944), pp. 10 and 27.   [2] Above, II: i : § 2.

In its general attitude to knowledge, to truth, to the interpretation of life, and therefore to the philosophy of history, Rome has known a very long period of empiricism, liberalism, indeed, one might say, of free thought. In the early centuries, and down to the Reformation, the orthodoxy of a doctrine was not determined by its coincidence with well-established canons, and less by its inherent value than by its survival chances in the sphere of ecclesiastical policy. Saint Augustine remained orthodox (after he abandoned Manichaeism) by formulating his doctrines only in the course of refuting acknowledged heresies. The Church swallowed the intellectual audacities of Saint Thomas Aquinas, who would appear to have believed that matter had existed forever, since it had been created by God of all eternity. To the end of the Middle Ages the real criterion of orthodoxy was less the doctrine itself than the temperament of the man: did he accept the Church as sole mediator between God and himself? The mystic and the witch, who made their own channels for communicating with the other world, were the real enemies.

With the Counter Reformation a desire for tidiness arose. The outside world would not have appreciated liberalism in doctrine. So, outwardly, an air of certitude was adopted. The Catechism of Trent solved every problem. But in actual fact the Church practised disciplined agreement and compromise. Many matters remained undefined, and this is true in particular of the difficulty about free will and Divine Grace, to which the Church applied a non-committal reticence. The philosophy of history contained in the works of Bossuet was orthodox, but its doctrine was not the only way in which a faithful son of the Church could look upon the course of past events. In the *Discours sur l'Histoire Universelle*, published in 1681, Bossuet set himself the task "of penetrating more deeply into the judgments of God under the guidance of His Scripture."[1] The great bishop took a very human view of the Immutable One: in his Providential aspect God was not free from change! He behaved in one way in the Old Testament, but "dans le nouveau Testament il a suivi une autre conduite."[2] Bossuet proclaimed his belief in free will as well as in Divine Providence. But he admitted that the whole problem presented

[1] Part II, chapter 21.   [2] *Ibid.*, Part II, chapter 27.

by these two incompatibles is a mystery which transcends human understanding. Rather naturally the Royal Bishop did not feel like giving excessive room to freedom in the world as he saw it. For him, the human soul enjoyed its shadowy freedom within a play-pen that was rapidly moved hither and thither by Providence. He tells us that "deux choses sont évidentes par la seule raison naturelle: l'une que nous sommes libres, . . . l'autre que les actions de notre liberté sont comprises dans les décrets de la divine Providence."[1]

The summary at the end of his treatise on the philosophy of history shows how completely Bossuet eliminated freedom. Directly addressing the Dauphin, for whom the *Traité* was written in the first instance, he declares: "Souvenez-vous, Monseigneur, que ce long enchaînement des causes particulières, qui font et défont les empires, dépend des ordres secrets de la divine Providence. Dieu tient du plus haut des cieux les rênes de tous les royaumes, il a tous les coeurs en sa main: tantôt il retient les passions, tantôt il leur lâche la bride, et par là il remue tout le genre humain. . . . Dieu exerce par ce moyen ses redoutables jugements, selon les règles de sa justice toujours infaillible. C'est lui qui prépare les effets dans les causes les plus éloignées, et qui frappe ces grands coups dont le contre-coup porte si loin. . . . C'est ainsi que Dieu règne sur tous les peuples . . ."[2] And this, surely, is the pure milk of determinism.

The happy period of free speculation behind a front of superficial and nominal agreement came to an end in the second half of the nineteenth century. Ever ready to change and adapt itself, the living organism that was Rome made a false move in the direction of rigidity. Hypnotized by the success of nineteenth century rationalism, the eternal Church bent its knee to triumphant reason. The Council of the Vatican, in 1870, condemned the pluralist philosophy which distinguishes between the realms of faith and of reason.[3] The mysteries of the faith, even if not yet

---

[1] *Traité du Libre Arbitre*, chapter III.   [2] *Discours*, Part XIV, chapter 8.

[3] "Si quis dixerit, disciplinas humanas ea cum libertate tractandas esse, ut earum assertiones, etsi doctrinae revelatae adversentur, tamquam verae retineri, neque ab ecclesia proscribi possint, anathema sit," Canon of the Council of the Vatican.

elucidated, became potentially capable of being rationally interpreted. Now, and until the subtle minds of Rome find an escape
from the prison they erected for themselves, their Church appears,
like that of Moscow, to be chained to one particular method for
acquiring knowledge. The logic of certitude has become the
essential ingredient of the Catholic's faith. It is the spoiling of a
fine, living work of art.

Those who believe in perennial values need not despair. Life is
change, and Rome is living still. Doctrine is never the basic fact
in human institutions: there I am with the Marxists. But I believe
it is the attitude that matters. That penetrating student of national
character, Paul Cohen-Portheim, wrote that Europe is divided
between two conceptions of life. The one is the slave or Christian
ideal, the other the Roman ideal, the conception of a *Herrenmoral*.
The former has been adopted by the Russians, but the latter is
kept alive by the Church of Rome.[1] So far Cohen-Portheim.
We may add the observation that certitude, as ungentlemanly as
enthusiasm, ill-suits the "Roman ideal." In his essay on conversation La Rochefoucauld wrote: "Il faut . . . ne laisser jamais croire
qu'on prétend avoir plus de raison que les autres, et céder aisé-
ment l'avantage." We may be sure that the growth of dogmatism
will find a compensation in the increase of the art of living in the
gentlemanly Church. Of this Rome shows every indication
already.

I have referred before to the studied reticence of the Church
of Rome. Nowhere is it practised as systematically as on this
subject of mutability. Where modernism is condemned, as it has
to be if the principle of an ecclesiastical monopoly of truth is to
be upheld, the necessary adaptation of dogma and morals to the
fluid demands of a *Herrenmoral* must in no circumstances be
exposed to the crude daylight. This means that it cannot be
shared by the mass of the faithful. It remains an esoteric doctrine
and an esoteric practice, reserved for the few. Dr. Marie Stopes
has revealed the existence of a double standard of sexual morality
within Catholic orthodoxy.[2] The difference is also to be found in
eschatological conceptions. Eternal bliss in the bosom of Abraham,

---

[1] *The Discovery of Europe* (1932), chapters on Post-War Europe.
[2] *Roman Catholic Methods of Birth Control* (1933).

touching family reunions in paradise are, like the bejewelled Madonnas with the legion of names, a consolation for the many. But the very few know that the real reward implied in eternal salvation is the *visio beatifica*, and that those occupied in the contemplation and the progressive but never to be completed understanding of the All-Perfect will have less and less inclination to bestow their attention upon family matters and friendly reminiscences. There is little difference between the *visio beatifica* and the Nirvana of the Buddhists.[1]

Rome puts water in its wine. The Calvinist takes his vinegar neat. Change, according to Calvinist thought, may occur in the individual soul when it becomes conscious of its election. Upon collective change, historical change, Calvinist ideology does not like to dwell. Being a new doctrine born of revolution, Calvinism is more interested in the antiquity of its origins than in the novelty of its philosophy. It insists upon the claim that it represents primitive Christianity. It minimizes the difference between the Old and the New Testaments, and quotes the Old, which is sterner and more truly reflective of its vindictive Deity, more readily than the New. Catholicism, on the other hand, likes to insist upon the break between the old and the new. No doubt, it does not encourage the reading of the Bible by laymen. Holy Writ is obscure, and, apart from the few who can read it in a dead language—another instance of esoterism—Catholics should accept their Biblical reading from the Church, duly selected and annotated. The method of selection greatly favours the humaner New Testament. Catholic hymnology dwells with delight upon the break between the old and the new, upon the renewal and change that accompanied the birth of the Church.[2]

---

[1] Mgr Duchesne and Lord Acton wrote for the few. They were not expelled from the Church. The Tsarist régime condemned no book that was sold for more than two gold roubles. "Il est avec le ciel des accommodements."

[2] The Blessed Sacrament is felt throughout the centuries to be a startling novelty, made possible only by the abolition of old ways and old conceptions. In his beautiful *Pange Lingua* Saint Thomas Aquinas says:

> Et antiquum documentum
> Novo cedat ritui.

The *Sacris Solemniis* jubilantly exclaims:

[*Footnote continued on page 214.*

A doctrine that is so conscious of mutability is bound to be a fertile serializer in the hands of an historian. It leads to the telling of novel stories which give rise to new questions and stimulate further research. With its exquisite indifference to facts it presents non-Catholic historians with new incentives to work, and since, their philosophic differences notwithstanding, all historians are members of one body of social servants, Catholic historians should not only be forgiven for their one-sidedness, but praised for it. They have a part to play. They play it very well. In Holland they have compelled historians of every school and opinion radically to revise their conceptions of Dutch history. W. J. F. Nuyens (1823–94), a doctor of medicine and a practising physician, devoted his leisure to the writing of several volumes on the history of the Revolt of the Netherlands. He exposed the narrow Little-Netherland racialism of current historical writing which was entirely under Calvinist influence, pointed out the unity of Dutch and Belgian history, and prepared the way for the later and better documented writings which have established the claims of the Catholics to full participation in the traditions of the Dutch people. The far-reaching innovations of the agnostic Geyl show a considerable kinship with the work of Nuyens. It is no longer possible to treat Dutch history as the story of the armed revelation of the God of Calvin in the Northern Netherlands. Success and the consciousness of their strength has, furthermore, induced Dutch Catholic historians to adopt canons of objectivity.

> Recedant vetera
> Nova sint omnia
> Corda, voces et opera.

While in *Lauda Sion Salvatorem*, the Holy Sacrament is described in these words:

> In hac mensa novi regis
> Novum pascha novae legis
> .Phase vetus terminat.
> Vetustatem novitas
> Umbram fugat veritas
> Noctem lux eliminat.

§3

MYTHOLOGIES

I have mentioned a few recognized and organized doctrines which contain within themselves complete philosophies of history. There are many more. Every religious or metaphysical system implies an interpretation of the human past. Every historian brings to his study of the past an interpretation of his own. Since the present work reflects conditions and trends of thought noticed during a life-time spent among English historians, I may not, in the remaining part of this chapter, omit a reference to two philosophies of history which have exercised a considerable influence upon these historians in recent years.

Of the teaching of the late R. G. Collingwood little remains to be said. I examined his doctrines when I dealt with the definition of the word history.[1] All I need do at this juncture is to remind the reader of Collingwood's intentional confusion of the two meanings of that word. His definition of the philosophy of history is unexceptionable: "a philosophical enquiry into the nature of history regarded as a special type or form of knowledge with a special type of subject."[2] Like Croce, Collingwood is "utraquistic," to use the word of the authors of *The Meaning of Meaning*. It is not clear when Collingwood's "history" refers to the past, and when it refers to the knowledge of the past. The essence of his epistemology is an identification of the one and the other by means of the use of creative historical imagination. Its main drawback is a pathetic belief in the possibility of indisputable knowledge.

A philosophy of history which has made a profound impression upon English-speaking readers is that of Arnold J. Toynbee, Research Professor of International History in the University of London. It has been presented to the world in six large volumes under the title of *A Study of History*. It began to appear in 1934, and has had several editions and impressions. More volumes are announced. The work bears palpable evidence of its author's profound erudition, of his immense knowledge of the past and

---

[1] Above, I: ii: § 2.　　　　　[2] *The Idea of History*, p. 7.

of the present. It contains many proofs of his knowledge of the world. It is varied, rich, always readable. To me it had, when I became first acquainted with it, the attraction of impish humour and of a joyful iconoclasm. Its description of the operations of a Board of Studies in History at an English University,[1] its reflections upon the mentality of English historians,[2] make it difficult for me to be entirely outspoken about its lovable author. Yet I consider the work to be based upon misleading arguments, intellectually dangerous, and totally false as a picture of the function of historical studies. It is the supreme embodiment of what I call left-wing deviationism, the confusion between history and the philosophy of history.

As an illustration of the way in which this work has conquered a place, not only in the minds, but in the hearts of some, I refer the reader to Mr. Tangye Lean's "A Study of Toynbee," in the periodical *Horizon* for January 1947. This article is the manifesto of a cult. Now Mr. Tangye Lean has, obviously, read *A Study of History*, and he believes that he has understood it. Many of the greatest admirers of the work have only browsed in it. It is immense. Unless one buys it one cannot keep it by one long enough to work one's way through it. As far as English historians are concerned, their admiration has been conditioned by the lengthy and numerous footnotes and the erudite apparatus served with the main dish. Every literature has been put under contribution. The author's omniscience frightened the scholar-tacticians who thought twice before attacking. It is a striking fact that the first really critical reviews of the system of Mr. Toynbee appeared when a less forbidding abridgment of the work was published in 1947.[3] This did not enjoy the immunity commanded by the *editio maior*. The barbed wire of annotation had been levelled, and word went round that the citadel was not impregnable.[4]

---

[1] Vol. I, pp. 163–4. [2] E.g., I, pp. 455–6.

[3] *A Study of History*, abridgment by Somervell, D. C., 1947.

[4] See Collingwood's severe criticism of the book, written before the publication of the *editio minor*, from his own specific point of view, in *The Idea of History*, pp. 159–65. Collingwood attacks Toynbee for failing "to see that the historian is an integral element in the process of history itself, reviving in himself the experiences of which he achieves historical knowledge," in other words, for not being a Croce-ite.

With that loyalty to Mandarin standards which characterizes him, Toynbee prints a letter from Dr. Edwyn Bevan explaining in a few words why Toynbee's whole scheme is wrong: "... While your attention and interest is directed mainly to the common characteristics, it is the uniqueness that impresses me. . . . The 'Hellenic Civilization' I see . . . as the unique beginning of something new in the history of Mankind. Never before that culture can we see a civilization of the same rationalist character . . ."[1] The publication, without comment, of this striking criticism is symptomatic of Toynbee. Even though he does not always make clear what it is he believes, he is unwavering in his belief. He is an absolutist. "So far, we have simply found that in the foreground of historical thought there is a shimmer of relativity," he writes, "and it is not impossible that the ascertainment of this fact may prove to be the first step towards ascertaining the presence of some constant and absolute object of historical thought in the background."[2] He pities those who have not been vouchsafed the revelation, treats them kindly, and has no desire to muzzle them.

I am not competent to criticize Toynbee's philosophy of history. But I may be allowed to mention two facts which make me suspicious about his method and his conclusions. The first is that wherever he deals with the history of the Low Countries he remains superficial and approximative, when he is not actually ill-informed. The other is Toynbee's use of myths and metaphors, not merely for the purpose of assisting thought, but as the basis for subsequent reasoning and classification. Faust, Job,—"let us open our ears to language and mythology,"[3]—Yin and Yang, Hippolitus and Phoedra, Hoder and Balder. Play with mythology leads us nowhere beyond mythology. It provides us with hypotheses—and what is there that does not?—but never with proofs. "For here we see the same 'great refusal' that the creators of the Egyptiac Civilization made in the age of the Pyramid-Builders, and *that Zeus would have made at the dawn of Hellenic history if he had not been saved from it, in spite of himself, by Prometheus.*"[4] There never was a Zeus! What Zeus said or intended is not evi-

---

[1] Vol. V, pp. 6–7. See the whole letter.   [2] Vol. I, p. 16.
[3] I, p. 271.   [4] III, p. 255. (My italics.)

dence. On the few pages that follow the statement I have just quoted, I underline the words "mythology, allegory, Epic, poet, poet, poem, feeling, anthropomorphically, allegorical imagery, allegory, hypothetical, a hypothesis which has to be taken on faith, parallel, the primordial images of Mythology, intuitive form of apprehending and expressing universal truths."[1] Why not just one single fact? And when there is an argument, it is too often formal and verbal: "A field of action—and, *a fortiori*, an intersection of a number of fields of action—cannot be a source of action. The source of action is other than the field of action *ex hypothesi*. And—to apply this truism to the case in point—the source of social action cannot be the society, but can only be each or some or one of the individuals whose fields of action constitute a society on the ground where they coincide."[2] A metaphoric argument like this, or an enumeration of myths—neither leads us to truth nor to knowledge.

As I said, I have no intention of discussing Professor Toynbee's doctrines. This has been done, adequately, and finally, by my compatriot Geyl.[3] My universal eclecticism leaves room for the message of Toynbee, if there be a message in his work. I condemn his condemnation of the treatment of problems of nationhood by historians because it is illiberal, and because any theory that attempts to expel from the ranks of historians men who have honestly attempted to carry out their social task is of necessity distorted and partial. I dislike Toynbee's method, because it dwells in the sphere of myth and allegory, outside rationality, and because the intense loyalties he inspires are equally innocent of rationality. The mentality of the Dutch theorist Romein, who manages to proclaim himself an adherent of the doctrines of Toynbee while remaining a believing Marxist, is typical, in my opinion, of the mentality that comes under the spell of *A Study of History*.

One aspect of Toynbeeism puzzles me. Toynbee's writing is magnificent. His style is Greece and the Bible and France, and the tongues of many peoples, with the quintessence extracted

---

[1] III, pp. 256–9.   [2] III, p. 230.
[3] See Geyl, P., "Toynbee's System of Civilizations," in *Journal of the History of Ideas*, Vol. IX, No. 1.

from them in a liberation from the tyranny of the *Logos* which leaves him in possession of the rhythm of all language. It is the style of a man whose soul is straight. This book cannot be a mystification. What is it, then? Though there is no deception of others, there is in it the nearest approach to self-deception. Sometimes we dream that we understand at last the mystery of life, that we have solved the riddle of human relationships. We awake, and say: "This is great, I must preserve it!" In the morning we remember the formula. It is inane. Toynbee had a vision. He dreamt that he could formulate the human universe. His mistake is that he remained faithful to the hypnological revelation and worked it out in millions of words. He should have sighed: "mirum somniavi somnium!" and written a poem about his experience. Preferably in Greek.

§ 4

A PRIORISM

In conclusion I may state once more that, while it is not the historian's task to formulate a philosophy of history, no historian approaches his task without certain preconceived and systematic generalizations about the course of the human past. He may owe these notions to his membership of a Church, to his approval of the doctrines of a political party, he may, instead, base them entirely upon his own reflections strengthened by his reading. He may derive them from both sources. The essential factor is that his philosophy is a prioristic, held before he set out upon his task of historical research, and that it provides him with a ready-made system for serializing into a story the events detected by research. But the conscientious historian must never forget that he is not writing to prove a theory or to make a contribution to the philosophy of history. He must remember, in consequence, that the a prioristic method, which is not his by choice, but by the nature of his work, presents a serious danger. It holds out a temptation to human weakness. Fustel de Coulanges warns us that if we approach a text with a preconceived idea we shall read in it only what we want to read. Nevertheless, this warning should not be taken by the historian as an invitation to turn his mind into a blank. Too many would-be historians have remained mere erudites because of the incurable blankness of their minds. The *a priori* method is not faulty, but it must be handled with care. The categories, the preconceived patterns presented by our personal philosophy of history, must rank in our minds as hypotheses, to be given up if they fail to produce a satisfying result, if the story to which they lead does not appear to be as accurate as is feasible. Once more, the historian is put on his honour.

Chapter V

THE "LAWS" OF HISTORY

§ 1

"LAW" AND RECURRENCE

WE have examined in the previous chapter a few among the many philosophies of history which compete for the historian's allegiance, and we have seen that, whether he accepts any of them or prefers to look at life in his own way, every historian holds a systematic and generalized view about the course taken in the past by human affairs. Is it possible to see how, in practice, these philosophies of history help the historian to formulate sets of rules that will help him in serializing the events known to him through his research?

It will be noticed in the first place that every philosophy of history implies a belief that things occur in the human world with some kind of regularity. Even Oman's cataclysmic conception of history postulates one regularity: the inevitable appearance of senseless interruptions which prevent orderly progress or evolution. Such regularities of occurrence, which form the substance of every philosophy of history, are called "laws of history." The word "history" here indicates the course of human experiences in the past. As for the word "laws," it has no legal connotation suggesting rules of behaviour provided with a sanction. It indicates, as it does in the expression "the laws of nature," the regularity with which certain events follow upon certain others. The formulation of laws gives concrete contents to the postulate of causation: not only is the principle accepted that certain sequences of events occur with regularity, but some of these regularities are noted and given a name. We say that each observed regularity is a law. The law is therefore a descriptive formulation of habits which we believe can be noticed in events, it obeys the events, and we have no logical ground for the belief that events obey the law (though we may have metaphysical or theological grounds for the belief). A law of history, like a law of nature, is an hypothesis of more than ordinary strength, but nevertheless one which like every other hypothesis may have to be discarded if it does not work.[1]

There is a significant, a fundamental difference, between the way in which use can be made of the laws of nature and of the laws of history. It is the difference which exists between the sciences of nature and the discipline which we call history. Science can and must predict; history does not predict. It is natural that we should ask whether, in the belief or maybe the knowledge that he is acquainted with the existence of certain regularities of occurrence in the past, the historian may not permit himself, or may not have the duty, to point out where in the future these regularities must present themselves once more. The answer to this question is that prophecy does not come within the historian's terms of reference, and is not within his power.

The task of the historian is simply and exclusively to keep available for social use the knowledge of the past experiences of human societies. As soon as he tries to use the knowledge of these experiences for any purpose whatever apart from putting them into the story that makes them generally available he ceases to be an historian.

> "I list not prophesy; but let Time's news
> Be known when 't is brought forth."[2]

What he does as an historian is to look at a portion of the past which would remain inexplicable unless one of those regularities of occurrence described in a law of history took place. "Generally speaking," he will say, "I know that a devotion to public duty operates more efficiently if it is spurred on by personal ambition. Can I apply this to the present case, where I have found traces of the existence of a sense of public duty and of activity applied with considerable efficiency? Can I presuppose that personal ambition was also at work in this particular instance? Let me see whether I can detect any traces of its existence." Or he may say:

---

[1] See Dewey on "timeless laws," in *Experience and Nature*, pp. 148 *sqq.* See Schiller on the Laws of Nature, in *Formal Logic*, pp. 310–37, and in *Logic for Use*, pp. 408 *sqq.*   [2] *A Winter's Tale*, IV, i.

"Crowds are at the same time more iconoclastic and more conservative than individuals. Here I have a crowd that acted violently and in an iconoclastic manner. It behaved, in fact, in a revolutionary way. Can I find traces that bear out my 'law,' traces of a conservative element which also influenced the behaviour of this crowd or mob?" The historian will not be looking for a confirmation of his law by events. He will be looking for events as yet unknown to him but suggested by the law which he believes to be true. What interests the historian is the *individual* case. He wishes to know a thing that happened, an event that took place. Science, on the other hand, goes beyond the individual, it tries forever to generalize as a preliminary to coping with every individual case that may occur.

The historian does not wish to predict the future. The historian cannot predict the future. Let us look once more at the "laws of nature" and at the part they play in science. Perhaps this will make the difference between the scientist's task and that of the historian more palpable. Two conceptions of science hold the field, nowadays. According to the first, the purpose of science and of the scientist is to know the physical and the living universe. This knowledge can be formulated in the shape of laws, which do not only describe the past behaviour of the universe, but which, being applicable in all circumstances, must necessarily also describe the way in which it will behave in the future. The laws of nature are therefore by definition prophetic. But since the scientist's task is to know, he may not rest in the passive expectation that his knowledge will hold good in the future. He must test his knowledge by experiment. The experiment will confirm his knowledge, till one day it fails to do so. Then the need will arise for reformulation of the law in such a manner that the new experience can be incorporated in it.

The other conception of science places the emphasis upon its practical aspect. Science is a technique, a systematization of methods for doing things. The very object of the scientist's work is achievement, and this achievement finds its expression in the experiment. The way in which experiments are carried out successfully, and therefore the way in which science achieves its purpose, is formulated in the shape of laws. The law predicts—if it is correct—the outcome of the experiment. So long as it does this it is accepted, but always provisionally. When it fails to carry out its real function, that of being the supreme instrument for the performance of actions, it must be modified, or scrapped.[1]

May I venture the opinion that there is no difference in practice between the two conceptions? Knowledge for the sake of the experiment, or experimentation for the sake of knowledge? For knowledge, unavoidably provisional, exists only in so far as it makes itself manifest through action. Experiments and the laws of nature live with and through each other. They advance hand in hand, even though they must progress ballet-like, each taking a step in turn, instead of marching behind a banner to the strains of a battle-hymn. Whatever the purpose of science, all scientists are agreed that there can be no scientific knowledge without experiments, or at any rate, without predictions. There lies the difference between scientific and historical knowledge. For there can be no historical knowledge dependent upon experimentation. History is the resurrection of that which happened once, and it is supremely indifferent to the issue whether the past occurrence will occur again. The scientist's interest, however, lies in the future. He wants to know that which must occur again.[2]

The question whether the historian could, if it were his task, foretell the future is often put in a different way: does history repeat itself? The word history is once more used in the objective sense, and refers to past collective human experiences. Do such experiences occur more than once? Can a specific set of occurrences take place more than once? Now it may be taken for granted as long as we accept the postulate of causation, that if *all* the circumstances which led to an occurrence are repeated, the occurrence itself will also be repeated, and that if this repetition is observed, the outcome may be predicted with safety. But since every occurrence is itself a sequence of occurrences of a lesser degree of importance, we can never be completely certain that

[1] I give this double formulation upon my own authority, but I have some confidence that my friends the scientists will not accuse me of a desire to caricature their position.

[2] Geology? A strong and effective alliance of the historical method with its indifference to future occurrence, and of the sciences like chemistry, physics, crystallography, etc. etc., which live by futurity only.

every single circumstance has genuinely presented itself a second time. The complete recurrence of circumstances must remain a matter of surmise. What is, perhaps, more relevant is that the complete recurrence of a set of circumstances is a contradiction in terms. The fact that a set of circumstances has occurred once necessarily influences a set of circumstances which resembles it and occurs later: it forms a circumstance which must be added to the second set. History *cannot* repeat itself.

The historian cannot prophesy.[1] As a private person, however, he is well qualified to express views upon the future. The habit of establishing causal sequences gives him powers of connected insight; he has acquired the practice of looking at public affairs on a large scale. He will have more chance of seeing permanent elements underneath the temporary accidents that strike the eye. The Dutch historian Blok described this limited gift of foresight very well when he said: "The knowledge, the detailed knowledge of the past cannot, of course, lead us, historians, to an infallible prediction of what will take place tomorrow or the day after, but it can and must serve to a better understanding of *the present*. And a good understanding of the present is one of the best guarantees of a wise treatment of this present with a view to the things which the future will bring us."[2]

§ 2

LIFE IS REASONABLE

If we believe that there are in the human past perceptible regularities of occurrence which the historian can formulate and use as tools for telling his story, we believe, by implication, that the historian's world, the human past, can be understood by him,

---

[1] Collingwood comes to the same conclusion. When eschatology intrudes, something has gone wrong, according to him, with the historian's fundamental conception of history. I cannot, however, accept Collingwood's reasoning. He bases it upon his well-known identification of objective and subjective history. Objective history = the past. Subjective history = objective history. *Ergo*, subjective history = the past, and has therefore nothing to do with the future (*cf. The Idea of History*, pp. 54–5, and p. 68: "The historian never prophesies").

[2] *Feestrede Historisch Genootschap* (1920).

that it is intelligible and that, figuratively speaking, it is reasonable. The scientist makes a similar assumption in dealing with nature. Whether it is inanimate, and studied by the physicist or the astronomer, or whether it takes the aspect we call life and provides material for the physiologist, the biologist, the zoologist, nature is assumed by these scientists to be reasonable. Reasonable, not rational. As Dewey observes, "the doctrine that nature is inherently rational was a costly one. It entailed the idea that reason in man is an outside spectator of a rationality already complete in itself."[1] It is a belief which leads to dogmatism and to totalitarianism. But we can understand nature, and that is an entirely different proposition. Dewey supports this view in another place: "The world is subject-matter for knowledge, because mind has developed *in* that world; a body-mind, whose structures have developed according to the structures of the world in which it exists, will naturally find some of its structures to be concordant and congenial with nature, and some phases of nature with itself."[2] All this applies with equal cogency to the human world, which is part of nature.

In this chapter, as I did in the chapter dealing with human behaviour, I want to go beyond, and a good way beyond, the rational and universally compelling (if there be such a thing). I wish to show how I exercise my own right to formulate laws of history. And before I enumerate a few of them, and explain how, for instance, I look upon change as an ineluctable law, upon momentum as a diabolical tempter of the good, upon class as a fundamental reality, upon revolution as a psycho-pathological phenomenon, and upon "greatness" as an ambivalent quality of certain men, I wish to explain how I draw from the reasonableness of the world a conclusion which my faith accepts while my reason allows it to pass with an apologetic smile. As William James observes, "Mankind is made on too uniform a pattern for any of us to escape successfully from acts of faith."[3] One of my acts of faith is a belief in what I like to call "the law of elasticity," which I derive from my rationally held conviction that the world of men is intelligible. Once we believe in this intelligibility we

[1] *The Quest for Certainty*, p. 202.
[2] *Experience and Nature*, p. 277.   [3] *The Meaning of Truth*, p. 257.

are entitled to assume that the human past cannot be mere chaos.
We have already noticed the universal belief in regularity, which
commands acceptance even in Oman's anarchistic system. Now
if we once agree that a certain degree of adequateness, of fitness,
of balance, may be postulated in the human world, we may
bring ourselves to believe that humanity need not be forever
baffled by the course of events. Had it always been proved
wrong and defeated, men would not have acquired their sense
of congruousness. Logically, this is a poor argument. But
the theory is amazingly productive of sound diagnoses of
social life.

Some three years before the outbreak of the Second World
War I was bemoaning the condition of public affairs in a conversation with the Scottish philosopher John MacMurray. "Yes,"
he said in the end, "but please remember that there is such a
thing as reality."[1] This remark impressed me, long before it was
justified by the course of events, and led me to formulate my law
of elasticity, which notes the habit of human affairs to resume
their reasonable shape after it has been modified by factors that
did not occur at the right moment in history. It is connected
with another law, the law of the appointed time, which I shall
describe later in this chapter. Tragic experience revealed the
existence of this law of elasticity to Oscar Wilde. In the days of
his triumphs he used to proclaim himself "a King of Language";
he persuaded himself that a great artist makes his own rules of
life and stands above common obligations and common morality.
After the débacle and while he was in prison Wilde composed
his *Epistola in Carcere et Vinculis*, extracts of which became
known under the title *De Profundis*. "One of the things one
learns in prison," he wrote in this essay, "is that things are what
they are."[2] Oscar Wilde had found out the meaning of the "law
of elasticity." The Greeks also knew it. They believed that
anangkè invariably overtakes *hubris*. The Chinese waited three
centuries for the overthrow of the Manchu dynasty. It came to
pass. "Things are what they are."

[1] See the concluding paragraph in MacMurray's *The Clue to History* (1938),
p. 237.
[2] See my *Oscar Wilde* (1933), p. 145.

§ 3

THE LAW OF CHANGE

When he is about to engage upon his task of telling the story of a part of mankind's past experiences, the historian asks himself a question that may be formulated in many different ways, but cannot be set aside by anyone who does not systematically preclude systematic thinking. Does Life, or at any rate human life, possess some single characteristic which will provide our story with its basic die? Must not everything in our universe, which is intelligible by definition, present itself to the spectator with a common mark, since the alternative would be ineffable and inenarrable chaos?

Does Dewey give us the clue when he writes: "Every existence is an event. . . . All structure is structure *of* something; anything defined as structure is a character of *events*, not something intrinsic and *per se*"?[1] This conception would, I imagine, receive the blessing of contemporary physical science, which looks upon matter, or, to be more accurate, deals with matter, not as a conglomeration of entities, but as a number of events. An earlier pragmatist, Alfred Sidgwick, wrote in the following terms about the continuity of nature: "We cannot escape the question how an actual thing called A came into its present form of existence; any actual thing called A must be either something permanent or something transient. But what things in Nature are really permanent when we come to close quarters with the question? That vague ideal entity 'matter' may be indestructible, but no actual (producible) form of it is so; and in the end we seem driven to admit that the only true 'substance' is something so indeterminate that nothing descriptive can be said of it. It 'exists' as the subject of change, and is only to be caught in the act of changing. Then A, if it be actual, describable, producible, verifiable, must be transient, arising out of non-A and passing into it again. So that A and non-A are each of them only passing forms of the other."[2]

These are ancient notions. We are merely a little more con-

---

[1] *Experience and Nature*, pp. 71-2.   [2] *Distinction and Criticism*, pp. 72-3.

sistent and thorough-going in the way we hold them nowadays.
Whether the Ionian philosophers of the sixth century B.C. were
already proclaiming that *panta rhei*, all things are in a flux, or
whether these words were put into their mouth by Aristotle in
the fourth century B.C.,[1] the impermanence of all things has
struck many human minds through the ages. Those who believe
that it applies to physical and biological nature realize, as a rule,
that the social human world, which is encompassed by nature
like the sponge by the sea (or better, like every cubic centimetre
of sea-water by the whole ocean), cannot escape the necessity of
change. Fundamentalist Christians believe in the total stability of
the human world, and Conservatives would like to persuade
themselves that they hold the same belief. But death and decay
are too much with us to enable anyone to be a consistent believer
in immutability. Whatever we may think of the physical universe,
life is inconceivable to us without death, its concomitant, and we
know in our hearts that societies of men are not singled out for
immutability in the midst of life.

How are we to imagine the ways of this permanent impermanence? All things flow, but they need not necessarily rush
down a cataract. Once again, we cannot begin to think of the
universe or of nature unless we suppose them to be intelligible.
Change must follow a pattern or leave us unaware of its existence.
Can we formulate a law of change, which will apply to the
physical world, the world of life, and the world of human
societies? It has been done, times without number, and through
formulas which have commanded a surprising amount of agreement. William James gave his formula when he wrote "Everything is in an environment, a surrounding world of other things,
and if you leave it to work there it will inevitably meet with
friction and opposition from its neighbours. Its rivals and
enemies will destroy it unless it can buy them off by compromis-
ing some parts of its original pretensions."[2] In other words,
there is a continual tendency for a thing to make concessions to
its environment without submitting entirely to it. Can we now,
without lapsing into metaphysics, express the law of change in a

[1] Collingwood, R. G., *The Idea of Nature*, especially pp. 29 and 82.
[2] *A Pluralistic Universe*, pp. 90-1.

more universal way, by taking as our point of departure the postulate of impermanence which is so generally accepted? We might attempt it by the following argument. Any object, any appearance upon which we fix our attention, is impermanent: it cannot continue to be what it is or seems to be. It is engaged upon becoming something which it is not. If this statement is untrue, we have met with an object or an appearance that is not subjected to the principle of impermanance. We may safely assert, therefore, that there is in everything a tendency[1] to cease being what it is. Our knowledge of the world warns us that the universal tendency to depart from the position or existence acquired at any given moment will not be carried out integrally. William James mentioned, in the passage I have just quoted, the fact that the surrounding world exercises a form of opposition to a thing's remaining what it is. But the same environment also thwarts the object's tendency to cease being what it is. Somewhere, in between the initial position and the integrally different position that would have marked the terminal point of the tendency's direction, a point is reached where the two environmental oppositions which pull in contrary directions reach a balance. But since this balance, like everything else in the universe, is subject to the principle of impermanence, it will itself become a starting position subjected to the environmental pull and repulsion: a new process of change sets in from the moment the compromise has been reached.

Here, surely, are the thesis, the antithesis, and the synthesis of Hegel and of Marx. But Hegel's dialectic process is transcendental, the environmental attraction and repulsion of Marx are exclusively "materialistic"—whatever that strange word may mean!—and economic. Our pragmatist dialectic is neither sacred nor universal, and therefore not a rule to be enforced by scorn or by concentration camps. Since we believe in a reasonable and intelligible world we are inclined to think that the world behaves in a way that satisfies our mind. Whenever, in our historical

[1] "The idea of tendency unites in itself exclusion of prior design and inclusion of movement in a particular direction, a direction that may be either furthered or counteracted and frustrated, but which is intrinsic" (Dewey, *Experience and Nature*, p. 373).

reconstruction, we meet a situation with clear-cut features we shall ask ourselves whether we can by any chance discover of which thesis and antithesis it is the synthesis, and also which antithesis it calls forth, and what are the chances of a synthesis arising in due course. Thus we shall be provided with hypotheses about the causes and origins of the situation upon which our attention has been fixed, and about the direction into which our narrative must now move if it is to be a life-like and accurate story. If the problems raised by this method fail to find an easy or acceptable solution, we shall know that a new heuristic task awaits us, or that our story cannot, in the present state of our knowledge, be liberated from obscurities that may legitimately prevent others from accepting it.

The knowledge of the law of change has given rise to a sociological doctrine known under the name of historicism. With this doctrine, and with its claims to predict the social future, the historian is not concerned.[1] A word must be said, however, about Mr. Collingwood's claim that the historical method can teach the scientist a way of improving his own methods.[2] I have throughout this book maintained the opposite view that the historian should approach his subject in the same way as the scientist, although the respective methods of science and of history are very different. Collingwood's doctrine boils down to the view—he should not be held responsible for my paraphrase—that each branch of human knowledge has, to speak figuratively, a metabolism of its own. There is continual absorption, with some assimilation and much elimination. On the whole, there is growth. Scientists will therefore provide better work if they are profoundly aware of the law of change as it applies to their own discipline. To be profoundly and vividly aware of the law of change is to think historically. Collingwood rightly felt that it would be useful for a scientist to be able to think historically. It is useful for all of us to be able to think historically. To think historically is to have a stereoscopic vision, not to perceive everything in two dimensions, like the blind man who, upon

[1] See Prof. Karl Popper's refutation of "historicism" in his articles on "The Poverty of Historicism" published in *Economica* for May and August 1944, and May 1945. [2] *The Idea of Nature* and *The Idea of History, passim.*

being imperfectly cured by Jesus, saw men walking like trees. To know and to feel the law of change is to realize that what was need not be now, that what is has not always been. It makes us understand that the morality of the past is not that of today, that in the early years of his reign Louis XIV may have been "a good thing," while Hitler was, at any moment of his public career, a baneful influence. The historian will be warned by the law of change not to accept the views of older writers uncritically. He will realize that Sparta cannot have lived for centuries under the iron rules of Lycurgus. He will look at Empires, even before they have reached their zenith, and seek for the causes of their dissolution. As Halphen observes, "l'histoire ne rend pas sceptique, mais elle est une merveilleuse école de prudence."[1] Yes, but of a kind of prudence which we bring to history and knew even before history tried to teach it to us.

§ 4

THE APPOINTED TIME

Time has its ups and downs, like wine that lives bottled in a cellar. There is an "optimum" moment for certain occurrences. Let us use this ugly word which is as neutral as a mathematical symbol. If we accept the law of change and the hypothesis of the reasonableness of the human world, if we believe that the course followed by events is not shapeless, we shall find no difficulty in adopting the view that one particular event may take place before, or after, the most suitable shape for it to fit into has been reached. Before the optimum moment there may still be too much fluidity, after it there may be an excess of rigidity, and the event cannot in those circumstances be absorbed into the general configuration of human experience.

I like to call this particular habit of events by the name of "law of the appointed time," using the word in the Biblical sense: "But it shall not prosper; for yet the end shall be at the time appointed" (Daniel xi. 27). There are moments when a community seems ready for a change, for a performance. At

[1] *Introduction à l'Histoire*, p. 9.

THE "LAWS" OF HISTORY

such moments the change or the performance occurs with a minimum of difficulty or friction. In Western European history there was a period when decentralization and regionalism had, for the good of each country, to give way before a centralized national government. England came first with the change, and at what was for that country the optimum moment, the end of the fifteenth century and the course of the sixteenth. That period was not yet the appointed time for centralization in the Low Countries: Philip II failed in his attempt to do there what the Tudors had done and were doing in England. The unification of Germany came long after the appointed time.[1] Statesmanship consists to a large extent in the ability to decide whether the appointed time has arrived for carrying out a given policy. The statesman cannot alter the appointed time, though it may be within his power to hasten its arrival or to delay its departure. A belief in the existence of this law is implied in the use of the expressions "moving with the times," "consonant with the spirit of the times." The *Zeitgeist* is the personification of the law of the appointed time.[2] It is the reflection, perhaps the distortion, of the appointed time in the minds of men living at a given moment. The English have no name for it. Living an undisturbed life behind their sea-barrier, they have enjoyed the occurrence of most of the significant events in their national existence at the appointed time. Little has happened so far to make them aware of the painful habit events have of misbehaving if prevented from taking place when the shape of things demands their occurrence.

The law of the appointed time has a corollary which I call the law of momentum.[3] Social life, like nature, treats us to the spectacle of energy being applied for the purpose of achieving a

[1] For applications of this law to Dutch history, see my *Dutch Nation*, pp. 80, 82, 212, 229.

[2] "The English and French bourgeoisie created a new society in their own image. The Germans came later, and they were compelled to live for a long time on the pale gruel of philosophy. The Germans invented the phrase 'speculative world,' which does not exist in English or French. While these nations were creating a new world, the Germans were thinking one up" (Trotsky, *History of the Russian Revolution*, Vol. I, pp. 202–3).

[3] The use of these home-made names has the advantage of underlining the fact that this chapter merely presents one individual interpretation.

result—or, if we prefer, of a result appearing subsequently to the application of energy. What happens to this energy when the result is achieved? If we consent to express ourselves in teleological terms, we shall say that, not being a careful or precise dispenser, nature produces means which exceed its requirements. If we prefer to use metaphors of a different nature we can say that the achievement of a result liberates a certain amount of energy which failed to be spent in the process of achieving this result. The same phenomenon can be observed in the activities of human societies and in those of human individuals. To achieve a purpose men build an organization, acquire habits, a mentality, loyalties, that help them towards the goal. When the task is performed these acquisitions cannot be immediately discarded. Once acquired, the momentum of occurrence tends to maintain itself. After he had performed the necessary task of giving to his country the unity and cohesion of which it was so badly in need, and of safeguarding it against outside interference, Louis XIV continued his absolutist rule and went on with his military conquests. From that moment—approximately 1685—the law of elasticity also began to operate. Things are what they are. And the continuation of absolutism did not correspond to the new needs of the age. The French Revolution gives us another example of the working of these laws. Threatened by a conspiracy between the royal Court and foreign powers, the Revolution went to war to defend its existence. When its safety was ensured, it continued to fight and to conquer. The career of Napoleon also shows the law of momentum in action.

§ 5

CLASS AND REVOLUTION

It must have become clear to every reader by now, that this chapter does not pretend to give an outline of the philosophy of history or even a systematic view of one person's philosophy. It is an attempt to illustrate how a belief in regularity in the course of human affairs leads the historian to establish certain types of sequences which will enable him to marshal events into a coherent story. Some of these typical sequences will be suggested to him by contemporary events. To formulate them as laws, to conceive the hypothesis that they will also apply to certain past occurrences, is yet another way of interrogating the past in the name of a living society.

Social classes form one of the main realities of the age in which we live. A number of countries, nowadays, are governed by dictators who proclaim themselves the caretakers of the proletariat. There are also countries where the government's aim is to achieve social justice for the working class. In other countries the government, by allowing, as much as they dare, the free play of economic forces, encourage the competition between various classes which is sometimes described as a class struggle or a class war. Throughout the world the competition between various social classes provides political and social life with its most striking aspect. It is natural that historians looking at the past experiences of societies should want to devote a considerable part of their story to the activities and the transformation of social classes.

In the absence of agreement among sociologists we may define a class as a group of human beings bound together by a similarity or a community of economic interests and by the notions and prejudices brought forth by these interests. We shall then observe that certain general tendencies which seem to be at work today and which appear to be slowly modifying the relative importance of various social classes were already in operation in the course of the past adventures of Western European societies. The historian's approach to the class factor is by no means exclusively based upon his observation of present society. He approaches the past with the view he takes of the past as much as with views he takes of the present. Let us not forget that there is, in this matter of extracting lessons from history, of generalizing about the past, a considerable amount of gentle and innocuous self-deception. What is the past about which we generalize, the past which leads us to construct theories *independently of our observation of the present*? It is very often a past seen at one remove, or even at a greater distance. It is the past narrated in accepted history. Accepted history occupies a considerable place in my theory. It is important and indispensable, but this does not mean that it presents us with secure knowledge.

I have stated that it is a gift horse we cannot look too frequently in the mouth.[1] Is it from the events narrated in accepted history that we derive our theories? Have they not been arranged by the narrators according to patterns that pre-existed in their minds? How could it be otherwise? We must admit that to our own subjectivity is added the subjectivity of our informant. On the other hand, if we work upon events which we have ourselves inferred from traces detected by our own research, our field will be restricted. Our individual "contribution" to knowledge remains too individual and too narrow to justify generalizations and the drawing of conclusions, at least as a rule.

With this important caveat we may now state a few laws that describe the occurrence of regularities in the class element of societies in the past and that also seem to belong to societies which we can directly observe at the present time. A first regularity may well be the fact that, in the long run, and if we compute not in years or decennia, but in units of one or even two centuries, the economic factors which determine class interests and class notions are more important in the life of societies than any other factor, including ideas, institutions, religion, psychological conditions, and heredity. This regularity will, if we observe it more closely, resolve itself into a number of regularities of a more tangible nature. One law of class history might be stated in these terms: political power tends to follow economic power. The class that controls wealth, i.e. economic power, will eventually also control political power. Strong factors may delay the operation of this law, but their veto has no finality.[2] The French Revolution began for a number of accidental and superficial reasons, but almost from the start the bourgeoisie, which had economic power only, struck out for political power. It defeated its competitors of the nobility and of the lower middle class and the proletariat, and emerged triumphant at the Restoration of 1815. The notion, by the way, that there are two classes only, the exploiters and the exploited, is a naïvety which finds no confirmation in the story of human experiences. The Dutch Republic was founded in the last third of the sixteenth century

[1] See above, II: i: § 1.
[2] For an example in Dutch history, see my *Dutch Nation*, pp. 16 *sqq.*

236

by proletarian revolutionaries who adopted the Calvinist faith (1572 onward). Here again our law of class power can be observed: the Calvinist revolutionaries had no economic power; this was in the hands of the liberal regents who represented the upper middle class. They plucked the fruits of the proletarian revolution and became masters of the Dutch Republic (from 1580).

Another regularity appears in the events that affect class relations. It belongs to the realm of ideas, of human consciousness, although the view that the ideas and states of consciousness that are involved are a direct reflection of economic conditions cannot seriously be questioned. This law may be universally applicable to the story of mankind, or not, but it is certainly observable in the history of Western European civilization. I would formulate it in these words: each successive class which holds both economic and political power comes nearer to equalling the totality of members of the society to which it belongs. As education spreads, as the working classes acquire a greater share in the control of production, democratic societies tend to become classless. It is still only a tendency. No classless society has yet arisen. To say whether, in Soviet Russia or elsewhere, a classless society may one day arise would be an attempt to prophesy. Historians are not prophets.

There is a matter which is bound at some time to claim the historian's attention and upon which light can perhaps be thrown if it is seen from the point of view of the class law which has just been formulated. Journalists and pamphleteers like to call the age in which they live "an age of transition." They are always right, since no age can fail to be a transition between that which came before and that which must follow. The notion of transition, however, implies something more: a belief that old possessions, including institutions, ideas and conditions are being abandoned more readily than is usually the case, and that the pace of social evolution has been hastened. It would be relevant to ask whether there are ages in which this pace is indeed faster or slower than in other ages. Now if class relations possess the paramount importance with which I credit them it is arguable that they will provide a measure of the speed of social evolution.

Whenever political power rests with the class which, in accordance with our law of class power, is entitled to hold it, society would appear to possess such stability as can be expected if the law of change is taken into consideration. Ages at which the class entitled to political power on the ground that it holds economic power is in fact still politically impotent can be called ages of transition. We would then call mid-Victorian society in England stable, and England in the nineteen-thirties unstable or living in a state of transition, while Britain under a revisionist socialist regime might be said to be tending towards stability.[1]

Are periods of transition necessarily full of revolutionary possibilities? It would be bold to assert this. For revolution presupposes not only a disequilibrium caused by maladjustment of power, but also the existence of a revolutionary doctrine. I doubt whether revolutions, as distinct from revolts or riots, are ever spontaneous. Nor am I satisfied that every revolution is concerned with class relations. It seems to me that what we call a revolution is the termination by means of force of the continuity of legality in favour of a group or class which is not in possession of political power. There exists a recognized difference between political and social revolutions. But is it not a fact that every social revolution is also political, while a political revolution is not necessarily social? Every revolution, however, has psychological, if not psycho-pathological, concomitants. Let us bear in mind, lest we fail to realize the essential aspect of revolutions, that to be a revolutionary is, nearly always—and I would prefer to say always—to be mentally unbalanced. Normal humanity is dialectical, it compromises forever between the natural conservatism by which the race preserves its existence and the natural adventurousness by which it secures progress. The revolutionary is non-dialectical: he is a creature whose evolution has been arrested at the stage of antithesis. Fatally impelled by the law of momentum, he remains the eternal no-man. Every revolutionary who

---

[1] A pure Marxist might tell us that never in the past has there yet existed a rational distribution of power. Since wealth and labour are synonymous to him, the dictatorship of the proletariat would be the only condition in which economic and political power coincide. All ages past and present must therefore have been ages of transition in the sense in which we use this expression.

has played a part in history and about whose early career sufficient data are available, can be reduced to type—invariably to a morbid type.[1]

In the course of a revolution a parental figure is dispossessed, and this is invariably accompanied by the exacerbation of the sense of guilt which is present in every human being. Every successful revolution in consequence contains, together with its thesis of justice and renovation, an antithesis which is the desire to restore the parental figure or to set up a substitute parent. The law of elasticity is also at work. Things are what they are. The fundamental conservatism of human beings cannot be suppressed completely while their adventurousness has its innings. The extreme revolutionary is a conservative.[2] It is not surprising, therefore, that we can lay down a law about revolutions, according to which they display an invariable sequence in which a dictator appears in the train of a revolution. This law was known to the European contemporaries of the French Revolution, who were looking for the appearance of a one-headed government in France several years before the emergence of Napoleon.

§ 6

OUTSIZE MEN IN HISTORY

The regular appearance of the revolution–dictator sequence in the human past brings us to the last of our generalizations. It deals with the behaviour and the significance of men of unusual stature. The large-scale experiments in dictatorship which have been made since the First World War provide

---

[1] The Gracchi suffered from a mother-fixation, Spartacus from an inferiority complex, Cromwell was a depressive maniac, Robespierre an obsessional narcissist, Danton an exhibitionist with an anal complex, Marat a schizophrene, Fouché an algolagniac. Edmund Wilson describes the nerves and bad tempers of revolutionary agitators, the waste of mental energies and emotions in sterile controversies and spiteful quarrels. He speaks of their diseased vanity, their jealousy and their suspicions (*To the Finland Station*, 1941, pp. 221–2). It is not surprising that once they achieve power such men find it difficult to accept the rules of common sense or of international courtesy.

[2] Sovietism is hierarchical, hieratic, conventional, puritannical, intolerant and nationalistic, in short, conservative.

actuality to the problems raised by the existence of extra-ordinary men.

We cannot exclude the human individual from history. He matters, he exercises social influence, but he is somewhat unaccountable, because he is unique. He cannot be caught by a formula. Yet he cannot be ignored, because there are things that are not achieved by the masses. Now and again the narrator comes up against the deeds of an individual as the ultimate factor that can be reached in a chain of events. He will, then, have to make up his mind whether, with Carlyle, Nietzsche, and many others including Oman, he will look upon the "great" man as the maker of the past, the present and the future. Certain philosophies, on the other hand, leave no room for the great man. Each historian must consider the claims of these schools, but there is no need for him to embrace either extreme of interpretation.

Let us avoid the expression "great men." It implies a favourable judgment of quality, and many people will find it impossible to use a term of approval in referring to every man who is entitled to a place in Madame Tussaud's exhibition. We are concerned with men of unusual stature, with those who are strikingly dangerous as well as with alleged benefactors of mankind, with Napoleon as well as with General Booth. This is why I prefer to talk of outsize men.

We must begin by setting apart outsize men who have achieved fame through artistic and intellectual achievements. Rembrandt, Michelangelo, Dante, Shakespeare, inventors, scientists like Newton. They may have "played a part in history," perhaps they did not; they may or may not have influenced the social experiences of their contemporaries and of posterity. There are men like Thomas à Kempis, Saint Augustine, Tolstoy, striking to all who behold the traces left by their passage upon earth. But are they not of interest to the psychologist rather than to the ordinary historian, to the student rather than to the historian of religion? It would be a mistake to legislate in this matter, but the view that they will receive from the ordinary historian reference rather than full treatment can be reasonably advanced.[1] There

[1] See above, I: ii: § 4.

are other men, however, who played a prominent part in the human drama, leading actors like Caesar, Napoleon, or Lenin. Did they influence, did they shape, the course of events, or were they merely the spokesmen of history (using the word in the objective sense)? Hegel has written: "der grosse Mann ist der Geschäftsführer des Weltgeistes." What do we really know about outsize men? The methodologist Bauer considers that we have little information of any value upon the subject. We do not know why Philip II of Spain imprisoned his son Carlos, or what made Antony stay in Egypt. But we believe that, if asked about the decline of the Spanish Empire, we can give some sound reasons for the event. Bauer is inclined to agree with Eduard Meyer and with Adolf Harnack, who wanted to remove biography from history.[1]

In sober truth we know far more facts about outsize men than the sceptics try to make out. About those who lived in classical antiquity we possess ample factual material, though it is not always equally reliable. We are well informed about those who lived in the modern period. Once, however, we try to connect our knowledge, and in particular, when we try to determine their influence upon the course of events in the midst of which they lived we feel baffled by the disagreement among those who wrote about them.[2]

The most important and fruitful generalization that can be made about outsize men is one which does not come readily to those who think or write about them. Yet it is obvious. Why should all outsize men who have arrested the attention of their contemporaries and whose memory is preserved by historians belong to one single type? Why should not some have influenced the world, some not, and some not very much? This differentiation is much more reasonable than the belief that when they appeared the world handed over the reins to them and looked on with bated breath while their task was being accomplished.

What, indeed, is this world of past events in which we wish to situate the outsize man? It is a world where all events are not of the same substance (this is a metaphor), where the one-ness which we presuppose without having proved its existence adopts

---

[1] Bauer, *op. cit.*, p. 68.   [2] Geyl, *Napoleon*, *passim*.

innumerable aspects. There are layers of occurrence, some deep and fundamental, others much nearer the surface, which cannot possibly affect the deeper layers. This is an old doctrine. It was formulated, but certainly not invented, by William James in 1909. "Nothing includes everything."[1] Naturally this applies also to the human past. Coming after many others, I formulated this doctrine in my book *The Dutch Nation*, published in 1944, in these words: "Power policy, psychological factors, religion even, may affect the march of mankind at every milestone of the road, but they are incapable of changing or determining the general direction of the march. In the long run, and by the reckoning of those who have the patient audacity to compute in centuries, social and economic factors are the only ones that count."[2]

How does our outsize man appear if we take the longer view of the past? There are several possibilities. If he follows the direction of the march of mankind, of the society to which he belongs, he may hasten it, he may plane away obstacles that are impeding the march, he may guide his contemporaries along a short cut that will save them from a tedious trudge along the meandering road. He is the servant of progress, an "instrument of history"; he carries out a social task, and exercises a fruitful and lasting influence upon the course of events. Instead, however, he may try to arrest the march. He may be strong enough to press back for a while the front ranks of the marchers. If he does, he will soon be swept off his feet and carried away. He may, perhaps, persuade or compel a detachment to stray from the main body of the advancing army, and lead it along byways till

[1] "Things are 'with' one another in many ways, but nothing includes everything, or dominates over everything. The word 'and' trails along after every sentence. Something always escapes. 'Ever not quite' has to be said of the best attempts made anywhere in the universe at attaining all-inclusiveness. The pluralistic world is thus more like a federal republic than like an empire or a kingdom. However much may be collected, however much may report itself as present at any effective centre of consciousness or action, something else is self-governed and absent and unreduced to unity" (James, W., *A Pluralistic Universe*, pp. 321–2).

[2] P. 134. In *The Use of History*, published in 1946, Mr. A. L. Rowse claims novelty for his theory about "the surface stream of history" and "the deep underlying tides and currents" (pp. 128 and 131). Cf. also Bauer, *op. cit.*, p. 68, on determinism and indeterminism.

it disbands or perishes in the wilderness. Such a man is neither a tool of history nor an active influence that affects the course of events in the long run. Most successful among outsize men is he who reads the signs of the age, who distinguishes lasting from passing factors, who notices the advent of the appointed time. He is what Koestler calls "the key that fits the lock."[1] He may be a spokesman of his people at a time of stress, like the younger Pitt, or like Winston S. Churchill. Not infrequently the outsize man belongs in part to the positive, in part to the negative class. Napoleon and Robespierre were such mixtures.

The upshot is that we cannot make a general statement about the nature of the influence exercised by outsize men. Instead, we can ask a set of questions about each of them. Did he hasten or retard the operation of fundamental factors affecting the course of events, or did his appearance fail to affect these fundamental factors? Did he waste his energy by undertaking the easier task of influencing the operation of some less fundamental factor like art or religion, with what measure of success, and in what direction? Did he read and understand the signs of the times? Was his activity conscious, was he aware of the fact that he was serving society, or was he trying to pursue his own interests and to satisfy his private passions? By asking these questions the historian will also discover new heuristic pointers and through them, perhaps, hitherto unnoticed traces of unknown events. Meanwhile he will give more "concatenation" to knowledge, and more body, but also more suppleness, to his story.

To conclude this chapter I may perhaps repeat that the actual nature of the theories which the historian holds about human behaviour and about regularities of occurrence in the human or social universe is of secondary importance compared to the fact that he has theories on these subjects at all. For sound theories do not always prevent men from making mistakes of judgment. But where intellectual integrity prevails there can never be obduracy in error. Vacant minds, however, cannot be saved by honesty—unless it be by the prudent honesty of silence.

[1] *The Yogi and the Commissar*, p. 44.

Chapter VI

HISTORY AS AN ART

In 1939 the Earl of Crawford and Balcarres told members of the Historical Association that "many of our own historians seem to fear that attention to prose, or rather the effort to make it attractive, must detract from the merit of the history—in short, that history is a picture which requires no frame, a precious stone which needs no setting."[1] The speaker was right, for the absence of elegance from the majority of English historical writings of the present day is deliberate. Most English historians want to make it abundantly clear that they are not men of letters. Some of them readily banish correctness as well as elegance for the sake of showing the world beyond a peradventure that history is not an art. The style of the late H. W. V. Temperley was invariably ugly, not seldom incorrect. Yet the Master of Trinity was a man of culture who knew what he was doing. G. N. Clark, one of the leaders of his profession, uses an impeccable style, but its leanness and its avoidance of flowers proclaims the deliberate intention of keeping his personality and his rich experience of life out of the severe reports in which he presents the results of his scholarly investigations. G. M. Trevelyan, a master of beautiful prose, does not enjoy the approval of the professionals of history in this country. His books are so clearly works of art that there are some who would gladly question his scholarship. Unhappily for them, *England under Queen Anne* and the Garibaldi series are as learned as they are readable.

Croce has stated that history is an art. Later, he recanted. In any case, his use of the word art was personal, and intended to suggest that there can be no history without a knowledge of the individual. But neither subtilization nor whimsicality can dispose of the problem of the relation between history and art. The question whether history is a science or an art can be left to students' debating societies. The methodologist, however, must

[1] "History and the Plain Man," in *History*, March 1939, p. 297.

make up his mind whether the art of writing may or may not be called to the assistance of the historian as he fulfils his supreme duty, that of telling a story. The theorist who supports what we have called right-wing deviationism and looks upon research as the essence of history, and upon the telling of the story as a subsidiary function, remains within his right. Wrong theories about history do not necessarily lead to the writing of bad history: Croce and Collingwood provide proof to the contrary. But the world will fail to show an interest in those who consider it their duty to write for the sole delectation of men whose hearts are as dry as their own. It will continue to read the beautiful writings of Motley which have long since been expelled from accepted history by the better informed, and it will look upon them as history. If history were an art, and nothing else, Motley would rank higher than any of the writers who have since gone over the same ground and have told his story anew and more accurately.

We know, however, that history, though not a science, is a discipline which approaches its subject-matter in the same spirit as science. It has the same way of looking upon the gradual acquisition of accurate knowledge; like science, it seeks knowledge for the sake of action, and tests the value of its knowledge in the process of acting. If art has anything to do with history, it will be when the stage is reached at which the historian communicates his results. Here is a difference with science. When the scientist takes to writing, he is drawing up a report of what he has done, and of the conclusions he has reached about the theoretical implications of his achievements. He states whether the forecasts he made have come true, and why. The writing comes after the scientist's work is done. In history the writing is the essential operation. It is the way in which the historian carries out his tems of reference, which are the fixing of some past experiences of a society. But the writing of the story is more than that: it is the ultimate test of the value of the trace-event inferences made by the historian at an earlier stage. In these circumstances it is reasonable that the historian, in whose work ethical standards and intellectual integrity play such a significant part, shall do his utmost to bestow upon his writing all the care of which he is capable, and give it every quality which he can possibly put into it.

The story told by the historian must, to begin with, satisfy certain requirements that can be made legitimately of every single piece of writing. Before all else, it must be clear. To write clearly, the historian must remember, like the engineer who composes a report, the civil servant who indites a letter, the scientist who draws up a paper, that language is an inadequate and primitive instrument. Without infinite care it will give rise to misunderstanding and contradiction. The use of ambiguous and undefined terms is to be avoided. Grammar must be respected. But language has other rules also, subtler than those of grammar or syntax, which preclude the use of certain constructions that are not theoretically incorrect.[1] These constructions are not necessarily obscure, but they contain within themselves the possibility of obscurity. A careless user of language is an intellectual road-hog. He may avoid accidents himself, but he exposes others to danger. Correctness is an aspect of clarity. So is tidiness. To pay no attention to the sequence of one's ideas and to the way in which they are connected is to court the danger of being misunderstood.

Since a superabundance of detail obscures any argument and hides the thread that must run through a story, there can be no clarity without conciseness. Detail rarely lends itself to concatenation. It tends to remain isolated. To amass details is therefore to throw upon the reader the whole burden of understanding, whereas it should be the writer's task to guide his reader towards the easy acceptance of his reconstruction. Elimination and generalization provide the two remedies against prolixity. Historical writing is particularly exposed to the danger of obscurity through overcrowding. The historian feels, rightly, that events should be allowed to speak for themselves. Generalization, on the other hand, is a risky business. But historians do not always know where to draw the line. They often attach undue importance to their own research work, and are loath to waste any of its results. The Dutch historian P. J. Blok was known for his reluctance to leave any item in his collection of cards unused: many of his

[1] Examples in Gowers, E., *Plain Words*, H.M. Stationery Office (1948).

sentences are unduly weighted by the last-minute addition of the contents of yet another *fiche*.[1]

The narrator of the story required by society should have the courage to shoulder his responsibility. We do not want to read the chef's recipe in our bill of fare. The flowery vagueness of French culinary jargon is the reason for the use of French on our "menu's," and not snobbishness. The historian must behave as one who is trusted. He must select, he must omit, he must see to it that he shall deserve to be trusted, he must demand the confidence which he deserves. Catalogues of slight events delight the research worker who has steeped himself in a period, but are wearisome to the reader. Footnotes exist for the purpose of satisfying the antiquarian who hides within the bosom of each historian. Maybe the pages of learned periodicals fulfil the same purpose.

Conciseness is more than the requisite of a good style. The famous ballerina Tamara Karsavina tells us in her autobiography that Serge Diaghileff once said to her: "Omission is the essence of art."[2] Omission or selection is not a purely logical process. It rests upon a sense of balance, an appreciation of fitness. The writer who bestows his care upon selection has already ventured into the realm of literature. There is no precise frontier between the story as a conscientious report and the story as a conscious effort to capture beauty. Art is the communication of an aesthetic emotion. The historian who loves his subject may easily experience this emotion, which is the sense of pleasure felt when perceiving physiologically unprofitable sensations. To see a fragment of the past taking shape as a result of our patient and skilful reconstruction can give us this unselfish glow, and make us desirous of communicating our feeling to others. If we do so successfully we are producing, or endeavouring to produce, a work of art. We shall feel it legitimate to bestow care upon the form in which we dress our communication. We shall feel that a consciously wrought style is the worthy medium of our expression. Gibbon, Macaulay, Motley, were artists. Their contributions are gradually eliminated from accepted history. But

[1] The obsession with waste and utilization as one of the inducements to historical research, above, I: i: § 3.   [2] *Theatre Street*, p. 258.

their works belong to the literature of the world. Their task of keeping the memory of mankind awake for a brief while has been fulfilled. Knowledge moves on, forever provisional. Knowledge is the groping of brave men in a dark world. Art is a perennial flower.

Chapter VII

HISTORIANS

Bonnard, me disais-je, tu sais déchiffrer les vieux textes, mais tu
ne sais pas lire dans le livre de la vie.
Anatole France, Le Crime de Silvestre Bonnard

HISTORY is action based upon knowledge. But the action which
is history is circumscribed, and limited to the accurate telling of
an important and necessary story. The historian is a social agent.
His discipline differs from the other branche of the humanities
and from the sciences of nature. Among intellectual workers the
historian is peculiarly situated: the methodological, ethical and
social problems that face him do not arise—or not in the same
way—in the exercise of other intellectual activities. These problems
are mainly concerned, not with the events that appear in his story,
but with the generalizations, explanations, and other elements
that belong to it, and with the various modes of serialization to
which the events must be submitted.

The exceptional and complicated nature of the historian's task
has given rise to a number of questions to which, in this final
chapter of my survey of the problems of history, I shall now
attempt to reply.

§ 1

OBJECTIVITY AND PARTIALITY

Should the historian remain impartial when he tells his story?
Here is a genuine problem: responsible historians and methodologists disagree about the solution. Absence of bias is not the
same thing as secure knowledge. We have noted more than once
that the historian's narrative cannot possibly be a faithful and
total reproduction of a section of the past. But in our awareness
of this limitation we have still to ask ourselves whether the
historian is allowed to take sides, or whether he must keep his
personality and his preferences out of the story. Ratzel, Helmolt,
Fustel de Coulanges, the Rumanian Xénopol, all favour complete

self-denial on the part of the historian. He must express no views. Langlois went very far in keeping his own notions out of his work. The four volumes of his *Vie en France au Moyen Age* are nothing but an anthology from medieval writers, novelists and moralists. Such an abdication of the historian, such a disregard of his duty to tell a story can only result from the mistaken belief that history is a science, or from a scepticism so profound that it restricts the historian's task to the collecting of facts.

No story can be told till a selection has been made among available events, and, as the Dutch historian Bussemaker observes, the selection of facts is a judgment passed upon their importance. Let us admit, therefore, that the impersonal story is inconceivable. This does not singularize our discipline. "Impersonal knowing should be admitted to be an abstraction, a fiction, and an impossibility," wrote the logician Schiller.[1] Hazlitt said, in his essay *On Genius and Common Sense*, that "in art, in taste, in life, in speech, you decide from feeling, and not from reason." Pirenne has explained why the historian cannot leave his personality out of the story. "The historian's subject is society itself. His task is to understand and recount events of which the factors are men like himself, nations like that to which he belongs. However impartial he may be, he cannot remain totally objective. However strong his personality, he cannot escape from his social environment. His own time necessarily expresses itself in his work, his point of view is determined by the level of civilization of the public which he addresses and of which he is a member."[2]

Clearly, then, the historian is present in his work with his whole personality, with his temperament and with his group-consciousness as well as with his reason. It would be absurd, it would be dangerous, to ask him to disguise this fact. Halphen points out that open partiality in an historian has the advantage of warning us against his limitations.[3] Trevelyan, who considers that bias is to some extent inevitable, says that it may sometimes help the historian "to sympathize with the actual passions of

[1] *Our Human Truths*, p. 11.
[2] *Revue Historique, art. cit.*, p. 51, slightly abridged.
[3] *Introduction à l'Histoire*, p. 30.

people in the past whose actions it is his business to describe";[1] which is a plea for imagination as a series-maker. Bauer explains in his treatise that the cult of objectivity presents serious drawbacks, since its object can never be achieved.[2] He considers that the historian should avoid with equal care tendentiousness and colourless impartiality.[3]

Bauer's *via media* is sometimes difficult to follow for a creature of flesh and blood. I find it impossible to observe the behaviour of the Dutch Counter-Remonstrants of the seventeenth century and their narrow-minded persecution of the Arminians without feeling, and expressing, disgust. I cannot read the story of the gentle, tolerant, over-prudent, humanly frail, and liberal minister Adolphus Venator and of the hysterical campaign of the orthodox against his charitable doctrines without taking the side of this anti-totalitarian of 1600.[4] And yet, a patriotic Dutchman may see the tragic greatness of Maurice of Orange as well as that of his victim John van Oldenbarnevelt; an historian who loves England may rise above a preference for Whigs or Tories of the eighteenth century. In doing so, however, the historian merely embraces a higher partiality which enables him to see the virtues of both sides in quarrels that belong to the past. By being a patriot before he is an admirer of one party the historian does not abdicate his personality.[5]

§ 2

ETHICS

The historian cannot keep his personality out of his story. It is better that he should openly admit his bias than let it work insidiously and put the reader off his guard. Does this mean that

[1] "Bias in History," Presidential address to the Historical Association (1947) (*History*, xxxii.)   [2] *Op. cit.*, p. 89.

[3] "Es wird schliesslich keineswegs schaden, wenn hinter die Schilderung vergangener Dinge eine scharf umrissene Persönlichkeit hindurchleuchtet, die von festen Gesichtspunkten aus Menschen und Welt betrachtet" (*ibid.*, pp. 90–1).

[4] See pamphlets nr. 1841 and nr. 1844 in Knuttel's catalogue, and the article "Adolphus Tectander Venator," by Vries, J. de, in *Oud Holland*, Vol. 40, pp. 124–60.

[5] See the discussion on "Bias in Historical Writing," reported in *History*, October 1926.

the historian may pass moral judgment upon the deeds of the individuals and groups with whom his story deals, that it is his duty to do this? His task is that of a social agent, and he is, as we know, under an obligation to practise intellectual integrity. This implies that ethical matters claim his attention at every turning of the road. What are his ethical standards? How has he acquired them?

Every historian was born blissfully free of all sense of right and wrong, combative, intensely resentful at the cessation of uterine nirvana, a greedy anarchist, though not unwilling to love his neighbour—for a consideration. His parents imposed upon him unwelcome rules concerning feeding, and later also concerning evacuation. The future historian suffered from frustration.[1] But he was a realist: he accepted defeat, adapted himself, and submitted to the rules. He knew that there are things one *must* do, even if one does not want to. At this point, however, habits arose, and complicated mental operations took place,[2] as a result of which the infant historian began to take the existence of imperative limitations of his freedom for granted. "Must" became "ought." He found himself in possession of a conscience and, at the same time, of an ethical sense.[3] His conscience told him that he ought to behave in accordance with an imperative that came from outside himself; his ethical sense was an attempt to give an objective and independent existence to the dictates of his conscience. They were the two sides of one coin placed by life in his private money-box.

The child has grown into an historian endowed with an ethical sense that operates in the same way as his aesthetic sense. It causes him to look with approval upon certain actions independently of the advantage he may reap from them, and induces him to disapprove, in the same non-utilitarian way, of certain other actions. He distinguishes between fine and ugly behaviour in himself and in others. Where did he find the contents with which he filled

---

[1] Menninger, Karl, *Love against Hate*, pp. 15 *sqq.*

[2] Incorporation in the self of qualities and moral attitudes of the environment. *Cf.* Flugel, *Man, Morals and Society*, pp. 41 *sqq.*

[3] And it is not inconceivable that this sense of "ought" was in due course registered in the "silent area" of the foremost part of his cerebral hemispheres. Nor is this proved, as yet. Like history, science deals in decreasing uncertainties.

the book he acquired in infancy? Education, no doubt, inscribed many pages. But while he adopted a number of rules handed to him by his educators, he inverted some of them, and imposed certain laws upon himself for no better reason than that his elders rejected them. Nor are the historian's ethics universal and current in every country any more than those of other adults. "Les tables de la loi sont éternelles, elles vivent en nous," wrote André Gide in his diary.[1] Within ourselves? Of course! Eternal? Most certainly not! No commandment is eternal or universal, except this one, that there ought to be obedience, on certain occasions, to certain rules. On which occasions, to which rules? "Why do this act if I feel like doing something else?" asks Dewey. "Any moral question," he observes, "may reduce itself to this question, if we so choose." And he continues: "In an empirical sense the answer is simple. The authority is that of Life. Why employ language, cultivate literature, acquire and develop science, sustain industry, and submit to the refinements of art? To ask these questions is equivalent to asking: 'Why live?' No one can . . . escape the problem of *how* to engage in life, since in any case he must engage in it in some way or other—or else quit and get out."[2] Ultimately, every historian sees life in his own way, and hears its injunction in a different version.

Here, then, is our historian with his categoric but personal ethics, and it is difficult to see how he can avoid judging by it every single deed which he recounts. May he express his inevitable judgment in the story which he tells; must he do so? Whether he is obliged to pronounce judgment, does not depend on him, but upon the nature of history. It has been asserted that history is judgment. In an eloquent passage the Dutch critic du Perron trounces the historian Huizinga for not condemning the Inquisition, the excesses of capitalism, and other injustices committed in the past.[3] The answer to du Perron is that the sole task of history is to reconstruct the past by means of a narrative. Society and its members are entitled to make whatever use they like of the narrative presented by the historian. The sociologist may deduce from it laws of social behaviour, the moralist may

[1] *Journal*, p. 55.   [2] *Human Nature and Conduct*, p. 81.
[3] *In deze Grootse Tijd* (1946), pp. 93-5.

draw lessons from it and pronounce upon the value of the deeds it recounts. But let us not command the weaver to cut and sew us a coat.

Nevertheless, as has been pointed out in the previous section, the historian is entitled to give free rein to his personality in the course of telling the story. If ethical considerations loom large in his spiritual equipment there is no reason for his keeping silence on the subject. His right to pronounce judgment is as clear as his right not to do so. Indignation may compel him to speak, moral disgust, or mere amazement. If he does, and if he is wise, he will remind himself of the law of change, and of the law of the appointed time. It will be foolish of him to reproach sixteenth-century capitalists for being blind to the liberalism which inspired young Karl Marx's *Communist Manifesto*, childish for him to deplore the fact that seventeenth-century Dutch ministers of religion have not read Voltaire. He will have to remember that actions are not in themselves good or bad, at least, can never be hallmarked good or bad if considered in themselves, but must be judged by the goodness or badness of their results. At the same time the historian cannot free himself entirely from the human impulse to judge, nor can he on all occasions resist the temptation to participate in the deeds he is recounting.

If and when he judges, the historian who takes a three dimensional view of the past, who wishes to see it in relief, will endeavour to judge past actions by the standards of morality of their own period. A narrator who is aware of the slender metaphysical foundation of morality and of the strength of its psychological roots will feel impelled to visit two sins only—inconsistency and stupidity. When all is said and done, these are our own besetting sins. And is not moral indignation mostly the expression of a desire to scourge our own shortcomings in others?[1]

The historian may judge, he must act. He must act by telling his story. His action will be measured immediately by his own standard of value. His personal ethics, therefore, the way in which he hears the injunction of life, will be his guide while he performs his task. Nevertheless the most subjective of ethical systems has to

[1] Cf. Flugel, *op. cit.*, on "Vicarious Punishment and the Projection of Guilt," pp. 164–74.

bow before a universal imperative which leaves no room for exceptions, admits no casuistry. This is because the ethics of history-writing resides in history, not in the historian. No one is obliged to choose history as a profession or a pastime, but he who chooses it must accept it with all its rules. History carried out without intellectual integrity is not history, but fiction. History possesses no infallible criteria: it lives in the brain and in the hand of its servants, it lives in their conscience. The morality of history-writing is exclusively methodological.

Historians who, like Edward Gibbon, cultivate the garden of history without having to sell their produce in the market have almost disappeared from England. Nowadays historians teach in a university, and receive a stipend. As academic personalities they will be wise to follow certain rules of conduct. Are these rules imperative? Only in so far as the historian's conscience conceives them as such. They can be ignored. But in ignoring them the academic historian will not help the reputation of his discipline. Can they be formulated? I am ready to make the attempt. We are back, as I hardly need remind the reader, in the sphere of the ultra-subjective.

§ 3

PRACTICAL ETHICS FOR ACADEMIC HISTORIANS

"Don't tell your friends their social faults; they will cure the Fault, and never forgive you."
Logan Pearsall Smith, *Afterthoughts*.

"Si j'étudie," said the great lexicographer Du Cange, "c'est pour le plaisir de l'étude, et non pour faire de la peine à autrui, non plus qu'à moi-même." Charity comes a little uneasily to scholars, because eye-strain is not eupeptic, and because they lack physical exercise. But the working of charity is curious. Directed towards others, whose path it smooths, it has a way of returning home to its owner, where it meets and pacifies his sternest judge, the critic who knows his shortcomings as no-one else.[1]

Fear and distrust are evil guides. The specialist who specializes because he knows nothing outside his speciality condemns others

[1] His wife or his super-ego? Let the reader decide!

for not specializing, because he hopes thus to cover up his own ignorance. But he who knows that history is one will recognize the value of work that is carried out in a manner not his own. He who knows that history is action will not condemn the action of those who act otherwise than he does. He will ask from them this only, that their action shall be the telling of a story which they honestly believe to be accurate.

The historian in authority will not treat his juniors as his own seniors used to treat him. Whatever the philosophy that dwells in his brain, his heart believes that the world in which we live is better than that in which he took his first steps.

Bearing himself among other scholars as though unaware of the fact that his discipline is Minerva's favourite, the historian will treat them kindly. He will never repeat to the victim an unkind word spoken about him in the Common Room, and will never fail to retail to a colleague a kind remark made about that colleague by another. Ethics has no rules, because it is subjective and empirical. But the laws of good taste are universal.

Appendix I

TWO DEFINITIONS OF HISTORY

Bernheim, p. 9:

"Die Geschichtswissenschaft ist die Wissenschaft, welche die zeitlich und räumlich bestimmten Tatsachen der Entwicklung der Menschen in ihren (singulären wie typischen und kollektiven) Betätigungen als soziale Wesen im Zusammenhange psycho-physischer Kausalität erforscht und darstellt."

Bauer, p. 17:

"Geschichte ist die Wissenschaft, die die Erscheinungen des Lebens zu beschreiben und nachfühlend zu erklären sucht, soweit es sich um Veränderungen handelt, die das Verhältnis des Menschen zu den verschiedenen gesellschaftlichen Gesamtheiten mit sich bringt, indem sie diese vom Standpunkt ihrer Wirkung auf die Folgezeit oder mit Rücksicht auf ihre typischen Eigenschaften auswählt und ihr Hauptaugenmerk auf solche Veränderungen richtet, die in der Zeit und im Raum unwiederholbar sind."

Appendix II

TRANSLATION OF QUOTATIONS

* The square brackets indicate footnotes.

PAUL VALÉRY, p. 5:

"History is the most dangerous product ever concocted by the chemistry of the intellect. Its properties are well known. It causes dreams, inebriates the nations, saddles them with false memories, exaggerates their reflexes, keeps their old sores running, torments them when they are at rest, and induces in them megalomania and the mania of persecution. It makes them bitter, arrogant, unbearable, and full of vanity."

[ANDRÉ GIDE, p. 7, n. 1:

"That habit of mine of always quoting those who are kindred to my mind. The more daring my thought, the more I take pleasure in the fact that it has also dwelt in other minds. They tell me I am wrong. I do not care. I take too great a pleasure in quotation and I am convinced, as was Montaigne, that fools only will consider me less original."]

HEGEL, p. 8:

"Just an ordinary historian!"

[HALPHEN, p. 20, n. 2:

"The most immediate purpose of history is to save the facts of the past from oblivion."]

GROTENFELT, p. 21:

"A not altogether pure science."

[DROYSEN, p. 25, n.

"Mankind's knowledge of itself, its self-awareness."]

HALPHEN, p. 27:

"To explain the facts of which we are witnesses."

PETRARCH, p. 30:

"To forget our own dreadful time."

BERNHEIM, p. 32:

"Man only is the object of historical science."

PIRENNE, p. 35:

"And the philosophy of history? Where do you put that?"

FRENCH ACADEMY:

"History is the story of things worthy of being remembered."

TAINE:

"To be as alive as nature the work must, like nature, contain nothing but events and actions. Let us not forget that history is above all a narrative."

CROCE:

"The story and the historical dissertation or reasoning."

AN. FRANCE, p. 39:

"Philosophy and ethics are not the essential part of the art of the historian."

DARDEL, p. 42:

"There is no object in itself, isolated from the subject who makes it objective. The modern prejudice which will look upon objective things as the only reality translates itself in history into an excessive growth of the most exterior modes of becoming."

BAUER, p. 53:

"Criticism should never become an aim in itself."

PIRENNE, p. 54:

"Without hypothesis and synthesis history remains a pastime of antiquarians: without criticism and erudition it loses itself in the domain of fantasy."

TAINE, p. 57:

"Ten centuries at the bottom of a black pit."

THE FRENCH, p. 74:

"Small history, history of customs."

[LA BRUYÈRE, p. 83, *n.* 1:

"Everything has been said and one comes too late after more than seven thousand years during which men have been thinking."]

BAUER, p. 88:

"All scientific investigation is fundamentally a further investigation."

SAINT-SIMON, p. 92:

"Such was the work of the loathsome Mazarin, whose wiles and perfidy formed his virtue, and whose cowardice was his prudence."

[BAUER, p. 95, *n.* 2:

"Every single historical fact presents a tissue of phenomena of the most diverse origin."]

HALPHEN, p. 97:

"Historical science gains nothing by wrapping itself up in mystery."

[BOSSUET, p. 112, *n.* 1:

"Just as for the sake of assisting one's memory to retain a knowledge of places, one preserves certain principal towns round which one places the others, each at its right distance: thus, also in the order of the centuries one must possess certain moments marked by some great event, round which one groups the remainder."]

MICHELET, p. 117:

"Before the fistula and after the fistula."

[CHATEAUBRIAND, p. 124, *n*. 2:

"It is, indeed, probable that the Author of Nature first planted ancient forests and young bushes; that the animals were born, some full of days, the others graced with the charms of infancy. When piercing the fertile soil the oaks, no doubt, were carrying at the same time old crow's nests, and the new brood of the doves. Caterpillar, chrysalis, or butterfly, the insect was crawling on the grass, or already suspending its golden egg in the forests or trembling in mid-air. The bee, though it had lived but one morning, already counted its ambrosia in generations of flowers. We must believe that the ewe was not without its lamb, the goldfinch, its young; that the bushes were hiding nightingales that were astonished at their own first song and warming the fragile hopes of their first voluptuous raptures."]

RANKE, p. 130:

"As it really did take place."

MONTAIGNE, p. 132:

"The pretence of certitude is a sure testimony of folly and extreme incertitude."

AN. FRANCE, p. 136:

"Thrown out lightly and by way of a jest" . . . "I see that they have some value."

[AN. FRANCE, p. 138, *n*.:

"I do not mean to say that there is justice in the world. Yet one does observe some strange turns of the tide. Force, the only judge of human actions, sometimes makes unexpected jumps. Its abrupt side-steps will disturb a balance that was considered stable. And its games, which are never without some hidden rule, display most unexpected throws."]

MONTAIGNE, p. 145:

"And truly, philosophy is but a sophisticated form of poetry."

AN. FRANCE:

"What is so admirable about metaphysics is that it takes away from the world that which it had and gives it that which it did not have."

[AN. FRANCE, p. 146, *n.* 1:

"Philosophic systems are interesting solely as tangible monuments that can enlighten scholars about the various states of mind through which men have travelled."]

[BAUER, *n.* 2:

"If one looks upon philosophy as the thought of an age worked into a system, every human being who does at any rate think independently up to a point is collaborating in the building up of the philosophy of his time."]

LANGLOIS, p. 147:

"Science is a way of economising time and effort by a process that makes facts rapidly recognisable. It collects slowly a quantity of detailed facts and condenses these into portable and *incontrovertible* formulas."

DE LA TOUR, p. 152:

"History has a great virtue of appeasement. I do not entertain the flattering thought that my solutions are definitive. History, like every discipline, recorrects ceaselessly, and every scholar ought to have before him the fine motto of Fustel de Coulanges: quaero, I am seeking."

[BERNHEIM, p. 176, *n.* 2:

"The investigator may use general categories only as a heuristic help, to make it possible to understand the relation of things, but he must be ready at any time to correct his generalisations by means of his factual material or to give them up in favour of more plausible connections."]

[BAUER, p. 177, *n.* 1:

"History cannot carry out its task without some conception of regularity, however restricted, and however empirically constructed. This enables the historian to build historical types and to see correlations on a large scale. It fills the gaps and makes it possible to make proper use of the testimony of the past."]

BOSSUET, p. 180:

"In this matter dates are everything."

[ARON, p. 185, *n.* 1:

"Historical research fastens upon the antecedents of a particular fact, sociological research looks for the causes of a fact which may occur again."]

AN. FRANCE, p. 189:

"There is within us a basic human substance which changes less than is sometimes imagined."

[BAUER, p. 189, *n.* 1:

"The individual as a psychological unity is the true crux of modern historical theory."]

[MONTAIGNE, p. 190, *n.* 3:

"Forsooth, man is a marvellously vague, varied and wriggly subject. It is uneasy to pass judgment about it. . . . In view of the instability of our customs and opinions I have often felt that it is a mistake on the part of our best authors to insist upon granting us a constant and solid texture."]

PIRENNE, p. 192:

"In so far as it interests the historian human nature does not change."

[BERNHEIM, *n.* 1:

"The identity of human nature is the basic axiom of all historical knowledge."]

[SEIGNOBOS:

"If the facts reported in documents had not been analogous to those we can observe we would be unable to understand them."]

[BAUER:

"It is possible to get in contact with historical data only upon the assumption that events in human consciousness take place in identical or similar internal and external circumstances."]

LA BRUYÈRE, p. 195:

"Physiognomy is not a rule given for judging men. It helps us to form conjectures about them."

MONTAIGNE, p. 203:

"For what we hate lies near to our heart."

SAINT-SIMON, p. 204:

"The sinew and principle of hatred and friendship, of gratitude and revenge, is the same."

BOSSUET, p. 210:

"In the New Testament He followed another line of conduct."

BOSSUET, p. 211:

"Two things are evident to unaided natural reason: one, that we are free, two, that our freedom is encompassed in the decrees of Divine Providence."

THE SAME:

"Remember, Monseigneur, that the long concatenation of particular causes which make and undo empires depends on the decrees of Divine Providence. High up in His heaven God holds the reins of all kingdoms. He has every heart in His hand. Sometimes He restrains passions, sometimes He leaves them free, and thus agitates all mankind. By this means God carries out His redoubtable judgments according to ever infallible rules. He it is who prepares results through the most distant causes, and who strikes vast blows whose repercussion is so wide-spread. Thus it is that God reigns over all nations."

[COUNCIL OF THE VATICAN, *n.* 3:

"If someone were to say that human disciplines are to be practised with such freedom that their assertions, even if they disagreed with revealed doctrine, must nevertheless be retained as true, let him be excommunicated."]

LA ROCHEFOUCAULD, p. 212:

"We must never create the impression that we pretend to be right against all others: we must easily give way."

HEGEL, p. 241:

"The great man is the business executive of the World Mind."

AN. FRANCE, p. 249:

"Bonnard, I said to myself, you know how to decypher old texts, but you cannot read in the book of life."

[BAUER, p. 251, *n.* 3:

"It will do no harm whatever if behind the picture of past things there shows up a sharply defined personality which looks upon men and the world from a fixed point of view."]

ANDRÉ GIDE, p. 253:

"The tables of the Law are eternal: they live within us."

DU CANGE, p. 255:

"If I study, it is for the pleasure of studying, and not with the purpose of hurting anyone."

INDEX